"Defense attorney Rudolf debuts with a searing look at systemic failures in the U.S. justice system. . . . Enriched by Rudolf's firsthand experience and heartfelt compassion for his clients, this is a harrowing call for change."

—*Publishers Weekly*

"Trial lawyers are storytellers, and when the trial lawyer is one of the very best, the stories could not be more riveting, or told with more passion. *American Injustice* is filled with compelling narratives, beautifully told, sweeping the reader along to the final conclusions. They are accounts of injustice and abuses of power that were not aberrant but seemingly embedded in case after case that Rudolf recounts. The impact is chilling. This is an important book not only for players in the criminal legal system, but for a public that truly needs to know."

—Hon. Nancy Gertner (ret.)

"David Rudolf has written a searing indictment of the American criminal justice system. This terrific book is neither a polemic nor an academic treatise. By describing the cases from his amazing career, Rudolf has written a very engaging and powerful first-person account of how justice and injustice are actually done in the United States."

—Erwin Chemerinsky, Dean and Jesse H. Choper Distinguished Professor of Law, University of California, Berkeley School of Law

"David Rudolf has been confronting injustice for decades. In this exciting book, his powerful voice for justice will inspire the new generation and inform us all."

—Michael E. Tigar, lawyer, teacher, author of
Sensing Injustice: A Lawyer's Life in the Battle for Change

AMERICAN INJUSTICE

ONE LAWYER'S FIGHT
TO PROTECT THE RULE OF LAW

DAVID S. RUDOLF

MARINER BOOKS

New York   Boston

A hardcover edition of this book was published in 2022 by Custom House, an imprint of William Morrow.

FIRST MARINER BOOKS PAPERBACK EDITION PUBLISHED 2023.

Library of Congress Cataloging-in-Publication Data

Names: Rudolf, David S., author.
Title: American injustice : one lawyer's fight to protect the rule of law / David S. Rudolf.
Description: New York : Custom House, [2022] | Includes index.
Identifiers: LCCN 2021036086 (print) | LCCN 2021036087 (ebook) | ISBN 9780062997357 (hardcover) | ISBN 9780062997364 (trade paperback) | ISBN 9780062997371 (ebook)
Subjects: LCSH: Criminal justice, Administration of—United States.
Classification: LCC KF9223 .R83 2022 (print) | LCC KF9223 (ebook) | DDC 345.73/05—dc23
LC record available at https://lccn.loc.gov/2021036086
LC ebook record available at https://lccn.loc.gov/2021036087

ISBN 978-0-06-299736-4

22 23 24 25 26 LBC 5 4 3 2 1

This book is dedicated to all who have lost their lives, their freedom, or their hope because of the abuse of power

CONTENTS

INTRODUCTION

But constant experience shows us that every man invested with power is apt to abuse it, and to carry his authority as far as it will go.

—Charles-Louis de Secondat, Baron de Montesquieu

On the night of July 27, 1990, Ed Friedland came home from a long day at work to find his wife bound with handcuffs and viciously slain on the dining room floor. The couple's ten-month-old adopted son, found in the nursery at the rear of the home, was unharmed but distraught after being left unattended for hours. Ed called 911 to report the murder. The police arrived minutes later and dutifully commenced their investigation into this unspeakable crime.

Even though Ed had no prior criminal record of any kind—in fact, he was a prominent physician—investigators soon began to focus on him as the killer. Every aspect of Ed's life was turned inside out by the police. Despite a lack of evidence, and at first based solely on Ed's demeanor and their intuition, they grew sure he had murdered his wife in cold blood. They just had to prove it—and that was what they set out to do. After an erratic and very public four-year investigation, Ed was indicted for first-degree murder. If convicted, he would face the death penalty.

Early in this process, which began with the murder and ended with Ed's indictment, the police lost sight of their true role as investigators. They stopped trying to solve the crime and instead focused all their energies on proving the culpability of a single suspect—Ed Friedland. Once the police had made up their minds that Ed was responsible for his wife's death, they misinterpreted facts and became blind to a mountain of evidence that pointed directly to another suspect: a longtime felon with a history of violence and drug use who lived nearby.

I represented Ed and defended him on the murder charge. During my investigation, I discovered that the police had not only chosen to ignore evidence that the murder had been committed by someone else, but they also hid this critical evidence *from the prosecuting attorney*. The police had become so entrenched in their theory that Ed was the killer, they seemed to be willing to do anything to have him prosecuted and convicted, even if it meant withholding information from the district attorney's office. As is always the case, the officers who were involved in the murder investigation denied all wrongdoing and suffered no consequences for their actions.

Willfully concealing evidence of a defendant's innocence is an egregious abuse of police power that comes with life-altering, and sometimes life-ending, consequences. Incredibly, this type of misconduct by law enforcement doesn't just happen in rare and isolated cases. It is common knowledge among criminal defense attorneys that police and prosecutors routinely engage in a variety of abuses of power to obtain convictions, and it happens in every jurisdiction in the United States.

Such misconduct by police and prosecutors takes several forms. The first involves the police concealing evidence of the defendant's innocence, as investigators did in the Ed Friedland case. Another common type of misconduct occurs when the police use highly suggestive procedures to make an eyewitness identification of a suspect more likely, which in turn has the effect of contaminating an eyewitness's true recollection of the crime and the perpetrator. Yet another occurs when the police fabricate or plant evidence for the purpose of implicating a suspect in a crime. A related abuse of power occurs when the police use interrogation tactics that coerce innocent defendants into giving false confessions and encourage incentivized witnesses, such as "jailhouse snitches," to give false testimony against an accused. Finally, in cases where forensic evidence exists and is relevant, investigators often resort to highly unreliable forensic disciplines, such as bite-mark and microscopic-hair-comparison analyses, to implicate suspects. Meanwhile, prosecutors routinely rely on unreliable evidence procured through police misconduct to obtain convictions or force plea deals with defendants.

Ironically, law enforcement misconduct is most often seen in cases in which there is a paucity of truly incriminating evidence—usually because the suspect in such cases is in fact innocent. Yet a strong belief by the police in their own ability to "know what really happened," coupled with the effects of confirmation bias and a desire not to let the perpetrator beat the charge, lead investigators astray and result in abuses of power that send innocent people to prison. It's not that the police set out to frame someone they know to be innocent, although that sometimes happens (if rarely). More often, the police feel the need to create or find the evidence necessary to convict where none exists. Those who work to correct injustices of this type have a name for it: noble-cause corruption.

Such abuses of power have resulted in the wrongful prosecutions of *thousands* of innocent people. Countless innocent people have likewise been imprisoned, and many have been sent to Death Row. Tragically, some of those sentenced to death were executed for crimes they likely did not commit. Racial minorities have disproportionately been the target and victims of police and prosecutor misconduct, particularly in the American South, where an enduring legacy of racial prejudice has long plagued the criminal justice system.

Just in the past thirty years, due in part to advancing scientific technologies, such as DNA testing, more than 2,800 innocent people serving prison sentences have been exonerated and freed from the shackles of confinement, their combined jail sentences adding up to more than 25,000 years of prison time. This number, however, represents only a small fraction of the number of persons wrongfully convicted over the same period, and it does not reflect those who were acquitted or granted a dismissal of the charges after being wrongfully arrested.

You would think that all the actors in the court system would happily work to correct erroneous convictions, but this has not proven to be the case. Prosecutors and judges have shown remarkable hostility to overturning convictions based on new evidence or evidence of misconduct by police or prosecutors, even when the new evidence includes reliable scientific data such as DNA comparisons that exclude the defendant as a perpetrator in the crime. Attorneys representing defendants who are challenging a conviction face steep uphill battles in winning exonerations, with the rare success often taking years and even decades to bring about. For each of the exonerees, there remain innumerable others still sitting in prison, praying for their day of justice to come. "It is better that ten guilty persons escape than that one innocent suffer": so said the English jurist William Blackstone in the 1760s. In the name of "law and order," however, police and prosecutors have turned this bedrock principle on its head.

As a criminal defense and civil rights attorney for more than forty years, I have spent my career fighting abuses of power in the criminal justice system whenever and wherever I found them. My work has been in America's courtrooms, where the state's mechanisms for the deprivation of liberty slowly grind, and where those responsible for wrongfully taking a person's liberty are all too rarely held to account. I have worked in the trenches as a public defender in the South Bronx, representing the poorest of the poor, and conversely I have represented the very wealthy, including entrepreneurs, politicians, and professional athletes. I have seen how the system works and how it fails. I have been privileged during my career to represent people in some of the most compelling cases imaginable, and in every case I have vigorously contested abuses of power and championed the cause of individual liberty. This has been the touchstone of my life.

This book contains the extraordinary stories of real people who lived through shocking abuses of power at the hands of the criminal justice system. Some spent decades in prison before finally winning their release. Many of the cases are from North Carolina, where I have practiced law since 1978, but they could have happened anywhere, and they have. The same stories, and the same travesties of justice, exist in every state. These stories and the people whose lives have been affected will illuminate the hidden systemic ills of our criminal justice system for inspection by all, and will call attention to common abuses of power that sacrifice the rule of law for a conviction at any cost, even if the cost is the life of another human being. I have seen it firsthand, and I have the stories to prove it.

Part I

THE ROLE OF THE CRIMINAL
DEFENSE LAWYER

1

DEFENDING THE RULE OF LAW

In the autumn of 1768, American colonists witnessed with alarm the arrival and mooring of two British warships in Boston Harbor. From the belly of the ships disembarked two orderly regiments of British soldiers, clad in their customary red coats and carrying muskets and powder. In rank and file, they marched into the city to the sound of fifes and drums.

American colonists in Boston had been in a state of heightened civil unrest since the enactment of the Stamp Act three years prior, followed by a second revenue measure imposed by the Crown in 1767. The new regiments of soldiers late arriving in the city had been dispatched to quell the growing unrest, impose order, and demand obedience from "his Majesty's dominions in America."* With the installation of the new regiments, some two thousand British soldiers would occupy Boston, a city of sixteen thousand people who had survived for generations without the yoke of British rule wound so tightly around their necks.

---

* The phrase "his Majesty's dominions in America," which appeared in certain Acts by the British Parliament directed at colonial America, such as the Townshend Acts of 1767, was a source of great umbrage among the colonists.

Many colonists viewed the British occupation as a profound degradation of their liberty, and the soldiers were seen as "instruments for fastening the shackles that had been forged"* by the king. Skirmishes between the colonists and the soldiers soon became commonplace. The Redcoats, quick to brandish cutlasses and bayonets in the face of protest, became an increasing source of ire and provocation. The winter of 1770 saw the fevered tensions escalate to bloodshed, with both sides crossing a boundary from which there could be no return.

The first day of a bitterly cold March that year brought several rounds of fisticuffs and name-calling between colonists and soldiers, and "neither side was sparing of insult."† The soldiers, having not made resort to their weapons, got the worst of it. Soon, rumors circulated through the city that the Redcoats would have their revenge the coming Monday. Four British soldiers were heard by a colonist to say that "a great many that would eat their dinners on Monday next . . . should not eat any on Tuesday,"‡ while the wife of a British grenadier ominously forecast that the soldiers would "wet their swords or bayonets in New England people's blood."§ The city had become a powder keg that would soon ignite.

All this angst and bitterness so long brewing came to a head on the evening of March 5, 1770. Boston lay under a sheet of ice, and snow was falling. For hours that day, townspeople had roamed the streets carrying cudgels and staves, seeming to invite conflict. On King Street, a single British soldier stood guard outside the Custom House, where the Crown kept its money. Earlier in the day, he had

---

* John Adams's contemporaneous notes of Josiah Quincy's argument to the court in the Boston Massacre trial.

† Richard Frothingham, *Life and Times of Joseph Warren* (1865).

‡ Statement of William Newhall, *A Short Narrative of the Horrid Massacre in Boston* (1770).

§ Statement of Daniel Calfe, *A Short Narrative of the Horrid Massacre in Boston* (1770).

cuffed a quarreling and sharp-mouthed barber's apprentice with his musket. Now the apprentice had returned with an angry mob.

The sentinel scrambled up the steps of the Custom House, away from the gathering horde, and hastily loaded his musket. Reinforcements from the British 29th Regiment were summoned to confront the townspeople, led by Captain Thomas Preston. With bayonets leveled, the soldiers pushed their way through the mob and formed a defensive half-circle. The colonists taunted the soldiers, assailed them with snow and pieces of ice, and cracked their sticks loudly together, raising a clamor. Surrounding the soldiers, the colonists dared the soldiers to shoot.

Samuel Gray, a rope maker, said, "My lads, they will not fire."* His mistake proved dire. In almost the same instant, someone in the mob struck a soldier's musket hard enough to knock him down. When the soldier found his feet again, he shot his gun into the crowd. This was followed in quick succession by the sound of another musket, and then another. The crowd fell back as the firing continued. Gray, contrary to his ill-fated prediction, was struck in the head and died instantly. Two more colonists were hit by the musket fire and perished there on the street. In all, five colonists were killed, and six were grievously wounded.

At the Old Brick Meeting House, a boy was lifted up to ring the fire bell, bringing people out of their homes and into the streets. Word spread that "the troops had risen on the people."† On a wave of anti-British sentiment, eight British soldiers, including Captain Preston, were arrested and charged with murder. If found guilty, they would face the death penalty.

The Boston Massacre, as the confrontation came to be known, had a profound and lasting effect on the people of Boston and throughout

---

* Frederic Kidder, *History of the Boston Massacre* (1870).

† Ibid.

the colonies. It was "the first blood flowing that was shed for American liberty,"[*] in the words of one patriot, and it set the stage for the eventual throwing off of British rule. News of the attack was spread far and wide. Samuel Adams, who would become a leader of the American Revolution, loudly proclaimed that a "bloody butchery" had occurred and demanded that the British occupation of Boston be ended lest more blood be imminently shed. Paul Revere, another American patriot, prepared and circulated an engraving of "The Bloody Massacre," depicting an orderly line of British soldiers firing on command into a crowd of unarmed men, women, and children, thus further stoking the flames of indignation.

Captain Preston and the other British soldiers, facing a trial for murder, sought representation among Boston's lawyers, but none could be found who would take the case. The lawyers feared that even associating with these soldiers, let alone defending them, would suggest a sympathy for British rule and subject the lawyers to opprobrium, scorn, and even harm from their fellow countrymen.

At last, word reached one young Boston lawyer that an increasingly desperate Captain Preston "wishes for counsel and can get none."[†] The lawyer was an idealist as well as a patriot. He believed that everyone, even a British soldier charged with murdering an American colonist, was entitled to a fair trial and a vigorous defense. The young lawyer saw this as a key tenet of the new country he hoped would soon be established. So at great personal risk to himself and his wife, who was pregnant, he undertook representation of Captain Thomas and the other soldiers on trial for their lives.

The trial began on November 27, 1770. In court, the lawyer for the soldiers argued that the killings had occurred because the actions of the unruly and aggressive mob had forced them to fire their muskets. In short, he argued the soldiers acted in self-defense.

---

[*]   Richard Frothingham, *Life and Times of Joseph Warren* (1865).

[†]   John Adams, *The Works of John Adams, Second President of the United States,* Vol. II (1850).

The lawyer told the jury: "Facts are stubborn things; and whatever may be our wishes, our inclinations, or the dictates of our passions, they cannot alter the state of facts and evidence."* After two and a half hours of deliberation, the jury acquitted all eight soldiers of murder. Two were found guilty of manslaughter, and for this crime they received nothing more than a brand from a hot iron on their right thumb (an "M" for "murderer").

Some colonists were angered by the outcome of the trial—but the story had a surprising conclusion for the lawyer. By maintaining his devotion to a strong and fair defense, he came to be respected by the citizens of Boston even more. In his later years, he said that defending the soldiers was "one of the most gallant, generous, manly and disinterested Actions of my whole Life, and one of the best Pieces of Service I ever rendered my Country."†

That young lawyer was John Adams, who would go on to be one of the leaders of the American Revolution, an original signer of the Declaration of Independence, and the second president of the United States. His statement demonstrates how a founding father of our country viewed the importance of the rule of law and the critical role of criminal defense lawyers in protecting it. And two hundred fifty years later, it is true now more than ever, when the rule of law has been so directly attacked by so many, and our country has become so bitterly divided against itself. The role of the criminal defense lawyer in defending the rule of law is just as critical now—if not more so—than it was in 1770.

---

* *The Adams Papers*, Legal Papers of John Adams, vol. 3, *Cases 63 and 64: The Boston Massacre Trials*, ed. L. Kinvin Wroth and Hiller B. Zobel. Cambridge, MA: Harvard University Press, 1965.

† Ibid.

2

HOW CAN YOU REPRESENT
"THOSE PEOPLE"?

Every lawyer who has done criminal defense work for any period of time has been asked one or more of these questions: "How can you represent 'those people'?" Or, "How can you represent someone who is guilty?" Or, sometimes, "How do you sleep at night?"

On a fundamental level, the answer for me is not that I am upholding "the adversary system" or that "everyone is entitled to a defense," although both of those answers are true enough. For me, it boils down to recognizing the humanity in my clients, no matter how horrendously they may have acted in a given situation. It's having some empathy for who they are, understanding the forces that shaped (and often twisted) them, and recognizing that they are not the sum total of the acts they have committed. The person who best exemplifies this notion is a young man I began representing in 1985, John William Rook, as he awaited execution for a murder he most certainly did commit.

He was at a cookout at a trailer park on Stovall Drive in Raleigh, North Carolina, when he ran out of beer. It was a hot, humid day in May, and the mobile home John was staying in didn't have air-conditioning. It was like an oven inside. He took off his shoes, socks, and shirt, leaving him wearing only a pair of old blue jeans. He pulled his long hair back into a ponytail to get it off his shoulders.

He didn't own a car, so he asked Ruby Howell, one of his neighbors, if he could borrow hers. Ruby knew he wasn't sober, that he was never sober, and that he'd been taking pills earlier in the day and washing them down with beer, but she gave him her keys anyway. The car was a 1972 Mercury that belonged to Ruby's mother, and she crossed her fingers that he'd bring it back in one piece. Half-dressed and fully stoned, John got in the Mercury and drove himself to the A&P grocery store.

He said he'd be right back. Ruby kept looking at her watch, wondering where he was. First one hour passed, then another. Maybe he'd been pulled over for drinking and driving. Maybe he'd wrecked the car. Her mother would kill her. How far could he go? She knew he probably didn't have enough money to buy beer *and* put gas in the car.

Just after twilight, John pulled back into the trailer park. As he returned the car keys to Ruby, his face was sickly pale. She noticed cuts on his face, and his arms and jeans were stained with blood. She asked John what on earth had happened to him, and he said nothing, he just got into a fight with a Black man at the A&P. As John went inside, she looked over the car. It had long grass caught up under it, like it'd been driven through a pasture.

The next night, a security officer with Dorothea Dix Hospital on a routine patrol came across a heap of blood-soaked women's clothes in the middle of a field. After breathlessly searching the area, he soon came across a naked female body lying about thirty-five feet away. It appeared she'd suffered massive blunt-force trauma almost from head to toe.

The investigation moved quickly. On the night of the cookout at the trailer park, four witnesses had reported seeing an altercation between a man matching John's description—hair in a ponytail, wearing only jeans—and a woman near the grocery store where

John had bought beer. One of the witnesses called the police, but when officers arrived, the car was gone, and no trace of it could be found. Fortunately, another witness had the presence of mind to take down the license plate number. It didn't take long for the police to connect this incident with the murdered woman. The police traced the car, a 1972 Mercury, to the trailer park where John lived, and he was soon under arrest.

The victim's name was Ann Marie Roche. She was a twenty-five-year-old nurse at a local hospital. When he was out to buy beer, John saw her walking home from work and pulled in front of her to block her path. Perhaps thinking that she knew him, she went to the driver's-side window of his car to speak with him. Things went south quickly. John pinched her arm (maybe trying to be flirtatious), and for this he got a slap across the face. He instantly became enraged and sprang out of the car. He attacked Ann Marie and began to beat her savagely. A witness described him "swinging her around by her hair," and another said he was hitting her with a stick-like object and that her face was cut and bleeding. In a flash, she had been forced into the car, where the attack continued. John struck her with such violence that "the steering wheel appeared to jar at times," according to another witness.

John drove Ann Marie to a grassy area near Dorothea Dix Hospital, where he beat her with a tire iron to the point of unresponsiveness and then raped her. He left her there in the tall grass, bleeding, and got back in the car. As he pulled out of the field to leave, he ran over her with the car. According to the court record, because of his small size, "He could barely see over the steering wheel, but knew he had run over her with the car because he heard a thump and the car got stuck. He spun the tires to free the car and then drove home."

The autopsy revealed grievous and frightening injuries—a broken leg, a fractured and separated pelvis, a broken rib, evidence of forcible sexual intercourse, and uniform, almost parallel, shallow cuts across the front part of the victim's body that had been inflicted with a knife. Ann Marie had survived for several hours after the attack; her body was still warm when she was found by the hospital security guard the next day.

After a short trial, the jury found John guilty, and also found that the rape and murder were "especially heinous, atrocious or cruel"—an aggravating factor allowing the imposition of the death penalty in North Carolina. On January 9, 1981, he was sentenced to die by lethal injection.

John's attorneys filed an appeal to the North Carolina Supreme Court and argued that John's culpability for crime was diminished due to his drug and alcohol use, as well as the abuse he suffered at the hands of his parents as a child. The Court denied the appeal, ruling as follows:

> *The record reveals that this defendant committed the most brutal, vile and vicious crime against Ann Marie Roche. . . . Defendant's sadistic and bloodthirsty crimes committed against this victim compel the conclusion that the sentence of death is not disproportionate or excessive, considering both the crime and the defendant. We, therefore, decline to exercise our discretion to set aside the death sentence imposed.*

I first met John in 1985, when he was on Death Row awaiting execution. He was in North Carolina's Central Prison, in Raleigh. I, along with Jack Boger from the Capital Punishment Project of the NAACP Legal Defense Fund, and Michelle Robertson, a young lawyer I had met while teaching at UNC Law School, undertook representation of John and fought to spare him from the death penalty, which we all believed to be immoral.

At first, John was sullen and non-communicative. He didn't trust me, or anyone, and did little to endear himself to us. It was difficult to get through to him and make him understand that we were trying, in earnest, to save his life. We explained to him what we were doing, and why, and we treated him as a human being. Over time, he slowly began to open up, and we came to learn what circumstances in his life and childhood had preceded his terrible crime.

John was twenty-one at the time of the murder. During his short life to that point, he had lived through, in the words of a justice of the North Carolina Supreme Court, "an abnormally deprived, if not depraved, childhood." Not one of us would be willing to trade our childhood years for the horrors that John endured. It left him, both mentally and emotionally, much more a child than an adult. He was a boy who never grew up.

John's early years were a living nightmare. He was one of seven children, and was always small for his age. His father, a chronic alcoholic and ne'er-do-well, beat the children regularly for minor things, or nothing at all. One of John's brothers recalled that their father would "grab the first thing he could get his hands on, light cord, water hose, stick, any damn—anything he could get his hands on, he'd grab it and that's what he'd beat us with." John and his siblings were forced to strip naked for the beatings, as the other children watched. The beatings would leave the children covered in blood and bruises. "That's the only way he believed in whipping anybody," according to John's brother.

His father enjoyed giving three-year-old John beer and liquor to drink—because he found it amusing to see John drunk. John suffered from significant cognitive impairment throughout his life—his IQ was measured at 71—and being forced to consume alcohol as a young child likely compounded his difficulties.

The abuse from his parents took all manner of forms. At times, Mr. Rook would line up the children in a tight circle and throw a heavy ashtray into the air to see which child it would fall on. He often beat their mother until she lay bleeding and unconscious, while the children cowered nearby. Every three or four weeks, John's father left the family for extended and unpredictable periods of time without food or necessities, and that neglect eventually led to his serving a two-year jail term for nonsupport when John was eight years old.

John's mother, unfortunately, was no better than his father when it came to caring for the children, and their lives did not improve with their father absent. A neighbor recalled, "I wouldn't beat a dog the way she was beating her youngins.... That was a beating. It was not a whipping." According to testimony presented at John's trial, she would regularly drink herself into an oblivion, getting "so drunk she didn't know if they [the children] were there or not."

With no one to look after him, John had to take care of himself, as did his siblings. It was not uncommon for them to stay out all hours of the night. John stole food because he was hungry, stole shoes because he had none, and stole wine because his mother demanded it. John was forced to survive by "living almost like an animal in the streets." He slept sometimes in Dempsey Dumpsters or cardboard boxes at a nearby apartment project, and other nights he just roamed the streets.

One entry in a Department of Social Services (DSS) file from that time describes the slovenly conditions in the Rook home, including the fact that "the children use the floor as a toilet." The principal at the elementary school once reported to DSS that "the children came to school filthy; and that they were taken to the shower for baths and were given clean clothing to wear while they were in school." None of the Rook children ever completed a full term at any one school facility.

North Carolina, as a result of its failure to help abused children like John, had been sued in 1979 in a class-action lawsuit on behalf of all minors who "now or in the future will suffer from serious emotional, mental, or neurological handicaps accompanied by violent or assaultive behavior and for whom the state provides no treatment." As a result, the state had established the "Willie M. Program," which provided funding for group homes and psychological treatment for such children. Although John clearly qualified, he was instead put into a foster home with no services.

Despite the extraordinary abuse and neglect John suffered, his first-grade teacher remembered him fondly. She recalled that he was extremely small for his age, looking more like a four-year-old than his real six years. And although he was "immature mentally and physically," she described six-year-old John as a "well-behaved child" who "responded to help." His foster mother, Frances Carter, described John at age eight as "a good child . . . a loving child. He liked to sit on my lap and liked to be talked to. He was just a good child."

When Mr. Rook was released from jail after serving his sentence for nonsupport, John was taken from the foster home and sent back to live with his parents, where he was subjected to the same horrifying regime of abuse and neglect as before. After he was returned "home," John would sneak back to Mrs. Carter's house for "hugs," as she described it.

Yet John could not overcome the ongoing circumstances of his birth, and his life soon veered toward destruction. At age twelve, when he was still very much a child, he was preyed upon by an older man, who exploited John for sexual gratification in exchange for providing John with food and a place to stay—an arrangement that John voluntarily accepted. He found it preferable to being at home. At trial, the state's psychiatric expert agreed that, for John, "living with a homosexual and engaging in homosexual acts . . . was a means of trying to find a more pleasant environment than he had elsewhere."

He then turned to drugs and alcohol to escape the brutality and deprivation of his family life. He had been exposed to alcohol consumption by his father when he was a toddler, and when he was nine, his brother taught him how to inhale lighter fluid. Evidence presented at trial showed that "since the age of 12, Mr. Rook [John] has been taking some form of drug *every day of his life* that he has not been incarcerated."

Predictably, as time went on, he got into trouble that was more serious. His juvenile record reflects more than a dozen charges and shows a pattern of increasingly violent offenses. John's school records from age fourteen state, "John on an unconscious level is preoccupied with family conflict, especially at his father. John uses denial about these problems, but it is not effective, as angry feelings erupt with slight provocation." Another teacher at John's school noted he was "very aggressive now toward females and would need some supervision." These were clear warning signs that were simply ignored.

By the time he was twenty-one years old, the age at which he raped and murdered Ann Marie Roche, he was completely out of control. He was drinking three to four six-packs of beer every day, injecting amphetamines, and generally impairing himself to the point of unconsciousness on a daily basis. At no point in his life had John ever received the benefit of any meaningful intervention from anyone. He needed care, help, and counseling throughout his youth, but it never came. Not from his parents; not from the community; not from the state or county government.

None of this excuses what John did to Ann Marie. His crimes were unspeakable, and he rightfully deserved punishment. But what all of this says to me is that John, as much as anyone I have ever met, deserved—and desperately, desperately needed—an advocate, and this was true his whole life. Despite the abject cruelty he experienced in his upbringing and his limited cognitive faculties, this child had been left to fend entirely for himself, and we know how it turned out. If anyone along the way in John's short life had stepped up and advocated for him, both he and Ann Marie might still be alive today.

John's execution, to occur by lethal injection, was scheduled for 2:00 a.m. on September 20, 1986. In our effort to stop the execution, we filed a petition for clemency to the governor of North Carolina, along with a motion to stay John's execution with the U.S. Supreme Court. The petition for clemency to the governor, Republican Jim Martin, argued that the state—indeed, all of us—had failed John. That it would be woefully unjust for the state to execute John when it was aware of all that he had been forced to endure but had done nothing to intervene.

In response to our petition, and following a meeting with the gov-

ernor, in which we argued for John's life, I received a handwritten
letter from the governor's legal counsel. It read:

> Please know that the Governor, Jim Trotter [the governor's legal
> counsel], and myself are all of the opinion that you did an out-
> standing job as attorney for John Rook.
>
> I would also like to express my deep respect for you not only as
> an attorney but as one who acts on strongly held beliefs.
>
> Although you and I may disagree on philosophical ideals, it was
> uplifting to work with an individual, who having determined what
> was right, proceeded to act without regard to costs or sacrifice.

Despite the kind words, Governor Martin denied our clemency
petition on Friday, just hours before the execution. John's life and
only hope lay in the hands of the U.S. Supreme Court.

I was at the prison with John in his final hours as we awaited word
from the Court. I was confident the Court would issue a stay in
John's case. It had recently agreed to hear arguments in two other
death-penalty cases, one from Florida and another from Georgia,
that raised the same constitutional issue we had asserted on behalf of
John. The Court certainly wouldn't allow a state to execute someone
before hearing and deciding other cases with the same issue, or so I
thought. I was wrong. Close to midnight, we received word from the
warden that the Court had denied the stay. The terse finality of the
Court's refusal to grant John a reprieve was abrupt and devastating:

> *The application for stay of execution of the sentence of death pre-
> sented to THE CHIEF JUSTICE and by him referred to the Court
> is DENIED.*

Four justices—William Brennan, Thurgood Marshall, Harry
Blackmun, and John Paul Stevens—voted to block John's execution,
but it wasn't enough. I told John he had less than two hours to live.
He didn't seem surprised by the news.

After several years on Death Row, John had a long beard, and his hair hung down almost to his waist. But inside, there was a part of John that was still so much a child. He'd never had a real chance to outgrow his childhood. For his last meal, he asked for twelve hot dogs "all the way" and two Cokes. He wanted to wear his favorite boots and his favorite shirt for the execution, which the prison allowed.

Heavyhearted and despondent, I left John's side that night just before the execution, before the state strapped him to a gurney and rolled him, flat on his back, into the execution chamber. He had asked me to be in the witness room, but I told him, as I had before, that I couldn't bear to watch, and I couldn't be in the same room with people who were there for the purpose of seeing him die. John told me he had an idea about how we could still be together even if I wasn't there with him physically. He said he would imagine, as he lay on the gurney waiting for the lethal drugs to be injected, that he was sitting on a Harley-Davidson motorcycle needing a jump start. He explained that while he was growing up, he loved to ride motorcycles, but he always had to start them by going down a hill until the engine kicked on. He asked me to imagine—at precisely 2:00 a.m., the scheduled execution time—that I was pushing him on a Harley, that I was pushing him down a hill to jump-start it. He would imagine the same. And that way, he said, we would be there together. At 2:00 a.m., I closed my eyes and pushed John down the hill on the Harley.

There was, in the end, a humanity to John, despite his horrendous crime. And there is a humanity to everyone charged with a crime. None of us wants that humanity to be forgotten or discarded, no matter what we may have done in the moment.

I left Central Prison that night and watched the hearse take John's body to the North Carolina medical examiner's office, although I had no idea why they had to do that. They knew what had killed him. As I left, a small group of death-penalty opponents outside the main entrance was singing softly—I can no longer remember the song. Up on a hill overlooking the prison, there was a large group of what appeared to be college students, laughing and drinking, wearing Wolfpack colors, singing, "Na Na Na Na, Na Na Na Na, Hey Hey Hey, Goodbye." I spent the rest of that night comparing that scene to the kindness John Rook had shown me a few minutes before he died. I didn't sleep that night, but not because I had represented John Rook.

Part II

RACE AND THE ABUSE OF POWER IN THE CRIMINAL JUSTICE SYSTEM

3

DUE PROCESS IN THE CRIMINAL JUSTICE SYSTEM

Most people today take for granted the rights afforded to those charged with crimes—such as the right to an appointed lawyer if you can't afford one, and even the right to remain silent. But those rights didn't exist in state courts prior to 1940. It took another young and idealistic criminal defense lawyer to lay the groundwork for many of the rights and civil liberties we now take for granted.

The 1960s and '70s were a time of intense cultural upheaval in the United States. The civil rights movement rightfully garnered most of the attention in the sixties, followed by the antiwar movement in the seventies. Less publicized, but as radical in its own way, was the transformation of the criminal justice system in the United States during those decades, led by the Supreme Court of Chief Justice Earl Warren between the years 1953 and 1969.

Earl Warren, a Republican and former governor of California, was appointed to the Supreme Court in 1953 by Republican president Dwight Eisenhower. The decisions of the Warren Court in criminal cases such as *Gideon v. Wainwright*, which required states to provide criminal defendants an attorney if they could not afford to hire their own, and *Miranda v. Arizona*, which gave life to the right to remain silent, would bring the concept of due process to the state courts and fundamentally alter how criminal defendants were *supposed* to be treated—although the actual process too often fell short of what was due.

These historic decisions of the Warren Court were made possible by another case—one that came before the Supreme Court two decades earlier—involving four young Black men wrongfully convicted of murder in Florida, and a courageous lawyer who fought for their freedom against impossible odds. The case would change the face of the criminal justice system in the United States forever.

In 1930, in the height of the Great Depression, a Black man from Maryland named Thurgood Marshall decided he would try to make a difference in the world. In some respects, he was a product of America's enduring history of racial injustice—Marshall's ancestry, on both sides of his family, included persons who had been owned as slaves in the American South. Growing up in the United States in the early twentieth century, he'd experienced firsthand the degradation and hatred of racial prejudice that was omnipresent in the social fabric of that era, and which continues still to this day.

After graduating from an all-Black college, Marshall applied to law school in Baltimore, the city where he lived, but was denied admission on the basis of his race. As he well knew, this was hardly unusual at the time, but it could not, and would not, lessen his trajectory. Steadfast, he applied, and this time was granted admission, to the Howard University School of Law in Washington, D.C. In 1933, he graduated first in his class. Before the end of his first decade of practice, when he was still a new lawyer, he argued what was to become a landmark case before the U.S. Supreme Court.

The case was *Chambers v. Florida* (1940), and it arose out of the murder of Robert Darcy, an elderly white merchant, in Pompano, Florida. There were no eyewitnesses to the attack, but it was believed by some that a group of transient Black men in the area were to blame. The murder ignited runaway racial hostilities that were then borne upon and heightened by the mob mentality of those wanting justice. A frenzied search was conducted for the killers, and hunting dogs were set upon their trail. Some in the community sought blood in retribution for the killing, and the specter of further violence increased pressure on the police to quickly solve the murder and identify the killers. More than three dozen Black men were rounded up and taken into custody by the police.

After five relentless days of questioning and abuse that culminated in an all-night interrogation session attended by vigilantes from the community, four men finally succumbed and offered confessions to the murder. Their names were Isiah Chambers, Jack Williamson, Charlie Davis, and Walter Woodward. Throughout the period of questioning, they had not been allowed access to an attorney or anyone other than their interrogators. Day after day, time and again, each man had been brought singly into a stifling room, where he was angrily confronted by several officers, the county sheriff, prison guards, and members of the community, all of whom were seething white men. Over the course of the week, the suspects were made to realize the inevitability of their circumstance and the futility of further resistance. They gave empty confessions to end the inquisition.

Chambers, Williamson, Davis, and Woodward were quickly convicted on the basis of their confessions and were sentenced to death. To many, the case seemed open and shut. The suspects had murdered a white man and confessed, so the argument went, and now they deserved to die, as so many of their brothers had, except this time it would be in the electric chair rather than at the end of a rope. The mere fact that the men were Black meant they were undeserving of sympathy and salvation. Sadly, this sentiment was implicitly embraced by the Florida courts, which saw no wrong in the manner in which the confessions were extorted from the defendants. The Florida Supreme Court upheld the convictions on appeal, which all but guaranteed the men's doom. They were left with no further recourse under state law in Florida.

Thurgood Marshall undertook representation of the four defendants, who were then prisoners of the state awaiting execution. He envisioned an unprecedented avenue of justice for the men, one that did not rely on Florida's laws governing the rights of criminal suspects, which were not offended by the barbarous treatment afforded the defendants. Instead, Marshall sought refuge for the men under the United States Constitution. Marshall believed there were broad due-process protections implicit in the Fourteenth Amendment that applied to the states, and that the Florida police violated the federal constitutional rights of the defendants in obtaining their confessions through terror and violence. It was this argument that was advanced by Marshall in his first argument to the U.S. Supreme Court.

Among the justices seated in stern contemplation on the venerable bench in front of Marshall that day was Justice Hugo Black. Prior to taking a seat on the Supreme Court, Black was not known for his support for minority rights. Indeed, in rural Alabama, where he had worked as a lawyer, he was once a member of the Robert E. Lee Klan No. 1. It was rumored that Black had even been given a lifetime membership to the Ku Klux Klan when he announced his run for the U.S. Senate. As a senator, he repeatedly opposed the passage of anti-lynching laws during a time when extrajudicial hangings and similar hate crimes were tragically prevalent and often ignored by law enforcement. Marshall surely knew about Black's questionable history with race as he stood for the first time from the counsel table and prepared to make his argument before the Supreme Court—an argument he made not only on behalf of his clients, but also on behalf of citizens in every state whose rights had been, and would continue to be, unfairly infringed upon, denied, and disregarded under state law. The case had the potential to change civil rights in this country forever.

If Justice Black remained hostile, or at least indifferent, to racial equality, it did not interfere with his receptiveness to Marshall's argument. Not only did Justice Black find the argument persuasive, he may have even been moved by it. He delivered the Court's majority opinion, which overturned the convictions of the four Black men and ensured they would receive a new trial.

In the opinion, the Court held—for the first time—that state officials were subject to the due-process clause of the U.S. Constitution. Justice Black wrote that due process of law is "preserved for all by our Constitution," regardless of "race, creed or persuasion," and that "all people must stand on an equality before the bar of justice in every American court." Black's opinion, in truly inspired rhetoric, helped establish an ideal for the American judicial system—to serve as a harbor, a fortress, and a sanctuary for all persons, including minorities and those marginalized by society:

> *Under our constitutional system, courts stand against any winds that blow as havens of refuge for those who might otherwise suffer because they are helpless, weak, outnumbered, or because they are nonconforming victims of prejudice and public excitement.*

The decision in *Chambers v. Florida*, which was announced on the anniversary of the birth of Abraham Lincoln, proved to be a watershed moment in American criminal justice. It made possible the historic string of Warren Court opinions articulating and expanding due-process rights that form the foundation of our criminal justice system today. In addition to *Gideon* and *Miranda*, between 1961 and 1969, the Warren Court decided multiple cases that extended protections to criminal defendants in state courts.

These included *Mapp v. Ohio* (precluding the use of illegally seized evidence in state courts), *Douglas v. California* (guaranteeing indigent state defendants the right to appeal their convictions), *Brady v. Maryland* (requiring state prosecutors to provide exculpatory evidence to criminal defendants), *Ker v. California* (holding that the Fourth Amendment protection against unreasonable searches and seizures applied to the states), *Malloy v. Hogan* (holding that the Fifth Amendment privilege against self-incrimination applied to the states), *Escobedo v. Illinois* (affirming the right to remain silent in state proceedings), *In re Gault* (providing that juveniles were entitled to due process in state courts), and *Duncan v. Louisiana* (extending the right to a jury trial in criminal cases to the states), among others. That all of these federal constitutional rights applicable to the states were not recognized by the U.S. Supreme Court before 1961 is difficult to comprehend. The Warren Court was the golden age of individual protections against the abuse of power by those in positions of authority. That it was largely contemporaneous with the civil rights movement was likely not coincidental.

After *Chambers*, Thurgood Marshall went on to argue and win an astonishing twenty-eight cases before the U.S. Supreme Court. In 1967, Marshall joined the Warren Court as the first Black Supreme Court Justice in history. He remained on the Court until 1991, when he resigned due to his failing health. He was replaced by Clarence Thomas, a Black conservative who was as much a polar opposite to Marshall as Amy Coney Barrett is to another iconic litigator who ascended to the Court after winning many arguments before it, Ruth Bader Ginsburg.

4

SOUTHERN JUSTICE

Charles Ray Finch, a Black man living in rural Wilson, North Carolina, was accused, tried, and convicted of killing a white man in 1976. Contrary to the many protections established by the U.S. Supreme Court for the benefit of criminal defendants, Ray was deprived of his liberty through an array of stunning abuses of power by police, prosecutors, and judges that spanned a period of more than four decades. I first met Ray in 2013, when I helped represent him at a hearing, ultimately unsuccessful, to vacate his conviction. Ray's long and storied journey through the criminal justice system began on February 13, 1976, on a brisk Friday evening in Wilson, a small city in eastern North Carolina known for its tobacco, barbecue, and local politics.

To tell Ray's story, you have to start downtown, on the east side of the railroad tracks, where poverty was visible in the storefronts and on the sidewalks, and on the lined faces of people walking the street as the day faded from light to dark. There was, I imagine, a feeling of angst in the air on this particular evening—a kind of low-boil anxiety felt in the gut with the coming of night after a hard week of work, with not enough of anything to go around.

In the stagnant back room of Tom Smith's Shoeshine Parlor,

Black men in blue-collar shirts were playing poker. An industrial light, rigged up with exposed wiring, hung from the low ceiling in a haze of cigarette smoke. Paper bags concealed six-packs of beer on the floor at the men's feet, and here and there was an empty bottle of wine. It was a low-stakes game: a dollar of the week's paycheck or a handful of change got you a seat at the table. Ray was one of the men playing cards that night at the shoeshine parlor. Soon he'd get a message from his girlfriend, the mother of his youngest child, telling Ray they were out of diapers. Ray would leave the game to run that errand before returning downtown.

Not far south, just past world-famous Parker's Barbecue on Highway 70, a man with a shotgun under his coat was standing watch on the porch of a tumbledown house hidden in a grove of trees. Inside, sheets of plywood lay over holes in the floor and boards covered the windows, but a fancy electric motor and switch controlled a sturdy metal door to the entrance, almost like something you'd see in a jail. The county sheriff, off work but still in his uniform, lounged at a table with three other white men, playing lowball and dice. Here, the ante was significantly higher than at the game downtown. They'd sometimes go as high as a thousand dollars a hand.

Five minutes farther down the road was a haphazard quartet of low-roofed, low-rent buildings known as the Forest Inn Motor Court. Behind windows illuminated by a neon sign, the girls of one of the local cathouses—and there were several—were dressing and getting ready for another evening of work. They were told to expect a busy night: in addition to the usual clientele, a few special customers, high-profile types, were being shuttled in from the state capital. Two patrol cars idled in the parking lot, but the girls and their madam knew they wouldn't get any trouble from the police.

Finally, another two miles south was Holloman's Grocery, one of the area's innumerable country stores, and the site where this tragedy began to unfold. Holloman's sat on a lonely stretch of road south of Wilson, surrounded by farmland and the occasional family cemetery. Barns and grain silos were more prevalent here than houses.

At 9:05 p.m. on this raw February night, Holloman's store was the scene of a violent armed robbery that left one man dead, one man imprisoned, and a trail of intrigue and deceit that took more than forty years to unravel.

Holloman's Grocery was owned and operated by Richard Linwood Holloman. People called him Shadow. His store was packed into a small whitewashed block building right up on the road, with windows shielded by bars of rusted iron and naked lightbulbs hanging from the eave. A hand-corrected sign outside advertised regular gas at 53 cents a gallon. Inside was a jumbled and dusty hodgepodge of grocery and convenience items, from hot dogs to belts for your car. A Bally Champ pinball machine sat unplugged and unused in the corner, except as one more place to stack things. Between the rows of shelves and drink boxes, there was hardly room enough to turn around.

Three weeks prior, Shadow had been in court on a charge of dealing in stolen goods. A couple of weeks later, someone broke out a high window in the back room of his store and tried to climb in, but didn't succeed. Shadow took to carrying a gun.

Lester Floyd Jones, whose nickname was Turnip Toe, worked for Shadow and pumped all the gas, but he wasn't allowed to handle any of the money. On this Friday evening, Jones and Shadow were talking about their plans for the weekend when Noble Harris came in and shook off the cold. Noble lived nearby and was a regular at Holloman's Grocery. He was known locally for two things: driving without a license, and an overly fond enjoyment of alcoholic beverages. He walked up to the counter and said to Shadow, "I need a beer and a quart of grapes." Shadow pretended not to understand about the grapes, but then handed over a bottle of cheap wine and a bottle of even cheaper beer. He then told Noble that he was closing the store early that night, to let him know he couldn't come back later to get more if he ran out, which was pretty typical for Noble.

At approximately 8:30 p.m., a car pulled out of the gravel parking lot of the Forest Inn Motor Court and drove in the direction of

Holloman's store. It slowed as it passed Holloman's, then turned off onto a narrow backroad that looped up and around to the west. Out of sight from the store, with woods in between, the driver pulled the car into the grass on the side of the road. Three men climbed out of the car carrying objects unseen. Without a word between them, they set off on foot into the woods toward Holloman's store, a faint glow of light half a mile away.

Just before 9:00 p.m., Shadow told Jones it was time to lock up for the evening. Shadow was closing early, he said, because he was going to a "steak party." He and Jones put on their coats and turned off the lights. They went outside together, and Shadow padlocked the heavy front doors. Jones noticed, without surprise, that Shadow had his gun drawn and visible.

As Shadow and Jones stood there talking in the cold, Jones noticed three Black men walking south down the road toward the store—which was odd, because the store was really too far from anywhere for people to be getting there on foot by way of the road. The three men left the highway and headed into the parking lot. One man stopped in the darkness, just out of clear sight, and remained there. The other two came right up to the door where Shadow and Jones were standing.

One of the men said, "Can I get an Alka-Seltzer?" He was wearing a red-and-white-checkered shirt and light-colored pants. The second man, who said nothing, had one leg of a woman's stocking over his head, according to the statement Jones later gave the police. Despite these unusual and concerning circumstances, Shadow replied, "I reckon so," fumbled in his pocket for the keys, took off the padlock, and reentered the store for the Alka-Seltzer—all the while clutching his gun. He was followed into the store by Jones and two of the men.

Inside the store, Shadow didn't turn on the lights. Instead, he relied on the faint illumination provided by a Budweiser clock above the pinball machine in the back. He went to retrieve the antacid, while Jones and the men waited on the other side of the counter. Jones was talking to Shadow's back, evidently oblivious to any possible dangers. Jones was close enough to the man next to him to "reach out and slap him," as he told the court and the jury at Shadow's murder trial.

Shadow asked if the man wanted water to go with the Alka-Seltzer, and the man said, "And your money, too." Shadow hotly responded, "Money, hell," and raised his gun. In a split second, all hell broke loose. The man standing next to Jones, like an outlaw in an old western, came out with a sawed-off shotgun from under his coat. He fired point-blank across the counter at Shadow, striking him in the chest. Jones dove to the floor and hid behind some shelves. He heard other shots being fired, shots ricocheting throughout the store, then heard the door banging open and closing again. Shadow, somehow still standing, was spilling blood between the pinball machine and the counter. He walked to the store's phone behind the cash register and picked it up to call the police. He then called for Jones, who came out of hiding and leapt over the counter to take the phone and call an ambulance. Shadow walked around the counter and fell face-first onto the floor.

Lester Floyd Jones was the only witness to Shadow's murder, and he was the person who provided all these intriguing details to the police. How he avoided being shot in such close quarters seemed miraculous and mysterious.

The paramedics were quick to arrive. They found Shadow lying unresponsive in the doorway, with his set of false teeth nearby. He was rushed to Wilson Memorial, where he was pronounced dead. In seeming contradiction to Jones's account, Shadow's body showed a single entry wound on his neck, near his collarbone, and a second entry wound high on his back right shoulder, as if the shooter had been standing above him when the shot was fired. A possible third entry wound appeared on his back, close to his right shoulder blade.

Word of Shadow's murder spread quickly, and locals, rattled by the news, began arriving at the store in droves to find out what happened. This was the third such robbery and murder of the owner of a country store in recent times in Wilson, and it sent multiplying waves of shock through the town. Before long, the roadside lot in front of Holloman's was full of cars, flashing lights, and citizens who were bewildered and frightened by another horrific murder.

A state trooper named Larry Richardson was the first law enforcement officer on the scene. He gave Jones a pen and paper and told him to write down exactly what happened. Jones wrote:

> We Had closed and 3 Black Males came up Walking and asked if They could get an alkaselsa and We Unlocked and Went in and The 1 Male With a Stocking over His Head said This is a Robery and drew a Sawed off Shoot Gun and Blasted at Mr Hollowman one Had a Black cap on The other Had a Tobogen on They were Walking.

Richardson took the paper from Jones and, after interrogating him for further details, wrote, "Checked shirt Toebogging." Below that, he wrote, "Black Pont / 1 Light Out on Back." "Pont" presumably referred to "Pontiac." Later that night, Jones augmented his account to add an important new detail—that the man with the sawed-off shotgun was wearing a long black coat.

After Jones gave his statement to Trooper Richardson, he went back inside the store. There Jones was captured in a photograph by a local newspaper photographer, who somehow got in the store before it was secured by the police. The photographer took a number of photos—one showing a mysterious gun resting in a chair, with a coat draped carefully over the arms of that chair—unknowingly capturing evidence that would become relevant in legal proceedings decades later.

Chief Deputy Tony Owens, the second in charge of the Wilson County Sheriff's Department, was for some reason parked only a mile away in his police car when the shooting occurred. He arrived within minutes. Once Owens was on the scene, there was no mistaking who was in charge. For many years, Owens was the law and order in Wilson County. He was tall and lean, but strong, with a helmet of dark hair and a dark mustache. He wore his uniform like he expected people to respect it, and they did. Even though he was only the chief deputy, he essentially ran the sheriff's department on a day-to-day basis. Very little happened in the county that Owens didn't know about. He wielded power over the police and criminals alike, born out of knowing how to exploit the system better than anyone else. He was damn smart, even cunning. People knew that you underestimated Chief Deputy Owens at your own peril.

Upon arriving at Holloman's store, before speaking with Jones or examining the crime scene, Chief Deputy Owens announced to everyone in earshot that he already had a suspect in mind: Ray Finch. Right away Owens put out an APB—an all-points bulletin—on Ray, who at the time was living half a mile through the woods from Holloman's store. Owens had known Ray for years, at least as far back as 1965, when Ray was the state's main witness in a murder trial that implicated Owens's uncle in a killing.

Owens later claimed the sheriff's department had a tip that Ray was going to rob a country store that night, so the sheriff's department was "staking out" various stores in Wilson County. He couldn't explain why, if the tip was specific to Ray and not to any particular store, he didn't just have Ray followed by an unmarked car. Wilson County had more than a hundred country stores in 1976, and only a handful of deputies, such that staking out all the stores would have been impossible. Owens later claimed that he was just lucky to have been so close to Holloman's store when the murder occurred.

After putting out the APB for Ray, Owens asked Noble Harris, who had returned to Holloman's in the midst of all the commotion, if he saw Ray at the store earlier in the evening. Noble thought about it and said he might just remember seeing Ray's car pulling into the parking lot when he (Noble) was leaving after getting his beer and wine. Noble said this would have been "just the edge of dark," when it was "just getting dark good." In February in North Carolina, this would have been around six o'clock. Noble thought maybe Ray had pulled in to get gas.

Nobody else on the scene seemed to know anything about the robbery and murder. It was time for Owens to go inside Holloman's store to collect the forensic evidence.

The store was a mess, but it always was. Merchandise was stacked and piled everywhere. Once inside, Owens carefully stepped over a pool of clabbering blood on the floor from where Shadow had fallen. Lester Floyd Jones had said that nothing was taken in the robbery, but Jones also said that Shadow was holding a money bag and fell on top of it when he went down. Now the money bag was nowhere to be found. Owens knew Jones from the two of them playing pool together from time to time, and he was aware that Jones wasn't the smartest or most reliable guy you'd meet. He also knew that Jones had a problem with alcohol and was only working at Holloman's because he lost his last job driving a truck after getting caught drinking and driving.

Owens walked slowly, deliberately, around the store. He found more blood at the far end of the counter, near the pinball machine,

Behind the counter at Holloman's store. In the chair rests a gun, and Shadow's coat is draped around the back of the chair.

and surmised this was where Holloman was shot. Under the pinball machine, on the ground, lay a single paper cup—the water cup for the Alka-Seltzer, most likely. Nearby, an open padlock rested in a spray of blood. A bottle of ketchup and other condiments sat on the counter, never having been put away for the evening. Owens observed another curious detail: the cardboard display boxes of Nabisco crackers in a wire rack on the counter showed numerous small, pinpoint holes. He made a note about this.

Owens then saw that the concrete-block wall behind the pinball machine had a cluster of pockmarks that he thought might be the result of errant buckshot from a shotgun. Using his pocketknife, Owens picked lead out of the wall, out of the lighted Budweiser clock, and from the floor behind the pinball machine, and bagged the fragments.

He then knelt down and discovered a handful of empty shells

from a .38 revolver littering the floor behind the counter. He guessed at a trajectory, followed it, and found an array of spent rounds across the back wall of the store—shots from the .38 that missed their mark. Owens bagged these, but they didn't come into evidence at trial, and in time they just disappeared altogether.

Owens then moved over to look at the cash register. Behind it, in the narrow, cluttered space between the counter and the wall, was the wooden chair Holloman sat in, day in and day out. Right there in Holloman's chair was a handgun, like someone left it there on purpose to be found. Owens picked it up, opened the cylinder, and counted the number of empty shells. It was the same gun that was visible in a newspaper photograph printed the next day. Incredibly, the photograph, when examined, contains a second clue: It showed Shadow's coat draped neatly around the back of the chair. Jones later told the court that, after being shot in the chest at close range by a shotgun, Shadow took off his coat and put it over the arms of the chair. Neither the gun nor the coat found by Owens were bagged for evidence or examined.

While Owens was taking his inventory of evidence, the Wilson Police stopped Ray Finch's blue Cadillac in downtown Wilson. In the car with Ray was a man named Charles Lewis. Charles was familiar to the police. He lived at the Forest Inn Motor Court and had had several previous confrontations with the law. He wasn't known to associate with Ray, but oddly enough, the two men bore a strong resemblance to each other. Charles was wearing a red-and-white-checked shirt and light-colored pants, and Ray was wearing a long black coat. What appeared to be dried blood was visible on each sleeve of Ray's coat. Both men were handcuffed and taken to the police station for questioning regarding the murder of Shadow Holloman.

THE LINEUP

Chief Deputy Owens, having seen enough, left Holloman's Grocery and escorted Jones, who was waiting in the back of a patrol car, to the police station to have him view Ray Finch and Charles Lewis in a lineup. Once at the police station, Jones heard on a scanner that the police had arrested Ray for the murder. He'd met Ray before and then recalled that he had pumped gas for Ray at Holloman's store as recently as Wednesday that same week. In fact, Ray had an account at the store, which he sometimes used when he bought gas or beer.

Just after midnight, and less than four hours after Shadow's murder, Owens set up a lineup in a hallway above the Wilson County jail. Jones, waiting downstairs at the station, saw Ray and Charles Lewis being taken upstairs in handcuffs. Owens then brought up five other men from the jail in various states of attire to serve as stand-ins.

Ray was put into the lineup still wearing his long black coat. Jones hadn't said anything about the shooter wearing a long black coat to Trooper Richardson just minutes after the murder occurred, when his memory was still fresh. This new detail about the coat had become part of Jones's account only after he spoke with Chief Deputy Owens. In the lineup, Finch was the only person wearing any kind of coat. The men pulled out of the jail for the lineup didn't even look like they'd come from outside.

Chief Deputy Owens took Jones in a room off the hall and told him what to do. After walking up and down the hall in front of the men, all of whom had been given a number to hold up, Jones identified Ray as the man with the sawed-off shotgun who killed Shadow Holloman: the man with the long black coat. He did not pick Charles Lewis out of the lineup even though Charles was wearing a "checked shirt" like in the description Jones had given to Trooper Richardson right after the shooting.

Chief Deputy Owens then rearranged the order of the lineup and had Jones look again. Once again, Jones identified Ray. For a third time, Owens reordered the lineup, and for a third time in less than half an hour, Jones identified Ray as the shooter. He was certain.

While Ray took part in the police lineup, Deputy James Tant of the Wilson County Sheriff's Department searched Ray's car for evidence related to the robbery. He returned with a shotgun shell he claimed to have found in an ashtray in the back seat. It fit perfectly with Jones's story of a man killing Shadow with a sawed-off shotgun, and it connected Ray to the crime. They had him dead to rights.

That night or the following morning, Chief Deputy Owens provided a detailed account of Holloman's murder to the *Wilson Daily Times*, the local paper of record, saying that Holloman was felled by a shotgun blast. The newspaper declared, "Quick action by local law enforcement officers and the eyewitness account by Jones led to the arrest of Ray Finch." A second newspaper article from that same day reported, "Following [an] interrogation and a lineup, Finch was charged with murder and placed in the Wilson County jail."

5

WHITE JUSTICE

Within a few hours of Shadow Holloman's murder, Ray Finch had been identified in three separate lineups by the one eyewitness to the shooting, and the police had found blood on his coat and a shotgun shell in his car. The next day, Ray's name appeared on the front page of the city newspaper as the man responsible for the killing of Shadow Holloman, as well as specific details about how the murder was committed, including the fact that Shadow had been felled by a shotgun blast at close range. Even the medical examiner concluded that the cause of death was a "shotgun wound." For all intents and purposes, before a single day had passed, Ray Finch had already been convicted for Shadow Holloman's murder.

That Saturday, Ray woke up in the Wilson County jail. He was in a cell by himself, lying on a thin mat on the concrete floor. The events of the preceding evening seemed like a bizarre dream. It was his birthday—he was thirty-eight years old—and he'd just been arrested for killing Shadow Holloman. He wondered if his family had heard what happened and if they knew where he was. His girlfriend hadn't been home the previous evening when he'd dropped off diapers for their young daughter, and he hadn't talked to her since earlier in the day.

Ray knew Shadow Holloman pretty well. Ray grew up in Wilson County, where everybody knew everybody. For several years Ray and his father drove a tobacco truck out of Wilson all up and down the East Coast, from New Jersey to Florida and west into Tennessee. They rode together and took turns driving until his father got too old for it, and then Ray did most of the driving after that. He also worked at a local garage. Ray loved cars and enjoyed working on them, and people said he was so good that he could "build one from scratch."

Ray was from a big family and had brothers named Jimmy, Rufus, and Robert, whom everyone called Spanky. Ray also had a younger brother named David, who passed away in 1965. Ray had six children of his own, including two daughters who were exactly two days apart in age, which is another story altogether. For the past year or so he'd been living with his aunt and uncle in a house back behind Shadow's store. It was only a five-minute walk to the store through the woods. Ray had a charge account at Shadow's store and once had to give his class ring as collateral until he could bring the account current. Ray even sold Shadow a car, a '67 Pontiac, and not that long before. Shadow and Lester Floyd Jones met Ray in a parking lot off Goldsboro Street downtown to pick it up. Shadow paid Ray all but $150 toward the car and said he'd pay the rest when he got it. Now Shadow was dead.

In his thirty-eight years, Ray had never been accused of doing an act as horrible or as violent as what happened to Shadow Holloman. He'd been stopped a couple of times for nickel-and-dime stuff, but nothing of any real consequence. Nothing that should have put him on the permanent radar of the police. Still, the Wilson County Sheriff's Department maintained a keen and constant focus on Ray.

In Wilson, you had to pay to play, so to speak, and Ray wasn't paying. It was well-known around town that the sheriff's department took payoffs from the several gambling and prostitution houses in the county, as well as from anyone else who wanted or needed to get away with something, but Ray had no part of that. He sometimes gambled at Tom Smith's Shoeshine Parlor on weekends, as he was doing on the night Shadow was killed, but he'd never paid off the sheriff's department for the right to do it. In his mind, Ray knew the whole system was corrupt. He'd seen it himself in 1965, when his younger brother was shot and killed by a white man in Wilson who got off scot-free.

In the 1960s, race relations in the United States were at a flashpoint, and cities all over the country, particularly in the South, saw violence between white and Black in cases that frequently wound up on the criminal side of the courts. Such cases often ended with unfair results and unequal justice due to the racial prejudice that was baked into the judicial system. In countless jurisdictions, the courts were run by white prosecutors and white judges, with juries of all white men handing down the verdicts. All too often, the people in these roles quietly harbored or openly displayed insidious racist hostilities and allowed the justice they dispensed to be directed or influenced by those hostilities. The notion of a fair trial in the American South during this era was more farce than reality.

There is a body of law in this country, starting with the Bill of Rights, that purports to provide equal justice to all persons, regardless of their race or ethnicity, and irrespective of the wealth or poverty of the participants. However, as someone who has experienced this system firsthand for more than four decades, I knew, well before the Black Lives Matter movement, that equal justice is more an illusion than a reality. Even criminal laws of comparatively recent memory from the Reagan and Clinton administrations, such as mandatory-minimum sentences, laws aimed at the "war on drugs," and the infamous three-strikes rule, may have seemed facially neutral as to race, but were in fact aimed at the so-called super predators and had a severe and lasting disparate impact on persons of color. Even in the best of systems, designed with the best of intentions, outcomes are tainted by abuses of power and biases held by the system's participants. This problem continues today, stoked during the Trump presidency and his dog whistles to white supremacists, but was even more pronounced in the 1960s and earlier, when racial prejudices were more overt and more virulent.

A look at the February 19, 1965, *Wilson Daily Times* and the articles that appeared in that day's paper provide some historical context for the state of racial tensions nationally and in North Carolina at that time. The banner headline of the paper read:

Reprinted courtesy of the Wilson Times, *formerly the* Wilson Daily Times.

The accompanying article began, "Negro youngsters marched again today in the Brooklyn section where a brick-throwing, window-smashing mob ran wild. . . ." Another article on the front page described a separate racial protest in Alabama, stating, "One Negro was shot twice and at least eight other persons, including three newsmen, were beaten during a clash between Negro protestors and police on the first night march of the present voter registration campaign."

A third article in the same paper ran under the headline "Negro-White Gun Fight Ends in Murder Charge." This article was about Ray Finch and his youngest brother. It's a tragic story of corruption and abuse in the criminal justice system.

Ray's youngest brother was named David, after their father, but he went by the name of Pete. Pete was several years younger than Ray. Despite their age difference, Ray and Pete were close. On February 18, 1965, Ray and Pete found themselves in a gun fight with two white men off Highway 42 in Wilson. There were markedly differing accounts as to how the altercation began.

Ray's story was that he, Pete, and three of their friends, all young Black men, were walking through neighborhoods picking up bottles.

They were carrying a .22 rifle, which they claimed was for protection from a man named Henry "Junior" Owens, who lived nearby. According to what Ray told the police, Junior Owens had, on a prior occasion, accused the Black men of stealing his liquor and had come after them with a gun. Ray said they brought along their rifle just in case Owens saw them walking and came out to accost them.

Ray said that as he and the other young men were walking down the road, Junior Owens drove by, and men in Owens's car shot at them from the car windows. The car then sped away, and the young Black men, who had scattered, came out from hiding and started walking home. Then, according to Ray, the car returned and pulled over onto a side road, and two men armed with a shotgun and a hunting rifle got out of the car and again began shooting.

Junior Owens, on the other hand, told a different story. He said he was out "inspecting his plant beds" in the garden when a gang of Black men came by and shot at his car. Luckily, he just happened to have a shotgun with him, he said, and was able to return fire. When asked why he was carrying a shotgun in the garden, Owens, perhaps euphemistically, said there were wild dogs in the vicinity.

A friend of Junior Owens named Robert Curtis Ethridge was either summoned by Owens or was close by and offered to help track down the men Owens claimed had fired at his car. Ethridge had a .30–30 hunting rifle at home and went to retrieve it. Owens and Ethridge then got in Owens's car and began pursuing the Black men, who were on foot. According to Ethridge's own sworn testimony, upon nearing the Black men walking down the road, Owens pulled his car off onto a roadside path, and that's when the shootout began in earnest. The Black men ran and took refuge behind an abandoned house.

At this point in the story, the divergent accounts come together, and there is little dispute about what happened next. While Ray, Pete, and the others were concealed behind the abandoned house, Ethridge slipped away from Owens's car and hid beneath an old tobacco-barn shelter with his .30–30 rifle pointed across the street. Owens then drove away, leaving Ethridge in position. As Ray and Pete emerged from hiding, believing the shootout to have ended, a pair of shots rang out. Pete convulsed and lurched sideways before collapsing in a heap. Ethridge was seen running out from behind the barn and into the woods.

The coroner's report showed that a round from Ethridge's hunting rifle entered Pete's left side and traveled all the way through him, coming out the other side, along with his entrails. A second round struck Pete in the arm. He died in Ray's arms on the side of the road. He was just nineteen years old.

Ethridge was charged with first-degree murder and taken into custody. Junior Owens, despite admitting to police that he shot at the Finch brothers with a shotgun, was not arrested or charged in connection with the killing. The case was scheduled for trial.

Everyone in Wilson knew about the murder of Pete Finch and the trial of Robert Curtis Ethridge, and it was starkly apparent exactly what was at stake. It was white against Black, Black against white. It had happened many times before, and would happen again. Would a local jury convict a white man for killing a Black man? Would there be justice for the Black man who was mercilessly killed at the hands of a white man? Would it be a fair trial? Would the prosecutor work as hard to obtain a conviction of a white man who killed a Black man, as he would have in a trial where the roles were reversed? It was an important moment for race relations in Wilson and the role of the courts in achieving equal justice in an otherwise imperfect system, and the system failed.

The esteemed Judge William Hyslop Sumner Burgwyn was summoned out of retirement to preside over the trial. Burgwyn was born in Jackson, North Carolina, in 1886. He had been practicing in North Carolina's courts for fifty-seven years, with twenty-eight years on the bench, when the Pete Finch murder case came before him.

Burgwyn, a venerable jurist, was outspoken, highly opinionated, and known to maintain absolute control of his courtroom at all times. He also had a reputation, well earned, of being thoughtful, astute, and more pragmatic than academic. In his very first appearance on the bench after being appointed to serve as a special superior court judge in North Carolina in 1937, he issued a written order, without a case before him, requiring all of the school buses in the county to be serviced annually by a mechanic. He justified this unorthodox use of judicial power by noting the importance of school buses to the county. It seemed unassailable.

The trial began early on a Monday morning. The jury was empaneled quickly: it was composed of twelve white men. Not a single woman nor person of color was seated on the jury. The records of the trial that remain do not disclose how this came about, but it is easy to speculate that the defense quickly excused any Black juror who was eligible to sit, which was itself a rarity. In some counties at that time, the sheriff himself was asked by the clerk of court to screen the prospective jurors and eliminate any he deemed unqualified to serve.

The courtroom was full, and tensions were high. Ray Finch was called to the stand as the prosecution's chief witness. He testified that Owens and Ethridge started the gun fight and that Ethridge ambushed Pete and murdered him in cold blood. The three other men who were with Ray and Pete also took the stand and corroborated Ray's version of events. On Monday night, after the first tumultuous day of the trial, the judge sequestered the jury and had them locked up for the night.

On Tuesday morning, Junior Owens testified first for the defense and gave his version of events—which, in a just world, should have proved damning for the defendant. Ethridge then testified on his own behalf, claiming that even though he and Owens pursued Ray and Pete Finch in an automobile while they were on foot, his killing of Pete Finch had been purely in self-defense.

The defense's final witness was a local Black man named Johnny

Franklin Williams. His sole purpose was to impugn Pete Finch's character and reputation. The gist was "Pete Finch was a Black boy who may have needed killing."

After deliberating for just over an hour, the all-white, all-male jury reported to Judge Burgwyn that they had reached a verdict. Judge Burgwyn promptly stationed officers throughout the courtroom and warned the onlookers in the gallery that he would not allow demonstrations or outbursts of any kind. After silencing the murmuring crowd with several sharp bangs of the gavel, he read the verdict to the packed courtroom: Ethridge had been found *not guilty* and would go free.

At almost the same moment, in an extraordinary turn of events, Ray Finch was arrested and charged with contempt of court. Judge Burgwyn issued a bench warrant for Ray after overhearing Johnny Franklin Williams, the Black man who had testified for the defense as to Pete Finch's bad character, tell Chief Deputy Wilbur Robin Pridgen that Ray had cursed and threatened him following his testimony. Ray's trial for contempt began as soon as the other trial had concluded. He had gone from being a witness in the trial for his brother's murder to a defendant in his own right. The man who killed his brother would walk free, while Ray might wind up in jail.

Nine witnesses were called on Ray's behalf to testify that Ray had not cursed or threatened Williams. Judge Burgwyn dismissed the contempt charges but sent Ray out of court with a stinging rebuke. "I'm sick and tired," said the judge, "of people flouting the law and trying to run the courts themselves."

This was what justice looked like for two Black men—Pete and Ray Finch—in Wilson, North Carolina, in 1965. Eleven years later, when Ray was arrested for Shadow Holloman's murder, not much had changed.

Junior Owens was reputed to be the uncle of Tony Owens, who joined the Wilson County Sheriff's Department as a deputy soon after the trial for Pete Finch's murder. Tony Owens would not soon forget, nor forgive, the indignity of Ray Finch implicating Junior Owens in a racially motivated murder.

In September 1975, Chief Deputy Owens arrested Ray for breaking into Ferrell's Supply Company but had to release him when the true perpetrator was identified by the owner of the store. Court records show that the money taken from Ray by Chief Deputy Owens during the arrest—$86.86—was never returned to him. Five months later, Chief Deputy Owens would arrest Ray for murdering Shadow Holloman.

6

SPEEDY JUSTICE

Ray's family couldn't afford to hire a private lawyer, so the Court appointed Vernon F. Daughtridge to represent him. Daughtridge was a native North Carolinian and World War II veteran who started practicing law in 1952. He was a well-known and notable public citizen in Wilson, and you'd be hard-pressed to find a civic organization in town for which he hadn't either volunteered or served on the board in some capacity. He was a Mason, an Elk, a member of the American Legion, and was involved with the Red Cross, the March of Dimes, the Boy Scouts, and the Shriners, among others. He was active in the state Democratic party and was on hand to greet John F. Kennedy when he came through North Carolina on a campaign stop in September 1960. But Daughtridge was perhaps best known locally for his voice. Sporting a bow tie and a straw boater hat, he was a frequent performer at the annual Eastern North Carolina Singing Convention, which brought crowds of more than twelve thousand people. Less well-known were the portraits of Confederate officers and Nazi banners on display in Daughtridge's home.

Daughtridge harbored and cultivated modest political ambitions and served for a time as the president of the local bar association and the larger district bar association. In 1962, he ran for district attorney against a lawyer with much less experience—and lost. After that, his enthusiasm for public office seemed to dwindle, although there was never a day when you couldn't find him at or near the courthouse.

Like many small-town attorneys, Daughtridge was overworked and underpaid. In order to make ends meet, he handled a wide variety of cases, including estate matters, simple business disputes, and traffic tickets. And whether to supplement his income or because he believed in the cause, he also took on the defense of court-appointed death-penalty cases.

When Ray was arrested in February 1976, Daughtridge was in the middle of representing two other defendants in separate death-penalty cases, in addition to his other legal work. Despite Daughtridge's overwhelming workload, the Court scheduled Ray's murder trial for May 3, 1976, *less than three months after his arrest.* In truth, it is impossible for any attorney to adequately defend a murder charge that quickly, as the prosecutor and the judge obviously knew. Ray was accused of killing a white man in the South, and justice for him would be swift, if not fair. The Court would make sure he got a speedy trial whether he wanted one or not.

Court records show that on April 6, less than a month prior to the scheduled trial date, Daughtridge asked the Court to allow him to withdraw as Ray's attorney, saying that he did not have time to prepare for Ray's trial in light of the other death-penalty cases he was handling. He informed the Court that he had just defended, and lost, one death-penalty case and now faced looming appellate deadlines on behalf of his condemned client that required his immediate attention.

Naturally, the prosecutor objected to any delay in the trial, and the judge denied Daughtridge's motion to withdraw, leaving him with the burden of three simultaneous capital cases while he struggled to find time to construct a defense on Ray's behalf.

On April 29, just four days prior to the start of Ray's trial, Daughtridge filed a motion to postpone the trial for the same reasons set forth in his motion to withdraw—namely, that he had not had enough time to prepare Ray's defense. By this point, on the very eve of trial, Daughtridge had met with Ray for only a fraction more than an hour. Although the prosecutor again objected, this time the judge granted the motion and postponed the trial—but not for long. It was rescheduled for June 28, barely four months after Shadow Holloman's murder.

Then something odd happened. On May 4, as Ray waited in the Wilson County jail to be tried the following month, the resident superior court judge for Wilson County, Judge Albert W. Cowper, issued an order transferring Ray from the Wilson County jail to Central Prison in Raleigh, North Carolina. No party had made a motion asking that Ray be transferred to Central Prison, nor did the judge give an explanation for his order, other than to enigmatically state that Ray was being moved for "safekeeping." The order did not disclose why the judge thought Ray wasn't safe in the Wilson County jail or who Ray needed safekeeping from.

The impact of this order on Ray's case was dramatic. Central Prison, a maximum-security penitentiary that houses Death Row inmates, is a good fifty miles or more from Wilson. Daughtridge, already overburdened, was now forced to travel back and forth between Wilson and Raleigh if he wished to meet with his client in person, making trial preparation more difficult and costly. Daughtridge did not visit Ray even once in Central Prison, nor does it appear that Daughtridge spoke with Ray on the telephone during this time.

On June 3, less than a month prior to trial, Daughtridge filed a motion to have Ray brought back to Wilson, reciting that "in order to complete the preparation of the defense to this criminal action, it is necessary that the defendant's court-appointed counsel confer with him many and numerous times prior to such trial and that said defendant be made readily available to said court-appointed counsel for conferences with regard to his said defense."

On June 7, Judge Cowper ordered that Ray be returned to the Wilson County jail. *It was now twenty-one days to trial.*

According to court records, it was only then—three weeks out from the start of the trial—that Daughtridge truly began working on Ray's case, a case that might well end with a death sentence. The time records show that the vast majority of Daughtridge's trial preparation occurred after June 8, with a flurry of short witness interviews done in the ten days immediately preceding the trial. Daughtridge met with Ray for a *total* of only three and a quarter hours between February 17, 1976, when he was appointed to represent Ray, and June 28, 1976, the first day of Ray's trial. That's half a workday for a client the state was trying its best to execute.

Daughtridge, having been appointed by the Court to represent Ray, was compensated at a rate of $30 per hour for in-court hours and $20 per hour for time spent preparing for the trial out of court. The rates didn't even cover his office overhead—not exactly an incentive for any lawyer, let alone one struggling to handle three death-penalty cases at the same time, to go above and beyond a minimum effort. In the end, Daughtridge was paid a grand total of $1,577.70 for representing a Black man facing the death penalty for allegedly killing a white man in rural North Carolina in 1976. It was a bargain for the state of North Carolina. Not so much for Ray Finch.

Mr. Vernon F. Daughtridge
Attorney and Counsellor at Law
Post Office Box 885
Wilson, North Carolina 27893

State vs. Charles Ray Finch

Dear Mr. Daughtridge:

I am returning Application for Payment for Legal Services signed in triplicate on appeal in the above entitled case. I forwarded your application to the Administrative Office of the Courts on June 16 to obtain the assistance of the Court of Appeals as to what fee should be allowed. Response to my letter of June 16 dated July 26, 1977 was on my desk this morning when I returned from Surry County. The fee suggested was $1,530.00 plus your expenses making a total of $1,577.70.

With kindest regards, I am

Sincerely yours,

Walter E. Crissman

WEC:mn

Enclosures

On the first day of the trial, Ray was brought into court in shackles. He sat alone at the defense table while prospective jurors shuffled into the courtroom, looked about uncertainly, and took seats in the gallery to await being called. The judge was still in chambers. Below the empty bench, the court reporter was setting up her stenotype machine, and clerks were busy sorting papers, as a handful of deputy sheriffs loitered in chairs along the wall opposite the jury box, talking in low voices.

Ray's family and friends had arrived early, dressed in their Sunday clothes. They sat behind the defense table, whispering about the injustice of it all. Shadow's family and friends were also in the courtroom, but on the other side, behind the prosecution table, hoping to see swift justice done. Along these lines, the courtroom seemed naturally to fall into sides of black and white. Outside the courtroom, the prosecutor and Chief Deputy Owens were seen going into a small conference room with Noble Harris, who would be the state's first witness.

The courtroom was at first loud and raucous, but people soon became settled. The courtroom gradually grew quiet in anticipation of the opening of court, and as the clock struck 9:00 a.m., not a sound could be heard. A few minutes after the hour, the door to the judge's chambers swung open. The bailiff shouted, "All *rise!*" Everyone present came to attention and slowly got to their feet. The judge, robed in black, moved in solemnly from the open door and ascended to the bench. The bailiff, now addressing the courtroom as would a chorus in a Shakespearean tragedy, called out, "Oyez, oyez, oyez! This honorable court is now open and sitting for the dispatch of its business. God save the state and this honorable court! You may be seated."

Next to Ray at the defense table, Daughtridge nervously scribbled last-minute thoughts on a yellow legal pad. After several minutes of reviewing documents and taking notes, the judge looked up and surveyed the courtroom. Daughtridge motioned for Ray to stand. Ray's heart was pounding out of his chest. He was praying this was all some kind of terrible dream.

With a nod from the judge, the clerk of court stood and read from a handwritten script, a formality in death-penalty proceedings left over from English common law: "Now say you, Charles Ray Finch, are you guilty of the felony of murder whereof you stand indicted, or not guilty?"

Daughtridge answered for him: "Not guilty."

The clerk of court called out, "How will you be tried?"

Daughtridge, with dignity, responded, "By God and my country."

The clerk of court then said, "May God send you a true deliverance."

So began Ray Finch's trial for murder on June 28, 1976. After a four-day trial, featuring Lester Jones as the state's star witness, and indeed the only eyewitness, upon whose account the state's case rested, Ray was convicted on July 2, 1976, by a jury composed of eleven white jurors and (surprisingly) one Black juror. He was sentenced to death. The death warrant signed by the judge ordered Sheriff Wilbur Robin Pridgen to deliver Ray to the warden of Central Prison to await execution. The death warrant, in haunting language, directed Ray to "inhale lethal gas of sufficient quantity to cause death, and to continue said inhaling of said lethal gas by you until you are dead." The final words of the death warrant read: "AND May Almighty God have mercy on your soul."

Part III

BLACK, WHITE, AND GRAY IN THE CRIMINAL JUSTICE SYSTEM

7

THE FRONT LINES

While Ray Finch was growing up poor and Black in rural North Carolina, I was growing up in suburbia on Long Island, New York, about three miles east of JFK Airport. My parents were part owners of a family manufacturing business. My public high school was located in a wealthy, mostly Jewish neighborhood. We had only one Black student; his father was the Haitian ambassador to the United Nations. It was not a diverse cultural experience.

I attended Rutgers University, where I obtained a BA degree in political science and graduated from New York University School of Law in 1974. While I was in college and law school, the Vietnam War was raging, college students were murdered by National Guard troops in Ohio, and the Nixon administration imploded into indictments, impeachment, and Nixon's resignation. It felt like government could no longer be trusted. It couldn't.

Upon graduation from law school, I was offered a clerkship with a federal judge in New Jersey, but I turned it down. I also declined to work for a big Wall Street firm, as many of my classmates with similar academic records had chosen to do. Instead, I applied to be a public defender in Washington, D.C., and in New York City. I wanted to be on the very front lines of the criminal justice system, which has always been, and likely always will be, an uneven playing field for criminal defendants, particularly those who lack the financial resources necessary to hire a private lawyer. I wanted to protect individuals against the power of the government.

My first job out of law school was with the Legal Aid Society's Criminal Defense Division's office in the South Bronx, at the grand salary of $11,000 per year (about half what the Wall Street firms were paying for new graduates at that time), which increased to $13,000 if I passed the bar exam. We worked on the second floor of an otherwise burned-out building near the elevated subway tracks on 161st Street and Third Avenue in the Bronx. There were five of us in one large office, with one telephone on a long cord, which was passed around from desk to desk as needed. One of my "roommates" was Barry Scheck, who would go on to be part of the O. J. Simpson defense team and, more importantly, start and lead the nationwide Innocence Project, which has been responsible for exonerating hundreds of innocent men and women convicted of crimes they had not committed.

There were too many cases and not enough resources, but we all felt like soldiers in a war for justice. It was, in many ways, the best job I've ever had. I was part of something important and larger than myself.

Seeking new challenges, I transferred after about eighteen months to the Federal Defenders office in Brooklyn. I represented defendants charged with federal crimes who couldn't afford to hire their own attorney. Typical cases involved bank robberies, drug possession, and transporting firearms over state lines. My caseloads were lower, and I had better resources. It was a choice assignment, and I was lucky to get it.

In the late summer of 1976, while Ray Finch was on Death Row in Central Prison in Raleigh awaiting execution, I was living in an

apartment on the Upper West Side of Manhattan. I had been working at the Federal Defenders' office for less than a year. Unbeknownst
to me, a progression of events had been unfolding in New York and
elsewhere that would lead to my advocating for someone fighting
abuses of power on an international and historical scale.

8

TERRORISTS OR FREEDOM FIGHTERS?

On Friday, September 10, 1976, a young American woman stood in the security line at LaGuardia Airport waiting to board a flight to Chicago. She was holding a large gift-wrapped present. It was a cooking pot, she told airport security. A wedding gift for some friends. A man next to her carried a bag containing a substance that looked like modeling clay. He spoke in an unusual accent that a security guard thought sounded Slavic. The young American woman and the man passed easily through the security checkpoint and boarded TWA Flight 355.

It would never reach Chicago.

Ninety-two people were aboard the plane, including several children. At 8:19 p.m., as the plane flew over western New York State, the young American woman and four men took control of the aircraft. The pot and clay had now been convincingly assembled into what appeared to be a homemade explosive device. Wielding the device, one of the hijackers gained access to the cockpit. The pilot informed air-traffic control that a man was on the flight deck "with a bomb ready to explode by just pressing a button." The plane was redirected north, away from Chicago.

Just after 9:00 p.m., the plane landed in Montreal and was refueled.

From the tarmac, the pilot, at the direction of the hijackers, radioed the Federal Aviation Administration that a bomb had been placed in locker 5713 in Grand Central Terminal, one level below the street. The bomb squad was called in. The FAA scrambled to set up an emergency command center in Washington.

Inside the locker, the police found a pressure-cooker bomb, a set of demands, and two lengthy political statements on behalf of an unknown group calling themselves "Fighters for Free Croatia."

The first statement, a typewritten, eight-page document, was an impassioned manifesto in support of Croatian independence from Yugoslavia. It spoke with surprising eloquence of the 1,300-year history of the Croatian people and their language, and ardently championed a universal right of national self-determination, which had been denied Croatia since its forced integration under Yugoslav rule in 1918. This was followed by a grim summary of atrocities committed by the Yugoslav government against the Croatian people, including targeted political executions and "sophisticated, diverse, and bloody forms of torture." This was, according to the statement, all part of the Yugoslav government's "sustained and intentional extermination of the Croatian nation." One passage stated poetically, "A whip is cracked over the head of suffering Croatia."

The second statement, styled as an "Appeal to the American People," lent further insight into the hijackers' motivations. This document was only a single page in length. It recited, in plain language, that the objective of the hijacking was "to present an accurate picture of the brutal oppression taking place in Yugoslavia." The hijackers had found inspiration in the American struggle for independence, the statement claimed, but these noble, founding ideals had since been abandoned by the United States in favor of political and economic expediency, and its support for a totalitarian Yugoslav regime. "If our goal is accomplished," the hijackers wrote, "we gladly accept all punishment and consider these ideas worthy of suffering for."

The demands accompanying the political statements were simple yet extraordinary: the hijackers wanted the two political statements to be printed the following day in five major newspapers—*New York Times, Washington Post, Los Angeles Times, Chicago Tribune,* and *International Herald Tribune* (Paris)—or else a second bomb that had been planted "somewhere in the United States" would be triggered.

For a major newspaper to be commandeered and used to disseminate political propaganda was unprecedented in the United States. Out of concern for the hostages aboard the plane, the FBI contacted each of the newspapers and urged them to print the statements in full. Benjamin C. Bradlee, the executive editor of the *Washington Post,* reached out to his counterparts at the other publications. While understandably reluctant to comply with the hijackers' demands for fear of setting a dangerous precedent, the editors believed their refusal would result in the death of innocent hostages.

At 11:00 p.m., as the five newspapers grappled with whether to print the hijackers' demands, Flight 355 left Montreal and headed east. Once in the air, the hijackers opened suitcases full of propaganda leaflets. Their plan was to drop the leaflets over various cities, first in other parts of Europe and then in Croatia, but the pilot—who was not rated to fly internationally—advised this wasn't feasible due to the location of the engines under the wings of the plane. The leaflets, he said, would be sucked into the engines and cause the plane to crash. The hijackers quickly made a deal with the FAA's emergency command center: the plane would land temporarily in Newfoundland and release some number of passengers in exchange for another plane equipped for the aerial distribution of leaflets.

Meanwhile, Sergeant Terrence McTigue, an experienced explosives technician, and other members of the New York City bomb squad opened locker 5713. For reasons unknown, McTigue was not wearing a blast suit. As the bomb was extracted from the locker, it dropped to the ground, falling three feet onto the concrete floor. It bounced and rolled to a stop but did not detonate. After heart rates returned to more normal levels, the device was taken to the bomb-disposal site in Rodman's Neck in the Bronx to be detonated or defused.

Officer Brian Murray worked with Sergeant McTigue on the bomb squad. Murray was married and had two children, both boys, ages four and two. In the air force, he trained as a bomb-disposal expert and had worked on the bomb squad of the police department for five of his six years with the force. He had recently submitted an application to transfer to a position with less risk, but his lieutenant asked him to stay on another week. Murray was at a bar when he got the call to assist McTigue in defusing the bomb.

September 11, 1976. 12:45 a.m. At the deactivation site, the bomb was lowered into a pit. Murray and McTigue tried to defuse the bomb for several minutes using Vigilite remote wire cutters. Murray, McTigue, and two other officers then approached the bomb—again, without protective gear—at which point it exploded in their faces. Murray was killed instantly. McTigue was rushed to surgery and would remain on the operating-room table for fourteen hours. He was horribly disfigured by the blast. He lost one eye and several fingers. "Nobody had time to touch it," reported a spokesman for the police department. "It just went off." New York police commissioner Michael Codd was furious. He said, "What we have here is the work of madmen, murderers."

At 1:00 a.m., by agreement with federal authorities, the hijacked flight landed in Gander, Newfoundland, and thirty-five hostages were released as a Boeing 707 entered the airspace, bearing U.S. marshals and FBI agents. The Boeing 707 would lead Flight 355 first to France, and then to Croatia. The hijackers were not aware, and were not made aware, that the bomb left in Grand Central Terminal had exploded and taken the life of a police officer.

With the Boeing 707 in the lead, the two aircraft departed Newfoundland and flew east out over the Atlantic.

Sometime in the very early morning, perhaps as a result of the bomb that killed Brian Murray, four of the newspapers agreed to print the political tracts in their Saturday papers, with the *International Herald Tribune* being unable to comply because its Saturday edition had already been printed. Ben Bradlee wrote in his memoir that he didn't want to wake up the next morning to the headline "Hijackers Kill 62 Americans after U.S. Editors Refuse to Publish Documents."

At 6:57 a.m., Flight 355 and the Boeing 707 landed at Keflavik Air Base in Iceland to refuel. As the planes sat one behind the other on the runway, suitcases containing the propaganda leaflets were hurriedly carried from Flight 355 to the Boeing 707. Both planes then departed for London.

That Saturday, happily unaware that all of this international intrigue was underway, I walked down the street from my apartment to buy some bagels at H & H on Broadway and Eightieth and some lox and cream cheese at Zabar's on the next block. On the way, I picked up a copy of the *New York Times*. The headline of the paper announced:

Jet Out of LaGuardia Is Hijacked; Bomb Left in New York Goes Off

Uncharacteristic for the *Times*, the accompanying article had entire paragraphs out of order and contained a hodgepodge of errors, suggesting a frantic race by the paper to address the hijackers' demands and meet publishing deadlines, as last-minute details of the chaotic story emerged. The hijackers' first political statement appeared without explanation on page 7 of the paper, under the enigmatic heading "Text of 'Croatian Fighters.'"

Later that morning, about 11:00 a.m. EST, Flight 355 and the Boeing 707 entered British airspace. Once over London, Flight 355 circled above the city as, far below, the Boeing 707 came in low and released a blizzard of leaflets that drifted down onto Trafalgar Square and Hyde Park and littered the city streets. At Heathrow Airport, hundreds of heavily armed police officers waited at the ready. Once the leaflet drop had been completed, the two planes circled briefly over Daventry and then flew on to Paris.

Over Paris, the Boeing 707 again descended in altitude and began bombarding the city with leaflets from above. Meanwhile, Flight 355, which was low on fuel, requested permission to land at Charles de Gaulle Airport. French aviation officials, who wanted no part of the hijacking, refused and directed the plane elsewhere. The FAA's emergency command center in Washington made an appeal to French prime minister Raymond Barre, who personally intervened and instructed the airport to allow the hijacked plane and its escort to land.

In the United States, passengers freed in Newfoundland finally reached Chicago. Incredibly, at the request of the hijackers, they voluntarily carried with them stacks of the informational leaflets. A helicopter hired by TWA then took the leaflets up and dropped them over Chicago. Other helicopters dropped more leaflets over New York and Montreal.

Federal investigators interviewed the freed passengers, who provided a puzzling, unexpected account of the hijackers. "They were so polite, it was ridiculous," said one passenger. "The girl, who from her speech appeared to be an American, a blond Aryan-looking girl, acted almost like a stewardess, walking up and down the aisle talking politely to people and calming them." Despite being taken against their will under the threat of violence, many released hostages seemed to be sympathetic to the hijackers' cause.

The government in Yugoslavia had by then become aware of the hijacking and was apoplectic. The Yugoslav envoy in Washington was given orders to protest the dissemination of the hijackers' statements in the United States, but the leaflet drops continued.

Shortly after 6:00 p.m. local Paris time, Flight 355 and its escort landed on a remote section of runway at Charles de Gaulle. French military snipers quickly moved in and shot out the tires of Flight 355, almost guaranteeing that the hijacking would end one way or the other on French soil. Dick Carey, the pilot of Flight 355, who had already been pushed to his limits after more than sixteen consecutive hours of flying with a bomb at his back, lashed out at French authorities in the control tower, outraged that shots were fired at the aircraft. He yelled into the radio, "I am in charge of this plane!"

The hijackers now needed a new plane to take them to Croatia, but this seemed increasingly unlikely. A communication came over the cockpit radio: the government in Yugoslavia had informed the French and American authorities that any plane carrying the hijackers would be shot down if it entered Yugoslav airspace, regardless of who else was onboard.

The aircraft by this time was out of food and anything to drink, including alcohol—which the stewardesses, with permission from the hijackers, had freely distributed to the passengers once the hijacking began. The toilets were full and unusable. The passengers were restless and frightened, and desperation grew among the hijackers. Outside the plane, row upon row of French security forces carrying military weaponry could be seen moving into position.

The hijacker with the homemade bomb continued to stand behind the pilot, directing the increasingly futile communications with French authorities. The French authorities, however, made it clear they would not negotiate.

What followed was a grueling twelve-hour standoff between French authorities and the hijackers. During the stalemate, arrangements were made for the young American woman to leave the plane to confirm that the political statements had been published by the newspapers. A French officer approached and handed her a copy of the *New York Times* containing the first statement. Her eyes fell on the headline—"Jet Out of LaGuardia Is Hijacked; Bomb Left in New York Goes Off." She read the article with disbelief and horror. She refused to believe that the bomb had detonated and that a life had been taken. She thought it must have been a trick.

The French government then issued a stark ultimatum: surrender and be expelled from the country, or face execution in France by firing squad. The hijackers surrendered. The hostages were released, and the hijackers were taken into custody. Dick Carey, the pilot of Flight 355, described the ordeal as "thirty hours of hell."

It was soon learned that the man primarily responsible for the hijacking was Zvonko Busic. He was a Croatian-born political activist the Yugoslav government quickly characterized as a "militant nationalist" operating out of one of the "little fascist groups" that were "rampaging" in the United States. The young American woman, it was learned, was his wife. Her name was Julie Busic.

Zvonko, Julie, and the three other hijackers, who were Croatian, were made to choose whether to be returned to the United States for trial or be sent to Yugoslavia. They asked to be returned to the United States.

Since the plane had taken off from LaGuardia, which was located within the Eastern District of New York, they were brought back to face charges in the federal courthouse where I worked. They were flown to the United States in a French government plane and were greeted at Kennedy Airport by no fewer than forty FBI agents.

Zvonko and Julie were charged with the federal crimes of air piracy and death in connection with air piracy—the former charge having a mandatory sentence of life imprisonment, the latter being punishable by death. They also faced the specter of a separate murder charge in state court, which in New York might have meant the electric chair.

Over the weekend, I watched the events unfold on the news and in the papers. On Monday at the Federal Defenders office, I was told that Julie Busic was my new client.

9

SHADES OF GRAY

I first met Julie at the Metropolitan Correctional Center (MCC), a high-rise federal holding facility in Manhattan, in one of the spartan, dimly lit attorney-client conference rooms on the third floor. She was young—only twenty-seven years old—but she was older than I was at the time. I kept this to myself. She sat at a small wooden table in the middle of the room, her hands shackled to a belt that went around her waist. Behind her was a heavy steel door with a thick pane of industrial security glass that distorted and darkened the light passing through it. The door I had entered, also steel, closed slowly and locked behind me with an unsettling finality, reminding me, if I had forgotten, that I was in a federal jail and that freedom was more fragile and more tenuous here than in the outside world.

The MCC, which is now sometimes referred to as the "Guantánamo of New York," was relatively new in 1976. Since then, over the years, it has housed a number of notable criminals, including John Gotti, El Chapo, Bernie Madoff, Ramzi Yousef (who was convicted in connection with the 1993 World Trade Center bombing), and, most recently, Paul Manafort and Jeffrey Epstein.

Julie was, predictably enough, dressed in the usual orange jumpsuit prison inmates are given to wear. Her blond hair was unadorned, except for a single flowered barrette that held her hair back on one side. She looked up and smiled when I came in, but her face showed worry and exhaustion. I could tell she'd been crying.

"I don't understand how this could have happened," she said. "Instructions were left in the locker on how to disarm it. It was never supposed to go off. No one was supposed to get hurt."

She asked if I had any more information about how the bomb had been detonated. I told her I was trying to find out. Police said initially that a remote detonator had been employed, but that story was inconsistent with other facts that had emerged about the explosion. Julie again began to cry.

In that first meeting, she told me she'd grown up in Oregon, where her parents still lived, and had worked as a teacher and a nurse's aide. Her father was a tenured professor at Portland State University and an avid book collector. She met Zvonko—whose nickname was Taik—while traveling in Vienna, Austria, in 1969, and they soon fell in love. His cause for a free Croatia soon became her cause, and she believed it a just and worthy cause—one worth going to prison for, if it came to that.

From Austria, Zvonko moved to Cleveland, Ohio, in 1969, to be with Julie. In November 1970, he dispatched Julie to Zagreb, the largest city in Croatia, with a plan to disrupt Yugoslav Republic Day—a national holiday—by dropping, from Zagreb's tallest building, leaflets that called attention to President Josip Broz Tito's human-rights abuses. The leaflets drifted down like snow on the people celebrating in the square below. She completed the mission successfully but was immediately arrested.

The law she violated by distributing the material—Article 118 of the Yugoslav Criminal Code, titled "Hostile Propaganda"—carried a sentence of up to twelve years in prison. Julie's brazen act, which came on the heels of a visit to Yugoslavia by then-president Richard Nixon, caused quite a diplomatic row between the United States and Yugoslavia. Julie was ultimately treated with leniency and expelled from the country. A U.S. State Department report about the incident suggests that Nixon's visit to Yugoslavia likely saved Julie from extended incarceration in a Yugoslav prison.

Zvonko and Julie were married in 1972 in Frankfurt, Germany. Later that same year, when the couple was residing in Austria, Zvonko was expelled from Austria for his political activities there. He was given only one day to leave the country. Thereafter, he and Julie returned to the United States.

Zvonko was born in a small Croatian village in 1946 and had long advocated for that country's independence. He believed, with good evidence, that he had become a marked man in the eyes of the Yugoslav government under President Tito, the Yugoslav strongman who held the disparate countries in the federation together through fear and violence. The Yugoslav secret police—known as the UDBA—had been targeting and murdering political dissidents living abroad, and Zvonko believed this had been done with the tacit support of the U.S. State Department. By September 1976, there had been no fewer than ten murders of Yugoslav political dissidents living in exile in that year alone, and Zvonko Busic believed he would soon be next. He felt he had to take significant action, not only for himself, but for all Croatians.

Zvonko, Julie, and the other hijackers knew they would go to prison for their actions, and that the prison terms might be significant. They did not anticipate, however, that the bomb left in Grand Central would kill Brian Murray and maim three other officers. This dramatically altered the calculus of their eventual punishment.

Over time, I came to understand and even respect Zvonko and Julie's motivations and goals, if not their means. If you just read the newspapers and looked no further, you would see Zvonko and Julie described repeatedly as remorseless terrorists and murderers. But, as is often the case, the reality was much more nuanced. The issues they fervently believed in and wished to publicize—not just the cause of

Croatian independence, but also American complicity in helping to keep Tito in power—were profound, historic, and important.

As history has established, Tito was a ruthless dictator who abused every aspect of his power. There was no rule of law in Yugoslavia, and what scant civil liberties existed were routinely abridged or done away with altogether. There were no avenues for obtaining legal redress for harms done against private citizens by the government, and anyone found to be publishing commentary critical of the government faced harsh punishment. The atrocities committed by Tito were eerily reminiscent of those inflicted by Stalin and Hitler—and it was disappointing and disheartening to learn that the United States had given its tacit approval of these abuses through military and economic aid. Julie and Zvonko's means had been drastic, reckless, and illegal, but I had sympathy for their objective. And they were willing to sacrifice their own freedom to advance the cause of freedom in Croatia—which finally came in 1995, following a bloody four-year war with innumerable casualties.

Julie and Zvonko's case went to trial in the spring of 1977. They were tried together with two of the other hijackers. The third had entered a guilty plea several months prior and was sentenced to thirty years in prison.

The trial lasted six long weeks. Each day, the courtroom was filled with people, often Croatian nationalists coming to show their support for the defendants. The Yugoslav government was also closely monitoring the trial, and members of the UDBA (the Yugoslav secret police) were frequently in the courtroom, noting the hijackers' supporters.

The federal prosecutor agreed just before trial not to pursue the death penalty against the hijackers. In a court filing, he wrote, "The bomb was not a time bomb; it was not set to go off, and the timing of the explosion was fortuitous. . . . [I]t is plain that evidence legally sufficient to justify the imposition of the death penalty will not be adduced." While this provided some measure of relief, Julie and Zvonko still faced life in prison if convicted.

The evidence at trial shed light on the plan devised by Zvonko in the weeks prior to the hijacking. He felt that hijacking an American plane, as opposed to a plane from some other country, would bring maximum attention to the plight of Croatian nationalists fighting for an independent Croatia under the brutal Yugoslav regime—as well as the role of the United States in giving aid to Yugoslavia, which to some extent allowed the atrocities to continue. Once on the plane, he would assemble a fake bomb out of conventional materials, such as a cooking pot and putty. The "bomb" would have a trigger that he would carry in his hand.

To ensure that authorities took the hijackers' demands seriously, the police would be pointed to an actual bomb in New York that would be identical in appearance to the fake one assembled on the plane. The bomb left in New York would be built so it could be detonated only by pressing the trigger and could easily be disarmed according to instructions left with it in the locker. Once on the plane, the pilot would be made to drop informational leaflets over France and then Croatia, and newspapers would be persuaded to print the group's political manifestos. Once these objectives had been achieved, the hijackers would surrender. But their plan, quite literally, blew up.

Michael Tigar defended Zvonko. Mike had been one of the leaders of the antiwar protests at Berkeley in the sixties. He had been hired as a law clerk to Justice William Brennan, a civil rights icon on the Supreme Court, but Brennan had rescinded the offer based on Mike's political activities. Mike had then joined the law firm of Edward Bennett Williams, the legendary Washington, D.C., criminal lawyer. But he was all in on defending those who were oppressed by the powers that be, whether in Croatia or Chicago. .

His defense of Zvonko focused on the political issues raised in the case: the gross abuses of power by the Yugoslav government, including political assassinations, and the desperation of the Croatian people under Tito's totalitarian control. As Zvonko explained to the court with conviction and remorse, "I did not do this act out of adventuristic or terroristic impulses. It was simply the scream of a disenfranchised and persecuted man."

But this did not justify what had happened, or even provide a legal defense. It was a political statement by a Croatian revolutionary, pure and simple.

For me, the question was how to represent a young American woman my age, who could have been someone I was friends with in college, whose parents and upbringing were not all that different from my own, but who had voluntarily participated in an indefensible act, where the facts were indisputable and the consequences devastating, not just for the police officers but for passengers and crew. It raised again the existential question every criminal defense lawyer is faced with: How can you sleep at night when your job is to get that person "off"?

The answer is that in the vast majority of cases, the goal of the defense lawyer is not to get the defendant "off" through some sleight-of-hand defense or technicality. The goal, rather, is to put the defendant's conduct into a larger context, so that they will not be judged and punished solely for what in many cases is the worst decision they will ever make. And to make sure that in reaching a fair and just result, the normal desire for revenge and retribution does not lead to an abuse of power by those in positions of authority, such as the police, the prosecutors, and the courts, and that the rule of law is protected.

So it was that in representing Julie, my job was to humanize her and to try to make her otherwise indefensible and incomprehensible act understandable to a judge and jury. Our legal defense was that she was merely a "knowing spectator" who did not "join in the venture in an effort to make it succeed." She was there only as Zvonko's loving partner. In putting forth this defense, the underlying goal was to educate the judge and jury about who Julie was and how she had come to such an incongruous and untenable position. She was a caring, thoughtful, and entirely selfless human being who ended up participating in a violent, callous act that she believed was motivated by selfless reasons.

The jury deliberated for twenty-seven hours before returning a verdict. Julie and Zvonko were both found guilty, and both were sentenced to life in prison. Over the course of the trial, the presiding judge, Senior United States District Judge John R. Bartels, a generally harsh sentencer, had gradually become convinced of Julie's sincere love for and belief in Zvonko, her basic good character, and her humanity. He was an elderly Southern gentlemen, albeit living in New York City, and the notion of a faithful wife in thrall to a domineering husband was the scenario he chose to believe. He concluded that Julie's participation in the hijacking was explicable, in large measure, based on her devotion to Zvonko and Zvonko's power over Julie as a result. At the sentencing hearing, Judge Bartels said, "While the analogy is not complete, Zvonko Busic's influence over her reminds one of the hypnotism that Svengali exercised over Trilby O'Farrell," a reference to the novel *Trilby* by British author George du Maurier. After sentencing Julie to life, he ordered that she would be eligible for parole after serving only eight years of her sentence. Zvonko would have to serve at least ten.

In the end, Julie spent thirteen years in prison before being paroled with some behind-the-scenes assistance by Judge Bartels. Following her release, she obtained a master's degree in German language, literature, and linguistics, with honors. In 1991, the Croatian War of Independence began, and from 1991 until 1992, Julie worked for a nonprofit organization, lobbying politicians in the United States with respect to Croatian independence and recognition. From 1992 until 1995, the year Croatia won its independence, Julie served as an advisor at the first-ever Croatian embassy in Washington, D.C. She then moved to Croatia and spent five years working in the office of the Croatian president. She still lives in Croatia. In 2009, without warning or explanation, she was placed on the U.S. no-fly list as a "terrorist," which makes it nearly impossible for her to return to the United States.

Zvonko Busic served thirty-two years in prison for his role in the hijacking and the death of Brian Murray. Julie was there waiting for him upon his release, her love for him undiminished during his period of incarceration. He died by suicide on September 1, 2013.

Bruno Busic, a Croatian political dissident and a relative of Zvonko's, wrote the political statements that were eventually printed in the major newspapers and dropped over cities in the United States and Europe. Bruno was murdered by the Yugoslav secret police in Paris on October 16, 1978.

Julie Busic with Rudy Bretz, a passenger on the hijacked airliner. Bretz visited Julie in prison following her conviction.

Ray Finch's father, David Finch, died on Monday, June 27, 1977, while Ray was on Death Row, awaiting his execution. Ray asked the Court for permission to attend his father's funeral, which was granted. He was brought by a sheriff's deputy to the service, which was already in progress. Ray had asked for a coat and tie that would be appropriate for the funeral, but instead he was left in his prison attire. One of Ray's sons was six years old at the time. His earliest memory of his father was seeing him at the funeral, brought out of a police car in an orange jumpsuit and shackles at the service, and then seeing his father taken away again by the police before he could speak to him or give him a hug.

The next month, while Julie and Zvonko were being sentenced to life in prison in New York, Ray's death sentence was commuted to life in prison in North Carolina. The U.S. Supreme Court found North Carolina's death-penalty statute unconstitutional in *Woodson v. North Carolina*, allowing Ray an escape from the gas chamber. He would spend the next forty-two years of his life behind bars, fighting to prove his innocence. Ray claimed that his arrest and conviction arose out of pervasive corruption in Wilson County involving the sheriff's department, but no one was listening.

10

LAW ENFORCEMENT OR CRIMINALS?

For a man to work as long as I have worked, and to go down in disgrace, there must be a hell on Earth.

—Wilson County Sheriff Wilbur Robin Pridgen, in 1979, speaking to the Court following his conviction on federal racketeering and corruption charges

Evelyn Watson leaned against the wall in a hallway of the federal courthouse in Raleigh. She had been summoned to speak to the grand jury regarding disturbing allegations that prostitution and gambling enterprises in Wilson County had, for several years, given the sheriff and his deputies monthly payoffs, including so-called carnal bribes, to allow the illegal businesses to operate in the county. As she watched nervously, other witnesses waiting on nearby benches were called one by one into the grand jury room to testify. She was terrified, and had good reason to be.

Evelyn began working as a prostitute at the Bel-Air Truck Stop in Wilson in 1976. The Bel-Air was located just off Highway 301, which, before the construction of I-95, was the main north-south thoroughfare in the eastern United States, from Florida, up through the Carolinas and Virginia, and on into Delaware. It was known as the Tobacco Trail, spanning between the large cigarette-manufacturing plants in Richmond and Petersburg, Virginia, through the bright-leaf fields of Durham, North Carolina, and on down south, as it followed "the original trails which were beaten through the wilderness by hogsheads of tobacco rolling to market behind teams of mules." By virtue of Highway 301, which ran through the heart of Wilson County, enterprising criminals could easily transport and receive interstate contraband, including narcotics and illegal cigarettes, the theft and sale of which were prolific in Wilson County. It was also how women working as prostitutes were ferried in from out of state to local brothels, including the Bel-Air, as part of an interstate prostitution scheme that ranged from Pennsylvania to Florida.

Evelyn, however, was not from out of state. She grew up in the mountains of North Carolina, in a town called Deep Gap. For the services she offered at the Bel-Air, Evelyn charged $20 for a "straight date," $30 for a "French date," and beyond that, it was "whatever she could get." Her clients were mostly long-distance truck drivers, not the high-profile types that other prostitution houses in town catered to. Her boss was named Rudolph Baker, a lowlife criminal from a neighboring county who'd served time and knew the ropes. The madam for the operation was Judy Bollinger, who began her work at the Bel-Air as one of the paid girls but now focused her efforts on scheduling the dates and collecting payment. Evelyn, Judy, and Judy's seventeen-year-old daughter, Sheila, were all romantically involved with Baker. It was a nightmare of dysfunction.

Evelyn made pretty good money, as much as $2,000 a week, but she'd be the first to tell you it was not an easy way to make a living. Once, she tried to leave the employment of the Bel-Air with one of the truck drivers, but Baker and another man reportedly pursued her in an automobile and shot at her with a machine gun. Judy Bollinger eventually persuaded Evelyn to come back to work and resume her duties, with a promise of no further violence from Baker.

The Bel-Air and the other brothels in Wilson County were not a secret to anyone. They were operating in plain sight, not even trying to hide what they were doing. How could they avoid prosecution year after year? Rumors began to circulate that the sheriff's department was on the take. People reported seeing police cars frequenting the brothels, but without any arrests being made. Based on such reports, the Charlotte office of the FBI initiated an investigation in late 1977 or early 1978, thinking they'd find small-time grift and shut down a prostitution house or two. Instead, what they uncovered was a nest of snakes and thieves, the likes of which the state had never seen.

On February 15, 1978, an FBI agent posing as a truck driver was scheduled to have a "date" at the Bel-Air with Evelyn. She led him by the hand into a bedroom at the truck stop and began to undress him, starting with his belt buckle—at which point he hastened to pull out his credentials, bringing the whole thing to a screeching halt. Evelyn gasped and nearly fainted. Agents who had been waiting outside and listening over a wire entered the building and began seizing records.

The agent encouraged Evelyn, now thoroughly mortified, to cooperate in the investigation, and she agreed. The next day, over a recorded line, she talked to Baker, who had learned about the FBI's raid on the Bel-Air. As expected, he rushed to the motel where Evelyn was staying. She'd been fitted with a wire and a tape recorder in the hopes of catching him making an admission. No doubt expecting this, Baker said nothing incriminating, other than to tell Evelyn not to say a word to the feds about what they'd been doing there at the Bel-Air.

The prostitution was one thing, but Baker needed to avoid any allegation that he'd been paying the sheriff's department for protection. He'd heard stories about what happened to people who talked, and damn if he'd wind up in a ditch. Baker told the other girls working at the Bel-Air to keep their mouths shut. Judy Bollinger, the madam, might have refused this instruction, if she had lived. Two weeks after the FBI's raid, and just hours after she was served with a subpoena to testify before the grand jury, Judy was found dead of an apparent drug overdose at the Days Inn East in Asheville, North Carolina.

For Evelyn, everything moved quickly after the raid. She was now waiting anxiously in the hallway of the courthouse, trying to decide what she might say to the grand jury when her turn came. Rudolph Baker, who would have been wise to be miles away, appeared suddenly around the corner and strode down the hall toward her. Without saying a word, he handed her a card with writing on it and a handful of pills. The card explained how to plead the Fifth Amendment, and the pills were ten-milligram tablets of Valium. She swallowed the Valium, walked unsteadily into the grand jury room, and refused to testify against Baker, pleading her Fifth Amendment right against self-incrimination. All of this was witnessed by a federal agent.

Baker was later charged with a litany of crimes, including obstruction of justice for witness tampering. Evelyn was called as a witness at Baker's trial despite her unwillingness to cooperate with authorities. While on the stand, she was asked if she had any regard whatsoever for the oath she had taken to testify truthfully in the case. Truthfully, she responded, "I also have a high regard for my life."

Evelyn survived this ordeal, but others, including Judy Bollinger, did not. And there were other casualties related to the corruption, including Obbie Gene Ward, a young man who was the father of several children and who was shot through the temple on September 1, 1973. At four in the morning, his body was deposited at the Southern 500 truck stop, where his wife worked as a waitress. His murder was investigated by Wilbur Robin Pridgen, at that time the chief deputy sheriff, and Tony Owens, still just a deputy, who called it a suicide even though the medical examiner vehemently disagreed and said it was obvious that the shooting wasn't a suicide. Even the county EMS logbook showed signs of tampering (see the

2	8-30-73	5:30	6:00	C.H.C. & W.M.H.	Ellis + Perry	1181			
2	8-30-73	7:00	7:36	2 Houses from Rock Ridge School to W.M.H.	Ellis + Woody	1182			
2	8-30-73	8:25	9:00	1306 Queen St. to W.M.H.	Ellis + Woody	1183	—		
2	8-30-73	9:45	10:55	201 E. Nash St.	1050	1022	Ellis + Woody		
4	8-31-73	7:00	7:30	Room 426 W.M.H. & Wake M.H.	Braswell Ellis	1201		REC	
3	8-31-73	12:05	12:05	713 E. Stantonsburg to N.C. Hospital	Lynn Johnson	1141		AOD	
2	8-31-73	11:25	12:06	510 W. Nash W.O.	Tomm + Perry	1276		AOD	
2	8-31-73	1:00	1:30	N.C. Hospital 47130 Stantonsburg St.	Tomm + Perry	1141		AOD	
3	8-31-73	1:00	4:30	Room 311 W.M.H. & Duke	Tomm + Perry	1189		AOD	
5	8-31-73	1:10	2:00	558 E. W.M.H. E.R.	DOA	Kitchen + Murphy	1253	AOD	
4	8-31-73	2:40	3:10	W.O. & 510 W. Jones St.	Braswell Ellis	12-76		AOD	
1	8-31-73	1:45	2:40	M.R.H.C. & W.C. & Return	Davis + Lucas	1254		W.M.H.	
2	8-31-73	5:50	6:30	600 Clark Ave.	Davis + Lucas	1142		W.M.H.	
2	9-3-73	7:15	7:20	42 West 1st Dist. Pol.	1025	Tomm + Miller		AOD	
3	9-3-73	7:30	7:45	Run Front apt. apt. D to W.M.H.	1022	Tomm + Miller		AOD	
2	9-31-73	10:15	8:15	Dunn Cross Rd. to W.M.H.	1022	Tomm + Miller	1143	AOD	
2	8-31-73	11:25	12:50	Pender St. to W.M.H.	1050	Tomm + Miller		AOD	
1	9-1-73	2:40	3:30	42 West to W.M.H.	1050	Tomm + Miller	1148	AOD	
2	9-1-73	4:00	5:10	Southern 500 Man Shot himself	Lynn + Lucas	1149		AOD	
2	9-1-73	8:55	9:50	Room 331 W.M.H. & Lutheran	Tomm + Lucas			AOD	
3	9-1-73	9:75	9:55	1 Riot Road on 1 Lord 264 E.	1022	Tomm + Lucas	1277	AOD	
3	9-1-73	10:35	11:25	Room 526 W.M.H. & 42 E. Thomas Farm	Tomm + Ellis	1150		AOD	
2	9-1-73	11:45	12:15	C.H.C. & W.M.H.	Lynn + Ellis	1186		AOD	
3	9-1-73	11:55	1:00	264 E. Stantonsburg W.O.	Tomm + Lucas	1186		AOD	

FOR OFFICE USE ONLY - DO NOT WRITE IN THIS SPACE

		Total figures To Date
Number Emergency Calls	12	400
Number Non-Emergency Calls	12	304
	24	
Grand Total		704

first entry for September 1, 1973, which does not match the other entries).

While Ward's murder remains unsolved to this day, I believe the evidence suggests that he planned to reveal the narcotics trade allegedly engaged in by Bobby Duke, a good friend of Owens's, and was permanently silenced for his efforts.

Because of such chilling violence, and the looming threat of retribution to anyone who might be inclined to talk, no one will ever know the full extent of the illegality in Wilson County during the 1970s. I suspect it goes far beyond what was ultimately uncovered by the federal investigation that began at the Bel-Air and ended, many months later, in the conviction of the sheriff, Wilbur Robin Pridgen, on racketeering and corruption charges, and which unearthed in the process evidence of illegality in nearly every form imaginable. The men profiting from the corruption were willing to do almost anything to conceal their misdeeds and preserve the spoils of their deceit.

THE SEEDS OF CORRUPTION

Some of the first bad seeds in Wilson were planted by Gerald Ayscue Frazier, a man from Lawrenceville, Virginia. Gerry, as he was known to his friends, met Billie Dean O'Barr in Virginia in 1966. He was an ambitious and talented con man with ties to illegal gambling; she was young, entrepreneurial, and made a living as a prostitute. It was the classic love story. Dreaming of ill-gotten riches, they moved to Wilson, where Gerry bought an old motel with plans to convert it into a house of prostitution.

The site chosen for the operation was a motel known as the Forest Inn Motor Court. It consisted of a dingy semicircle of squat, one-story cabins off Highway 301, a site fitting for a low-rent bordello, and a few miles south of where the Bel-Air would one day operate under Rudolph Baker. The cabins were sad little duplexes and quadplexes, with mossy concrete front patios and a shingled awning over each door, set back in a straggly copse of trees. It was just far enough back off the road that you could visit the motel without everyone seeing your car from the highway.

The Forest Inn Motor Court

Despite the bleak setting, the prostitution business soon began to flourish, but it made up only a portion of Gerry's income. He had his fingers in a lot of pies, allegedly including, at one time, an interstate cigarette theft ring. This was big money and extremely high stakes. The business model involved stealing trucks full of cigarettes marked for overseas distribution. Pulling heists of this magnitude required payments to a lot of people, but there were fortunes to be made. In 1970, Gerry reportedly got caught red-handed with a stolen tractor-trailer containing more than a thousand *cases* of cigarettes, but the charges were later dismissed, leaving him free to engage in further illegalities in Wilson.

Gerry's next big venture was to open a gambling house not far from the Forest Inn. He learned about an old cinderblock building hiding in the trees behind the Beefmastor Inn restaurant (also on Highway 301). It was owned by a local attorney and was currently unused. Gerry rented it, boarded up the windows, installed a heavy automatic door with one-way glass, and started running poker and dice games out of it. For Wilson, it was high-dollar gambling, and an armed guard was stationed to keep watch at the door. On a particularly bad night, one player there lost $10,000, according to court testimony. Gerry called it the Clubhouse, and it was indeed an exclusive club. One member of the club was the county sheriff.

Wilbur Robin Pridgen was the chief deputy before becoming the sheriff of Wilson County during its heyday of corruption. He'd been in law enforcement (if you could call what he did law enforcement) for practically his whole life, starting off with the Wilson city police department, and thereafter spending decades in the sheriff's department before advancing to chief deputy and, finally, sheriff. He was, as they say in the South, as crooked as a dog's hind leg. He didn't mind illegal activity in Wilson County as long as he got his share. Pridgen and Gerry Frazier were friends, but friendship apparently went only so far. Pridgen required Gerry to pay in order to keep the gambling activities at the Clubhouse away from the attention of law enforcement, and Gerry paid like a slot machine. Pridgen would come to the Clubhouse to gamble, often in uniform, and the payoff money would be slid across the table to him under a bottle of whiskey.

It was the same for the prostitution at the Forest Inn. At first, Pridgen's payment was just $100 a month. Then, when he moved from deputy sheriff to sheriff in 1974, the number went up to $400 a month. For this fee, the sheriff's department would not only overlook the prostitution, but it would also notify the Forest Inn in the event of a raid by another law enforcement agency. This was done using the telephone and prearranged code words. It was understood that the payoff precluded other houses of prostitution from operating in the area, but that was before the other houses of prostitution started paying Pridgen more than what he was paid by the Forest Inn. Before long, the prostitution house at the Forest Inn was joined by another at the Rainbow Motel, and then by the Bel-Air. For these latter two cathouses, to use the vernacular of the day, Pridgen was paid $700 a month by each. That was a fair amount of money back then.

Sheriff Pridgen and several of the deputies took full advantage of the services offered at the Forest Inn, which included "free dates" for the officers. Sometimes the deputies would be given girls from the Forest Inn to accompany them on trips to the beach. Sometimes they'd bring their own dates to the Forest Inn in order to use the rooms, their wives being none the wiser (or so they thought). Chief Deputy Tony Owens was one of the deputies who availed himself of the free dates at the Forest Inn and the other houses of prostitution, according to multiple witnesses interviewed by the FBI.

Much of the foregoing was uncovered by the FBI's investigation and came out at Pridgen's trial. Incredibly, this was just the tip of the iceberg. The investigation also found evidence that the sheriff's department indulged in and even *sponsored* other criminal activity in Wilson County, including a theft ring made up of local criminals who would participate in burglaries identified and coordinated by members of the sheriff's department. Country stores were robbed;

safes were taken. The thieves were given police walkie-talkies to use in the heists. Guns were stolen and appropriated by sheriff's deputies for their own use. Contraband was taken out of the evidence locker and used by the sheriff and his deputies. Steak houses were robbed of their steaks. Cigarette stores were repeatedly robbed of large quantities of cigarettes. Narcotics dealers were allowed to traffic throughout the county, and competitors were framed to put them out of business. If someone close to the sheriff's department was arrested, steps would be taken to ensure he received favorable treatment from the prosecutor's office to keep him from informing. It was like the wild west, and corruption and illegality were rampant. It was truly an "anything goes" atmosphere. For years, the sheriff and his deputies were untouchable.

During this time, the Forest Inn was a locus of Wilson County's corruption. It was a "police-free zone," off-limits to law enforcement by virtue of the payments made by Gerry Frazier and the relationship between Gerry and Sheriff Pridgen, and it became a haven for lawlessness. A cast of undesirables lived in the rooms not used for prostitution. They included a notorious gambler who was a close friend of Gerry's, an escaped convict, a man described by one witness as a "hit man," a prostitute's husband—who was later murdered, according to what another witness told the FBI—and, finally, Charles Lewis, the man who was in the car with Ray Finch when Ray was arrested a few hours after Shadow Holloman's murder.

According to court documents and public records, Lewis began living at the Forest Inn Motor Court as early as 1974. His arrest records suggest he was participating in organized theft. In one arrest, for example, he was caught with thirty-seven commercial truck tires and related equipment—not the kind of stuff you can get away with under your coat or in the back of your sedan. Not the kind of stuff you can unload at the local pawnshop. He seemed to have friends in high places. For this crime, Lewis walked into court, posted a $5,000 bond, and walked right back out. He served no time for the offense.

Because he lived at the Forest Inn, Lewis knew what was really going on behind the scenes in Wilson County. He knew about the payoffs for the prostitution; he knew about the payoffs for the gambling. He knew about the organized theft, the narcotics, and the cigarettes trafficked up and down Highway 301. And he knew all the heads that would roll if anyone ever found out. He could bring the whole glorious enterprise crashing down.

11

THE COVER-UP

As the FBI investigation into the corruption in Wilson County gathered steam in 1978, I accepted a teaching position at the UNC School of Law in Chapel Hill, North Carolina. In July of that year, I moved from New York to North Carolina to establish and run a criminal law clinical program at the law school. I taught trial advocacy and supervised third-year law students who were assigned to represent federal prisoners at parole hearings and indigent defendants charged with state misdemeanors. One of my goals was to show the students how to use the law to help people who were facing the power of the state, with the hope that some of them would choose this important, but less than lucrative, career path. As it turned out, a number of my students became public defenders. One of my first students was Jerry Buting, whose representation of Steven Avery would be featured years later in the Netflix documentary *Making a Murderer*.

While I was settling in to my new role in Chapel Hill, Ray Finch was busy trying to prove his innocence. In early 1979, Sheriff Pridgen had been convicted in federal court of running the Wilson County Sheriff's Department as a RICO (Racketeer Influenced and Corrupt Organization) enterprise and was sentenced to three six-year terms, to run concurrently, in federal prison. Chief Deputy Owens was luckier. Although he had been indicted for perjury and obstruction of justice, he had been found not guilty of those crimes. Yet as a result of the FBI investigation and the federal prosecution, the corruption in Wilson County had finally been exposed, and the citizens of Wilson County had elected a new sheriff named L. G. Taylor. The old guard at the sheriff's department, who had been around for years, even decades, were sent packing.

In May 1979, after Pridgen's and Owens's federal trials, Ray wrote a letter to the new sheriff. In his letter, Ray alleged that Pridgen and Owens had framed him for the murder of Shadow Holloman. According to Ray, this was because the true killer knew all about the corruption in the sheriff's department and would have implicated the sheriff and chief deputy if he'd been arrested and charged with the murder instead of Ray. The true killer, according to Ray, was Charles Lewis. Ray alleged that when he gave Lewis a ride on the night of the murder, Lewis admitted to having just had a "shoot-out" in Holloman's store. Lewis was in a separate prison facility on charges unrelated to Holloman's murder, so he was easy to find.

Ray also wrote and filed a post-conviction motion with the Court, in which he again alleged his innocence and asked the Court to vacate his conviction. He was hoping the new sheriff would help him prove his allegations of corruption against the former sheriff and chief deputy and establish that he'd been set up to take the fall for Holloman's murder. The Court appointed a lawyer to represent Ray on that motion.

Sheriff Taylor, upon receiving Ray's letter, appears to have taken it seriously, or at least wanted to protect himself from being accused of a cover-up. He sent Ray's letter on to the N.C. State Bureau of Investigation (SBI) with a request that Ray's allegations be investigated.

The SBI assigned Special Agent Alan McMahan to look into Ray's extraordinary allegations about the setup and the reason for it specifically because Agent McMahan was familiar with Wilson County. On August 7, 1979, Agent McMahan drove to Central Prison to interview Ray and dutifully took notes of the interview. The following day, Agent McMahan went to the prison where Charles Lewis was incarcerated and interviewed him. Although Ray had given McMahan the names of a number of witnesses Ray said could confirm his allegations, McMahan didn't interview any of them. He also never contacted the lead FBI agent to get the benefit of all that the FBI had uncovered in its investigation in Wilson.

Instead, after talking to the two men, Agent McMahan concluded that Ray's allegations of corruption on the part of the former sheriff and chief deputy were baseless. This was close to absurd, given the FBI investigation, the resulting publicity about the Wilson County corruption, and Sheriff Pridgen's conviction for corruption. My instinct and experience tells me that McMahan was covering for something or someone. Perhaps he was covering for his own failure to report the corruption to his superiors. Perhaps he was covering for other law enforcement officers, such as a colleague at the SBI who might have gotten mixed up in the corruption.

Whatever the case, in his SBI report, Agent McMahan concluded: "In reporting agent's interview with [Ray Finch], Finch was unable to substantiate the allegations he made in his letter to Sheriff L. G. Taylor concerning corruption on the part of The Wilson County Sheriff's Department, especially on the part of Former Sheriff Robin Pridgen, and Chief Deputy Tony Owens." McMahan's report came less than five months after Sheriff Pridgen had been convicted of corruption in federal court.

McMahan knew that Finch had a post-conviction motion pending in the Wilson County Superior Court. McMahan sent his report to the assistant district attorney handling Finch's motion and then closed the investigation and his file.

Shortly after McMahan had ended his investigation, a hearing was held on Finch's motion to vacate his conviction. Lacking any independent evidence that he had been set up to protect Pridgen, Owens, and others in the police department, the Court summarily denied Finch's motion. At the time, Finch had served four years. As a result of what I believe was a cover-up by McMahan, Finch would spend an additional thirty-eight years in prison before the truth of his allegations would finally be established.

Part IV

FIGHTING THE ABUSE OF POWER BY PROSECUTORS

12

THE MOST POWERFUL PERSON IN THE SYSTEM

The prosecutor has more control over life, liberty, and reputation than any other person in America.

—Robert H. Jackson, U.S. Attorney General (1940–1941); U.S. Supreme Court Justice (1941–1954)

Justice Jackson's observation, written more than eighty years ago, remains undeniably true today. Prosecutors, of all the players in the American criminal justice system, including judges and juries, exercise the greatest level of control over the lives and destinies of the ordinary individuals with whom they interact in that system. Prosecutors wield extraordinary power, including the ability to initiate and direct investigations of individuals, bring or withhold criminal charges, and control the resolution of any charges they do bring.

The mere announcement that someone is a "person of interest" in a criminal investigation is enough to change that person's life forever, as Richard Jewell found out during the Centennial Olympic Park bombing investigation in Atlanta. An indictment, even if followed by an acquittal, forever taints that person's reputation. It's the modern-day equivalent of a scarlet letter.

Prosecutorial discretion for these life-altering decisions is nearly unlimited. State and federal prosecutors enjoy absolute immunity from civil liability for all acts undertaken in connection with initiating a prosecution and in presenting the State's case, regardless of whether the prosecutor was negligent or acting in bad faith in prosecuting the case. This means that if an innocent person is wrongfully charged, tried, convicted, imprisoned, and subsequently exonerated, that person cannot sue the prosecutor for damages, even if the prosecutor *knew* the person was innocent and *intentionally* chose to prosecute her anyway, and even if the prosecutor *knowingly and deliberately* withheld exculpatory evidence that might have led to the defendant's acquittal. It's an extraordinary shield for a person exercising such enormous power in an adversary system that too often emphasizes results (i.e., convictions) over justice. And criminal charges against prosecutors for obstruction of justice or subordination of perjury occur almost never. After all, it is one prosecutor who decides whether to charge another prosecutor, and the thin blue line doesn't just protect police officers who engage in misconduct.

THE FEDERAL CRIMINAL INJUSTICE SYSTEM: THE "TRIAL PENALTY"

A secret that everyone who works in the federal criminal justice system knows, but only criminal defense lawyers openly talk about, is that the jury trial in criminal cases in the U.S. District Courts is essentially extinct. The system has been skewed so that severe penalties are imposed on anyone who insists on a trial rather than pleading guilty and "cooperating." It's not just that those who plead guilty and/or cooperate are given some modicum of credit for accepting responsibility. That has always been true and appropriate. And it's not just that prosecutors have the discretion to determine what charges are filed, which has also long been true.

The problem stems from the adoption of more and more severe federal punishments, including mandatory minimums for many crimes, and the adoption of the United States Sentencing Guidelines, enacted in 1987 ostensibly to provide "fairness" and "consistency" to federal sentencing. Dramatically demonstrating the law of unforeseen consequences, however, over the past three decades the federal guidelines have morphed into a draconian system of super-harsh punishments that intimidate defendants and keep them from asserting their right to trial. Although federal judges may "vary" from the guidelines, they are required to start their analysis of the appropriate sentence from the guideline range, which is based primarily on the offense of conviction, plus specified "aggravating" and "mitigating" factors.

This means that if the prosecutor allows the defendant to plead guilty to a lesser offense before he is indicted, the initial guideline calculation by the Court will be greatly reduced. If the defendant insists on pleading not guilty, the prosecutor may indict on the most serious charges, causing the initial guideline range in the event of a conviction to be much greater. The guidelines have thereby served to substantially increase the leverage prosecutors have to force defendants to plead guilty rather than go to trial. Defense lawyers call this the "trial penalty." It often results in a race to the U.S. Attorney's office to be the first to plead guilty and cooperate. Fewer and fewer defendants go to trial these days.

As a result, criminal defense lawyers have become simply a cog in the federal criminal justice processing machine, there to grease the wheels while the prosecutors run the engine. Their role is now primarily to explain to the defendant the incredible cost of being convicted after a trial and the great benefit of pleading guilty as soon as possible, especially if one is willing to "cooperate" by providing testimony against other people—as long as that testimony is consistent with the prosecutor's theory of the case. Federal prosecutors possess virtually unlimited discretion to determine if someone who has "accepted responsibility" for his conduct and agreed to cooperate has done so "fully" and "truthfully." If someone does not truthfully provide all the information the prosecutor believes he or she possesses, the prosecutor can simply void any agreement to mitigate the person's sentence, even though the person cannot withdraw their guilty plea.

Once the client agrees to plead guilty and cooperate, as the vast majority choose to do, the defense attorney then serves primarily as a facilitator, helping his client cooperate with the prosecutor as effectively as possible. He in essence becomes part of the prosecution team. This role is necessary, given the way the system works, but dedicated criminal trial lawyers see this as a sellout of the traditional role and chafe at the new paradigm.

My law partner (and wife) Sonya Pfeiffer experienced this when she was the defense attorney for Michael Boughner, whose job at a debt-collection company was supervising the telephone operators who called debtors to collect money they owed to various businesses for goods or services they had gotten. When the Department of Justice decided to "crack down" on collection agencies for using language in these calls that violated the Fair Debt Collection Practices Act, Michael, along with almost everyone at the company, was charged with "conspiracy to commit wire fraud."

He believed he had just done his job of helping to collect debts that were *legitimately* owed to the businesses, and he wanted to fight the charges by going to trial. So did Sonya, but she had to tell him that the United States Sentencing Guidelines would make him responsible for the total amount of debt *the entire company had collected over several years*—not just for the debt he had been responsible for collecting. He could be sentenced to decades in prison.

Instead, Michael reluctantly pled guilty to limit his prison exposure and cooperated with the investigators. Sonya requested home detention and supervised probation for this first-time offender, but despite Michael's cooperation, the prosecutor insisted on prison, and a federal judge sentenced Michael to forty-one months. A year later, he was diagnosed with a brain tumor and stage-four cancer and given only months to live. He was transferred to a Bureau of Prisons medical facility with hospice care. At his mother's request, Michael became eligible for compassionate release so he could die at home. But the prosecutor needed permission from his supervisor to file a perfunctory motion, and the permission was never granted. Almost six months passed, and Michael died in prison, alone. He had in essence been sentenced to the rest of his life for working at a debt-collection company.

Cases like Michael Boughner's are all too common because the guidelines have given prosecutors such enormous leverage in plea negotiations, which is how approximately 97 percent of federal criminal cases are resolved. While most federal prosecutors no doubt believe they are exercising their vast power righteously in order to deter crime and punish offenders, the adversary system is supposed to exist as a check and balance on the exercise of prosecutorial power, however well-intentioned it might be.

It is axiomatic that absolute, unchecked power leads to abuses, and abuses of prosecutorial power, even if well-intentioned, often lead to grave injustices. I experienced this firsthand early in my career, and it shaped me forever thereafter. I felt what my clients felt—the absolute power of the government to upend your life, regardless of your guilt or innocence.

13

CAUGHT IN THE CROSS FIRE

By 1981, I had settled into an academic routine, although I missed the work I had done in New York, being part of a group of lawyers and fighting for those who were up against the power of the system. One of my faculty colleagues, a labor law professor named Dan Pollitt, came to me that spring with an intriguing opportunity. A friend of his, Wilbur Hobby, was a union leader in North Carolina, a state historically hostile to unions. Wilbur had been indicted in federal court on corruption charges in the midst of a pitched political battle between North Carolina's Democratic governor, Jim Hunt, and a political action committee controlled by Republican North Carolina Senator Jesse Helms, and he was in dire need of an attorney.

I immediately knew to whom Dan was referring. The case had been all over the news for months. Dan said, "There's one more thing. I should probably mention that if you do this, you'll be working for free. He can't afford to pay you much of anything. I'm not sure if he can find his own checkbook."

When I met Wilbur Hobby in early 1981, he was the president of the North Carolina chapter of the American Federation of Labor and Congress of Industrial Organizations (AFL-CIO). At the time, the AFL-CIO was a robust and influential organization nationally, and Wilbur, as the state union chief, wielded significant political influence within North Carolina.

At first impression, Wilbur's most notable characteristics were his large size and unkempt appearance. He was stout but not overly tall, with an enormous round face and a nearly bald head. He had dark, unruly eyebrows that appeared mismatched with his gray-white hair, and doleful, furtive eyes that were deep-set in his face. His clothes were invariably rumpled, and his suit coats carried a frenzy of permanent wrinkles. It was plain that he gave little regard to his appearance, and it was hard to imagine, just looking at him, that Wilbur might be successful at anything.

Upon closer inspection, a more complex picture of Wilbur emerged. The Wilbur Hobby I came to know, notwithstanding his disheveled presentation, was a deeply principled person of keen intelligence and formidable memory who understood the value of personal relationships and was masterful when it came to developing and using them to achieve his goals. He had supported integration in the South and opposed the Vietnam War when many other national union leaders opposed integration and supported the war. He was a maverick who resisted the abuse of power by business owners and others in positions of authority. I liked and respected Wilbur immediately and agreed to represent him, notwithstanding Dan's caveat about payment. I was joined by a colleague from Duke Law School, a clinical law professor named Don Beskind, who was another recently transplanted northerner.

Next to Jesse Helms, Dean Smith, and the state governor (and not necessarily in that order), I expect that Wilbur was one of the most well-known North Carolinians at that time. As he walked down the street, people approached him and shook his hand, and Wilbur talked earnestly to them about jobs and politics. On one occasion, I saw Wilbur pull money out of his own pocket and give it to someone who was out of a job and down on his luck. He was a friend to everyone he met. His upbringing probably had something to do with this.

Wilbur grew up in a poor section of Durham, North Carolina, in the 1920s and '30s, a majority-Black city in an area where textile and hosiery mills provided most of what employment there was to go around. Wilbur's father, a brickmason, absconded when Wilbur was seven years old, which left Wilbur's mother to look after him and his five brothers. They moved constantly from house to house in the same mill town, sometimes unable to pay the rent. Wilbur's mother, while waiting on paltry alimony payments that seldom arrived, had one job cleaning chickens for a little grocery store on the corner of Angier Avenue and Elm Street, another job working at the WPA sewing room, and a third job in one of the hosiery mills in town. She worked her fingers raw, but never had much to show for it.

Wilbur quit school in the ninth grade and spent the summer working as a batboy for the Durham Bulls. Then, with his mother's permission, he enlisted in the navy at age seventeen and served in the South Pacific during World War II. After three years in the navy, Wilbur returned to Durham, where he got a job oiling cigarette machines with the American Tobacco Company at a rate of 75 cents an hour. One evening after work, he attended a union meeting and almost by accident found himself the head of the American Tobacco night-shift union: no one else wanted the position, so Wilbur volunteered for it.

By 1949, despite his inauspicious start, Wilbur had become heavily involved in local politics and served as the president of Voters for Better Government, which counted many Black citizens among its membership. Through this organization, he advocated for Black workers at a time when it was politically perilous to do so, and in a state that was slow to relinquish long-held, discriminatory racial attitudes.

Wilbur went on to become the secretary and treasurer of the state Democratic party in 1955, just one year after the U.S. Supreme Court declared school segregation unconstitutional in *Brown v. Board of Education*, and in 1960, he became the director of the AFL-CIO's Committee on Political Education (COPE). After serving for nine years as the director of COPE, Wilbur was elected state president for North Carolina's AFL-CIO. In this position, and to the chagrin of the Republican establishment, Wilbur wielded significant political clout that he readily threw behind Democratic political candidates in the state. He was quite successful at this until 1981. Then came his indictment.

Despite Wilbur's good intentions and his tireless advocacy for laborers in the state, he had one big shortcoming: in contrast to his success in organizing workers, he was totally disorganized in his personal affairs. He was as slovenly with his accounting as he was with his attire. Wilbur believed that if you meant well, people would assume you were acting in good faith and overlook minor discrepancies in regard to how money was handled. This was naïve in the toxic political climate of the 1970s, and it proved to be Wilbur's downfall.

In 1979, Wilbur formed a nonprofit corporation with an office across the street from his union office at the AFL-CIO. He then applied for, and received, two large federal grants in excess of a million dollars under a program known as the Comprehensive Employment and Training Act (CETA). The money was to be used to hire and provide training to people in the job market who lacked job skills. Wilbur's nonprofit was awarded the federal money through two state agencies headed by Democratic candidates Wilbur had vocally supported in prior political campaigns, and this triggered all sorts of alarms.

The grants came under intense scrutiny. Republicans called it a "political payout" to Wilbur in exchange for the support he lent to the political candidates, and demanded that then-governor Jim Hunt investigate the payments to Wilbur. Hunt was slow to take action. In fact, Hunt personally intervened and stopped a federal audit of Wilbur's use of the CETA funds, which might well have made matters worse.

Wilbur and the CETA funds became *the* central issue in the 1980 North Carolina gubernatorial campaign between Jim Hunt and his opponent, Beverly Lake Jr., a racial reactionary and Helms-approved candidate. The Raleigh *News & Observer* alone ran nearly one hundred articles on Wilbur and the CETA funds, many of them unflattering. A political action committee known as the Congressional Club, controlled by Jesse Helms, ran endless political advertisements targeting Jim Hunt and featuring Wilbur. One TV commercial paid for by Helms's group was so offensive that only one television station in all of North Carolina agreed to air it. Another political ad played on Wilbur's well-known obesity, showing $100 bills being laid into a notably obese palm with a voiceover saying something like "Governor Hunt is giving away your tax dollars to Wilbur Hobby for his political support." It was ugly.

At the direction of the U.S. Attorney for the Eastern District of North Carolina, the FBI launched an investigation, and in October 1980, Wilbur received a target letter from the U.S. Attorney's office.

For those who have never received a target letter from a federal prosecutor, it is a singularly heart-stopping experience. The purpose of a target letter is to alert you that the government has reason to believe you have committed a federal crime and, more importantly, that you are likely to be indicted as a result. It signals that a complex machinery with unlimited investigatory resources has been activated and directed at *you*. It means that experienced FBI agents are out on the streets collecting information that may be used *against you* in a trial. It means that a grand jury has likely been convened to hear evidence against you, and a federal prosecutor is seriously considering whether to issue a felony indictment with your name on it. In short, it means you may soon be facing serious criminal charges, and your freedom is in imminent peril. For Wilbur, all of this was true.

Close on the heels of his target letter, Wilbur was indicted in February 1981, not long after Ronald Reagan moved into the White House. Wilbur was quoted as saying it was "no surprise" that federal charges were brought against him within a month of Reagan's swearing in. Wilbur was defiant in claiming his innocence and believed his indictment was the direct result of the political campaign run by Helms and the Congressional Club, bitter and long-standing adversaries of Wilbur and the labor movement generally, in the 1980 gubernatorial election. It was, he rightly believed, a proxy fight between competing political forces. And while there is no question that there was a significant, and perhaps decisive, political component to Wilbur's prosecution, an audit of his use of the CETA funds suggested he had likely run afoul of federal regulations. The abysmal state of his accounting records—which were scattered about, and sometimes just kept in shoe boxes—did nothing to aid Wilbur's defense.

The first major development in the case came with the resignation of the U.S. Attorney who brought the charges against Wilbur. At the behest of Jesse Helms, Reagan nominated Samuel T. Currin to fill the open post. Currin, who was Helm's chief legislative aide, was in lock-step philosophically with Helms's conservative agenda, and he no doubt had marching orders to take over the Wilbur Hobby prosecution with all due speed and enthusiasm.

At that time, I knew Currin only by his growing reputation as a Jesse Helms clone—someone who seemed to harbor certain antebellum attitudes on race and an uncommon zeal for conservative ideals. One judge subsequently said of Currin, "I can conceive of no more dangerous a person than a fanatic with power. . . . I personally believe Sam Currin would use any method for any purpose he thought was right." He was now our opponent in Wilbur's case.

Wilbur's trial was only three months away. Don Beskind and I were working hard on Wilbur's defense, interviewing witnesses, preparing trial exhibits, and drafting legal motions to be filed with the Court. One afternoon I received a call from Don. "Did you get any mail today?" he asked. He sounded short of breath and one step away from outright panic. I told him I hadn't, and he told me I'd better sit down. He said, "You're not going to believe this."

Don read me a letter he'd received from the U.S. Attorney's office. It was a target letter *to us* notifying Don and me that *we* were now the targets of an investigation by the federal government related to Wilbur's case. It was signed by Sam Currin.

"What's he claiming we did?" I asked. Don said, "The letter says we violated federal law by giving Wilbur a copy of the grand jury transcript of a witness's testimony." As we well knew, the grand jury had taken testimony against Wilbur prior to issuing his indictment, and a transcript had been made of the proceedings. We had shared part of the transcript with Wilbur, who had then allegedly made use of it for some improper purpose we knew absolutely nothing about.

Currin's target letter made reference to a federal rule regarding the secrecy of grand jury materials, such as testimony by a witness or other evidence provided to a federal grand jury, that prohibits the disclosure of such materials. A stenographer taking down a witness's testimony, for instance, cannot reveal to anyone what the witness said, nor can a member of the grand jury who hears the testimony. The letter indicated we had violated this federal rule and were therefore being personally targeted for prosecution.

Don and I were stunned. A federal indictment, whatever the ultimate outcome, would likely result in us being suspended by our respective law schools until the matter was resolved, and perhaps even terminated. It would forever taint our reputations and undoubtedly interfere with our ability to practice law together in the future, something we were seriously considering. I was married and had a two-year-old son, and Don was married and had a one-year-old daughter. We were both in a fragile place in our careers, and it crossed our minds that defending against this charge might bankrupt both of us. We also knew it would be sensational news, and Wilbur's detractors, including Jesse Helms's political organization, would have a field day. We imagined the headline: WILBUR HOBBY'S ATTORNEYS INDICTED.

I called Wilbur immediately. "Wilbur, we're being threatened with indictment by the U.S. Attorney because of something he claims you did with the portion of the grand jury transcript we gave you! What the hell is that about?"

After a frantic afternoon, we learned that after we had given Wilbur a partial transcript of the grand jury testimony so he could help us investigate and rebut what a particular witness had claimed he had done, he had taken a page from that transcript and used it in a flyer for his ongoing campaign for president of the union. Wilbur had discovered, to his dismay, that his challenger for the union presidency, who had worked for him, had quietly given testimony against Wilbur before the grand jury. Wilbur felt very much like he and the union had been betrayed and wanted to let the voting union members know that his challenger was the kind of person who would stab someone in the back. So Wilbur made a copy of a page of the transcript we had given him to help us prepare his defense and passed it out during the union convention. We knew nothing about this, but his challenger reported it to the government, and that's what led to Currin's target letter.

We quickly determined that neither our giving Wilbur a portion of the grand jury transcript, nor Wilbur's act of distributing it, was in any way illegal. This was obvious just by reading the language of the rule we had allegedly violated. The prohibition on the dissemination of grand jury materials did not apply to defendants or their lawyers. In fact, defense attorneys routinely disclose grand jury testimony to their clients to prepare a defense.

By using the law to antagonize us in this way, Currin was, in my opinion, plainly abusing his power as U.S. Attorney. He was apparently trying to disqualify us from representing Wilbur by creating a conflict between our interests and Wilbur's. After all, Wilbur was the only person who could establish that *we* gave him the transcript—meaning Wilbur would have to be subpoenaed by Currin as a witness in any grand jury proceeding or trial against us. And how could we prepare for Wilbur's trial and fight the government vigorously while we were under investigation by the same prosecutors? It was an impossible situation. Don and I were both feeling intimidated, which we felt sure was the whole point. We decided we couldn't represent ourselves; we needed to hire our own lawyers.

We took the threat seriously and hired not one but two lawyers to represent us. The first attorney we hired was Earl Silbert, a widely respected prosecutor from the Watergate case. He was a Republican, well-connected in the Reagan Department of Justice (just in case those connections were useful), who had recently gone into private practice in Washington, D.C. The second attorney we hired was Eugene Boyce, a well-known and accomplished trial lawyer in Raleigh, North Carolina. Gene had also been involved in Watergate, having been one of the chief investigators whose work helped uncover the existence of the Watergate tapes. He also had a long-standing and good relationship with the federal trial judge assigned to the Hobby case. In other words, we weren't taking any chances, regardless of the cost.

With our attorneys, we developed a risky but necessary strategy. We couldn't try Wilbur's case while being threatened with prosecution ourselves. That much was clear. We decided to ask the judge to postpone Wilbur's trial until the investigation of Don and me had either been terminated or we had been indicted and tried. In short, we were going to test how far Currin was willing to take his threat.

It was a frightening time. I now understood exactly how powerless and unsettled my clients felt in the face of possible criminal prosecution. My fate was no longer in my hands. Upon what appeared to be nothing more than the whim and caprice of a politically appointed federal prosecutor, I was facing criminal charges in federal court and could do nothing but rely on my lawyers' advice and hope for the fairness and impartiality of a federal judge.

About a month prior to the date on which Wilbur's trial was to begin, we received a message from the judge who was scheduled to preside over Wilbur's case: "The Honorable W. Earl Britt would like to see all the lawyers in chambers today at 4:30 p.m."

I called Gene Boyce and asked him what was up. Gene said, "I don't have any idea, but I suggest we get our tails down to the courthouse."

We waited in Judge Britt's courtroom until he had recessed court for the day. Don and I, along with Gene Boyce, waited on one side of the courtroom, while Sam and his chief assistant, Doug McCullough, waited on the other. Judge Britt then stood wearily and motioned for us all to precede him into the back hallway of the federal court-house. I felt a little like a teenager being brought into a meeting with his parents to discuss his fate for something he hadn't done.

Once we were all in the judge's chambers, he motioned to Gene to close the door. Then he said, "Mr. Currin, I've been thinking about this situation we have with Mr. Hobby, and with these two gentle-men here"—indicating Don and me. "I don't think it's fair, based on what I've seen, to make these lawyers take Mr. Hobby's case to trial with a federal investigation hanging over their heads."

Currin said, "Your Honor—" but Judge Britt cut him off with a wave of his hand.

"So I'm going to tell you what I'm inclined to do, and then you all can tell me if you agree or disagree, but I'll tell you that my mind is pretty well made up. What I think I've decided is that I don't believe I'm going to have these lawyers defend Mr. Hobby at trial while you continue to investigate them at the same time. That wouldn't be fair to Mr. Hobby or to them, would it? So—we've got a trial date set for Mr. Hobby on December 7. You can go ahead and indict these lawyers and we'll try *them* on that date instead of Mr. Hobby. And after that we can decide when we can get around to trying him. Really what I'm saying is that it's one or the other. I need to know by the end of tomorrow what you plan to do." I couldn't read the ex-pression on Currin's face, but he seemed to seethe from head to foot before marching out of the room. Don and I left feeling sick to our stomachs. It was beyond surreal to hear a federal judge tell a federal prosecutor he needed to decide quickly whether to indict us so we could be tried the following month. But Judge Britt knew exactly what was likely to happen, even if we didn't.

The next week we received a "no prosecution" letter from Cur-rin's office in the mail, signaling that the investigation against Don and me had been dropped, and reinforcing our belief that the target letter and claims against us had been frivolous.

We tried Wilbur's case for three weeks in December 1981. The jury was out for fifteen hours before returning a disappointing verdict: Wilbur was found guilty on all charges. The judge fined Wilbur $40,000 and sentenced him to eighteen months in prison, but he served less than a year.

Following his conviction, Wilbur continued to proclaim his innocence, although much of the fight and courage he'd shown in his life had dissipated. As Wilbur left the courthouse following his sentencing with his wife, his sixteen-year-old son, and his nine-year-old daughter at his side, he smiled and said, "I don't know anything I've done that I wouldn't do over again, except maybe a little tighter bookkeeping."

Wilbur never recovered from his indictment and conviction. He was not what I'd call a broken man, but he wasn't the same afterward. He didn't return to the AFL-CIO, and he slowly disappeared from public view. After getting out of prison, he went back to his job as a machine oiler at American Tobacco, where he remained until 1986. His health gradually worsened, and he died in 1992.

As for me, I recovered from the experience, but it strengthened my commitment to fighting the abuse of power by those in positions of authority in the criminal justice system. It was not just an abstract concept anymore; I had experienced what I perceived as an abuse of power directed at me personally, and it became much more of a mission. For the rest of my career, I understood exactly how my clients felt when they came through the door looking for help in facing the power of the government.

14

THE ATTACK ON CONDOMS AND THE
FIRST AMENDMENT

*The effect of this cursed business on our youth and society, no pen
can describe.*

—Anthony Comstock, Special Agent, U.S. Post Office; Secretary, New York Society for the Suppression of Vice (1844–1915)

Perhaps no freedom protected by the Bill of Rights has a more storied or important role in our history, or is more cherished by our citizens, than our First Amendment right to freedom of speech. From lofty pamphlets like the Federalist Papers, to protests and marches during the sixties and seventies, to topless dancing, it all comes under the protection of the First Amendment. Despite serving as a bedrock principle in our democracy, it has frequently been subjected to abuses of power by those in positions of authority in the criminal justice system, both recently and in the past.

In the early years after the American Civil War, an enterprising fellow named Henry Hunter owned and operated a modest yet diverse publishing company in Hinsdale, New Hampshire, under the name Hunter & Co. Its principal publication was a periodical titled *The Star*

Spangled Banner, which in 1870 boasted a robust monthly circulation of thirty thousand copies. Hunter & Co. offered a variety of items for sale to younger audiences, such as "dialog books," how-to guides for ventriloquism, and copies of *Robinson Crusoe*, which sold for 12 cents. For their more mature customers, Hunter & Co. advertised that *any* order would be filled, including requests for "fancy articles." In the vernacular of the day, this term referred to merchandise of a more adult nature.

In August 1873, Hunter & Co. received an order from a new customer with a post office box in New Jersey. The customer was seeking a product of relatively recent origin and availability in the United States known as a "French safe." Hunter & Co., true to its word, filled the order. It was the first India-rubber condom Hunter & Co. ever shipped, and it would prove to be the last. A raid by federal agents on Hunter & Co. would soon follow.

Hunter & Co. had fallen prey to a decoy letter sent by a special agent for the U.S. Post Office. The purpose of the letter was to induce Hunter & Co. to send a contraceptive item through the mail system of the United States, which at that time (and for many years thereafter) constituted a crime under federal law.

The special agent's name was none other than Anthony Comstock, a self-appointed knight-errant of public morality and a tireless crusader against "indecency." Comstock, born in the biblically named New Canaan, Connecticut, in 1844, had an early life that was unremarkable until his twenty-eighth year, when he discovered, to his horror, that a coworker at the dry-goods store where he worked had taken to reading, and *enjoying*, what was considered "erotic literature" in that bygone era. Truth be told, Comstock himself was readily aroused by salacious stimuli, according to his diary, which too often plunged him into a self-gratifying practice that he loathed, causing him crushing shame. He therefore viewed all things tending to excite sexual interest as the very worst of abominations and sought their suppression. So Comstock hatched a plan to save his colleague at the dry-goods store from the libidinous clutches of tawdry books. Still blushing, he marched down to the bookstore where his coworker purchased the "erotica," bought copies for himself, and promptly tattled to the police—who straightaway arrested the book merchant for peddling obscenity.

Comstock's spontaneous sting operation was widely and favorably reported in an America that still retained much in the way of Victorian sensibilities. Being a man of heightened religious zeal, to put it mildly, he interpreted his success as a directive from on high that his destiny was to identify all peddlers of "fancy items" and run them out of business, thereby ridding the world of all that stirred the loins and warmed the coals of desire. He wouldn't rest until he had "drawn an indictment against this horde of blasphemers and revilers of the ever-living God," and this became his life's mission and his life's work.

Comstock soon discovered that existing federal law was not sufficiently stringent for his purposes, as some subsequent arrests he orchestrated failed to result in convictions. In 1873, with the support and underwriting of the YMCA, Comstock went to Washington by train to prevail upon Congress to draft more expansive legislation that would better suit his purposes and allow him to lay his snares and traps far and wide. Congress responded by passing Section 3893 et seq. of Title XLVI of the U.S. Code, which criminalized the use of the U.S. mail to send:

"Obscene, lewd, or lascivious" publications of any kind.

Publications of an "indecent character."

"Any article or thing designed or intended for the prevention of conception."

"Any article or thing intended or adapted for any indecent or immoral use or nature."

Any advertisements of any kind (including catalogs) telling where or how to obtain such items.

Violation of the statute was punishable by a fine of up to $5,000 (in 1873 dollars) or imprisonment "at hard labor" for up to ten years, or both.

This law, which could be construed to cover nearly anything relating to sex, would bring ruin and dishonor to many an honest publisher, bookseller, distributor, author, artist, and photographer under its capricious terms. It soon became known as the Comstock Law, and this was fitting. As if by divine providence, Comstock was given a unique dispensation by the federal government. He was named Special Agent of the Post Office Department of the United States, and was singularly empowered to enforce the provisions of the new postal "obscenity act." In his position as special agent, he could travel anywhere in the United States by rail free of charge to cleanse the states of indecency. It was thus that Anthony Comstock, in a fever of pious monomania, began to police the nation's public morality.

Comstock, we now know, abhorred lust. Lust "defiles the body, debauches the imagination, corrupts the mind, deadens the will, destroys the memory, sears the conscience, hardens the heart, and damns the soul," Comstock wrote in 1880. He used the new law to censor anything that was apt to excite lust, and Comstock saw lust everywhere he looked. He brought prosecutions against mundane literature with only cloaked allusions to sex, pencil drawings of classical nudes, depictions of fully clothed women with dresses that fell just above the ankle, textbooks with frank discussions about reproduction, advertisements for contraceptives, and circulars promising cures for "private diseases." He abused his power by using the law to criminalize anything that *he* found personally offensive—including materials protected by the First Amendment to the Constitution.

The Comstock Law included no definitions of the material terms, so it was impossible for any citizen to know what might be considered obscene or indecent, and what might be merely a tad immodest. A petition prepared and circulated by a number of publishers, professors, authors, and artists circa 1874 regarding the Comstock Law makes the point well: "A learned jurist has said that 'no legislative body in making laws should use language that has to be defined and construed by others. Every crime should be so clearly defined that there can be no mistaking it. Murder, homicide, arson, larceny, burglary, forgery, and so forth, are so defined that they cannot be misunderstood. It is not so with obscenity; the term is left to be construed by judges, lawyers, juries, and whoever chooses to decide what *is* obscene, and what is *not*. If obscenity is a crime punishable by fine and imprisonment, it at least ought to be correctly defined so that it may be known in what it consists, and so, that an accused person shall not be at the mercy of a man or a number of men who construe what is obscene, what is indecent and immoral by their own particular opinion or notion of morality and immorality. What is obscene to one man may be as pure as the mountain snow to another, and one man ought not to be empowered to decide for other men.'"

Even when a jury voted to acquit a merchant or artist, in many cases the damage had already been done. The defendant had been publicly identified as a "smut peddler" and had received the community's disdain accordingly. Some had to close as a result.

It was, of course, Anthony Comstock himself who, using a false name and address, had requested the fancy French-styled condom by mail, a tactic that Comstock described as a "process of excusable deception," and one that he would employ hundreds if not thousands of times during his period of inquisition. It was also Comstock who raided Hunter & Co. on September 22, 1873, with a federal marshal, to arrest Mr. Hunter and take him ignominiously into custody. By unwittingly mailing the condom to Comstock, Hunter & Co. had violated the new postal law and faced prosecution and opprobrium as a purveyor of obscenity.

After arresting Henry Hunter and four of his clerks, who had nothing to do with the affair, Comstock then turned the offices of Hunter & Co. upside down in his search for more licentious materials, and seized all manner of merchandise that was impounded and later destroyed.

Comstock loved to crow about his arrests, and he soon announced the raid on Hunter & Co. to the *Boston Daily Globe*, which ran a story that was likely ghostwritten by Comstock. It described, in obsequious, exaggerated terms, how the mighty Comstock, wielding power under the 1873 law, had "worked the destruction of hundreds of thousands of vicious productions which are all-potent in undermining the morals of the young." The story averred—well prior to trial—that Hunter had for years carried on a "gigantic business in swindling and obscene publications," and that he was a notorious trafficker in "obscene books" that were sold out of his "lair" in New Hampshire. (Most newspapers today would at least have thrown in the word "allegedly" in front of the accusations.)

The case against Hunter & Co. was eventually dropped, according to one source, but the harm to Hunter was nevertheless extreme. As one observer wrote, "Though the case was not pressed against [Hunter & Co.], it cost them thousands of dollars, to the almost utter ruin of their business and an amount of trouble and intense anxiety on the part of themselves and families that never can be fully estimated." This was a common and recurring theme with Comstock's obscenity prosecutions. He accomplished his goal even if he ultimately lost the case.

E. M. Grandin, who Comstock described as "a true villain," was another casualty of comstockery. To Comstock, Grandin was the worst sort of scoundrel. He operated the Sporting Man's Emporium, whose advertisements claimed, "We have on hand, and will forward at the shortest notice, all articles used by THE SPORTING MAN, THE MAN OF LEISURE, THE MAN OF TASTE." The company also offered "Books, Books, Books, the newest and gayest out!" along with "rubber goods of the highest quality." As should be evident, all of this innuendo hardly concealed the true nature of the goods being sold, and Comstock was right on to them.

Using a pseudonym, Comstock wrote to Grandin from Bedford, Ohio, asking for a catalog of the "sporting books" Grandin advertised in an admittedly salty periodical known as *The Days' Doings*. Grandin, in reply, sent Comstock a catalog of available books. Grandin was forthwith arrested, tried, and convicted on the basis of the *catalog* alone and was sentenced to prison.

In the first seven years following the enactment of the Comstock

Law, Comstock was responsible for the arrest and prosecution of more than four hundred people. During this time, by his own count, he seized and destroyed more than twenty-four thousand pounds of books and materials, including 202,679 "obscene pictures and photos"; 14,420 pounds of stereotype plates for printing books; 64,094 "articles for immoral use," such as condoms and lord knows what else; 6,072 indecent playing cards; more than a million circulars, catalogs, songs, and poems; and 22,354 newspapers containing unlawful advertisements. All of this was done for the purpose, as Comstock wrote, "to crush out [the] business" of obscenity.

Almost exactly one hundred years after Comstock's reign of terror, a renewed inquisition against the business of selling sexually explicit images and related objects began anew in America with tricks, traps, and decoys that would have made Comstock proud.

15

ADAM & EVE FIGHT BACK

The enormous disparity between plaintiffs' resources and the resources of the government means, as a practical matter, that plaintiffs could be swiftly driven out of business before they ever set foot inside a courtroom.

—U.S. District Court Judge Joyce Hens Green, *PHE, Inc. v. United States Department of Justice* (1990)

A middle-aged man named David was at work on a Sunday. With a furtive glance over his shoulder, he pulled a brown paper bag from his briefcase and poured its contents carefully onto the desk. What emerged was a faded, dog-eared catalog that appeared to have seen some use. On the cover, which he flipped quickly past, a model in red lingerie posed hipshot and seductive below the words *"Adam & Eve."* He sighed and shook his head. This was not the sort of thing he could have at home.

David swallowed hard. There were so many choices. You really couldn't tell much from the video titles, all of which had predictable names like *The Sex Goddess* and *The Ultimate O*. It was too bad the harder stuff wasn't set out in its own separate section. After several minutes of searching, he placed a hesitant check mark next to four movies, a couple of magazines, and, as an afterthought, a large, flesh-colored item known euphemistically as a "marital aid." He exhaled and took another look around, then copied the items onto the order card and added up the total. A whopping $290.86. It seemed excessive, but if he was going to place an order, he might as well get what he needed. Go big or go home, as they say.

On the envelope, he wrote out the return address, a discreet post office box under the name "David Hunt." He obviously couldn't use his real name and address when ordering adult merchandise. After all, he thought, at least some of this stuff was illegal, and you could go to jail just for buying it.

In due course, Adam & Eve, one of the nation's largest distributors of contraceptives and sexually explicit merchandise, received the order from "David Hunt" and promptly filled it. It was almost Valentine's Day in 1986. This might have been a romantic gift from one spouse to another. Sales always ticked up around the holidays.

Adam & Eve would soon learn that David Hunt was in fact David Hedgecock, and that David Hedgecock was in fact a special agent of the North Carolina State Bureau of Investigation. By sending what amounted to a decoy letter to bait Adam & Eve to send something explicit through the mail, Hedgecock had taken a page right out of Comstock's playbook and thrust Adam & Eve into a multistate legal controversy that would go on for years.

Agent Hedgecock received the large package from Adam & Eve and shared the contents with other state and federal authorities. In darkened rooms, with blinds drawn, prosecutors and postal inspectors in several jurisdictions took turns inserting the videos into their respective VCRs and watched as paid adult performers engaged in consensual sexual acts. The authorities soon came to decide that all the materials provided by Adam & Eve were legally obscene, and that a military-style raid on the Adam & Eve headquarters should be made to disrupt the company's operations and land a heavy blow against the pornography industry.

This picking up where Comstock left off was due, in no small part, to President Ronald Reagan announcing in 1984 that his administration would make it a priority to put pornographers out of business. To this end, Reagan tasked Edwin Meese, the attorney general, with the imperative of studying the effects of pornography on society and ways in which "the spread of pornography can be contained, consistent with constitutional guarantees." Meese, in turn, created the Attorney General's Commission on Pornography, which was comprised of luminaries like Dr. James Dobson of Focus on the Family, and Rev. Bruce Ritter, the founder of Covenant House, a home for wayward teenagers.[*]

The commission's conclusions,[†] while not well supported by science, purported to find causal links between pornography and crime. This was enough to give state and federal prosecutors an incentive to direct truly obscene levels of government resources toward the prosecution of sexually explicit magazines and videos.[‡] In a special ceremony attended by two hundred "anti-obscenity leaders," Reagan put the pornography business on notice by saying, in his inimitable John Wayne style, "Your days are numbered."

---

[*] Years after the Meese Commission had closed its books, an investigation found "extensive" evidence of inappropriate contact between Rev. Ritter and some of the children lodged at Covenant House.

[†] The commission's 1,960-page report contains, among other pieces of useful information, unforgettable deadpan play-by-play descriptions, written by commission members, of popular adult films like *Debbie Does Dallas* and *The Devil in Miss Jones*, as well as the names of nearly every explicit magazine, book, and movie in existence at that time, and the cities in which the works could be purchased.

[‡] Make no mistake—obscenity and pornography prosecutions have been a mainstay of American jurisprudence since the days of Comstock, and the 1970s and '80s saw countless prosecutions in jurisdictions all across the country in cases like *United States v. One Reel of Film* (1973) and *United States v. Various Articles of Obscene Merchandise* (1981). But it wasn't until the Reagan federal anti-pornography initiative that federal and state governments engaged in a concerted, focused campaign to destroy the pornography industry as a whole through the use of a "multiple prosecution" strategy.

This was a clarion call to my old nemesis, U.S. Attorney Samuel T. Currin, who, like Comstock, had a keen interest in pornography prosecutions, and who believed that companies like Adam & Eve were ruinous to public morality. Currin and North Carolina Attorney General Lacy Thornburg, a Democrat from western North Carolina, joined forces to create the nation's first federal-state task force on pornography, and its first target was Adam & Eve.

On May 29, 1986, following a six-month investigation, *thirty-seven* federal and state agents, including postal inspectors from North Carolina, Utah, Arizona, and California, descended on Adam & Eve's headquarters in Carrboro, North Carolina, with guns drawn. Armed guards were stationed at each door of the facility, and no one was allowed in or out. When the receptionist questioned whether the agents had the right to enter the building, an officer threatened to kick down the door.

Once inside, the agents swarmed over the premises and shouted at people to put their hands up, as if instead of putting adult videos into envelopes, the employees were drug lords readying heroin for shipment to area elementary schools. The agents demanded to be taken to where the sex videos were made and appeared surprised and perhaps disappointed to learn that Adam & Eve did not actually film any of the videos it distributed.

The switchboard was shut down, and employees were corralled and marched into the warehouse, where they were divided into lines, intrusively photographed, and interviewed by the agents. Some were taken off into private rooms.

Some employees objected to being interviewed but were informed they could not refuse. All 118 employees present that day were issued a subpoena to appear before a federal grand jury and were made to display the subpoena before they were allowed to leave. Agents refused to allow employees to speak with any attorney, including a company attorney who came to the premises specifically to advise employees of their rights. It was an incredibly frightening experience for many employees, as well as an egregious abuse of power by the government.

When the workers, all of whom were rattled and dismayed, were finally allowed to leave, agents searched their briefcases and pocket-books at the exits. In another nod to Comstock, agents then turned Adam & Eve's offices upside down and confiscated all manner of books, magazines, videos, financial records, and even documents labeled as attorney-client communications. Grainger R. Barrett, a former town attorney for Chapel Hill, and a man not known for hy-perbole, arrived on the scene in the midst of the raid. Describing the scene later in court, he said quite seriously, "I would call it a concentration-camp atmosphere."

Phil Harvey is the president and owner of Adam & Eve, whose corporate parent is PHE, Inc. (Phil Harvey Enterprises). He was in New York when the raid occurred. When he arrived back at PHE, he saw that agents had been in his office, broken open his desk, and examined everything in it. It was an extraordinarily unsettling and invasive experience.

Sam Currin, in justification of the raid, claimed to the press that complaints about Adam & Eve had come from as far away as Utah, and that his office had received hundreds of complaints about Adam & Eve from all over the country. "We've probably gotten more com-plaints about Adam & Eve than any other matter we've dealt with," said Currin. What he failed to mention was that it was federal and state agents who had registered most of the complaints.

Federal and state grand juries were hastily convened to consider whether to bring charges against Phil Harvey, PHE, and various em-ployees. The first indictments to be handed down came on August 4, 1987, from Alamance County, North Carolina. Harvey, the com-pany, and two employees faced twelve felony counts of distributing obscenity, one for each item shipped through the mail. The individ-uals faced maximum sentences of forty-five years in prison.

It would be easy to imagine that the president of a major adult-film and sex-toy distributor would be an unsavory character of low morals who exploited workers and debased women for his personal gain. When it comes to Phil Harvey, this could not be further from the truth.

After growing up in Illinois, Phil graduated from Harvard College in 1961, and two years later he went to work in India for CARE, a global charity dedicated to ending poverty and promoting social justice. His work for CARE in India involved large-scale feeding programs for needy and impoverished children. While working for CARE, he astutely observed the critical need in India, and elsewhere around the world, including the United States, for adequate family-planning services, which were sorely lacking the world over.

In 1969, Phil entered the School of Public Health at the University of North Carolina at Chapel Hill, to work toward a master's degree in family-planning administration. In connection with his thesis work, Phil and another graduate student named Tim Black secured permission from the university to make a foray into providing contraceptives to the public through the mail. Phil believed that people ought to have ready access to birth control and that the government should not pose obstacles to consenting adults making their own reproductive choices. He foresaw that millions of lives could be saved by making contraceptives widely available, and that is precisely what he did.

Incredibly, though, under the Comstock Law, it was still illegal in 1969 to send contraceptives, or information about birth control, through the mail. In 1965, in the landmark case *Griswold v. Connecticut*, the U.S. Supreme Court struck down a Connecticut law prohibiting the sale of contraceptives to married couples. Phil surmised that under the ruling in *Griswold*, it should be possible to lawfully provide condoms to married couples through the mail, and this formed the basis of his first business model.

With Tim Black, Phil formed two entities known as Population Planning Associates (PPA) and Population Services International

(PSI) in 1970 and began to run ads for mail-order condoms. "Because the Comstock Law had deterred virtually everyone else from selling condoms through the mail," Phil said, "we found a ready market."

In the early 1970s, PPA and PSI were warned by the state of New York that its advertisements and mail-order condoms violated a New York law that prohibited the sale of contraceptives to anyone under sixteen, allowed only licensed pharmacists to sell contraceptives, and, similar to the Comstock Law, prohibited all advertisements for contraceptives. At the time, several states had similar laws on the books. Phil filed suit against the governor and attorney general of New York, claiming that the law was unconstitutional and in violation of the First and Fourteenth Amendments. The case made its way to the U.S. Supreme Court. In 1977, in *Carey v. Population Services International*, the Supreme Court agreed with Phil and struck down the law denying minors and other persons in New York reasonable access to contraceptives and related information. This was an important case that further expanded the right of individuals to be free from government interference in their private reproductive choices.

Between 1970 and 1986, the year the federal government raided Adam & Eve and charged its owner and employees with a laundry list of felonies, PPA and PSI sold and distributed millions of condoms in the United States and to poor countries abroad, which helped avoid millions of unwanted pregnancies and saved an untold number of lives.

At some point along the way, PPA—whose name was changed to PHE, Inc. (PHE) in 1982—began selling other sexually explicit merchandise. This was a business decision by Phil and the other owners of PHE, who believed the change was necessary to support the growing company. PHE initially had tried to get people to buy ship-building kits, digital watches, and women's leisurewear, but it was the "erotic magazines with soft-focus nudity" that really took off. When VCRs hit the market in the early 1980s, adult videos became a popular form of sexual expression, and this became a big part of Adam & Eve's business. It was what the people wanted; and customers could watch the videos in the privacy of their own homes.

Under U.S. law, "obscenity" is not protected by the First Amendment. The states and the federal government may, without running afoul of the Constitution, pass laws suppressing and even *punishing* "obscene" speech—which can include works as diverse as songs, poems, books, magazines, photographs, videos, and other forms of expression. The big question is how we determine, under our laws, what speech is "obscene," and therefore subject to regulation, and which speech is not obscene, and thus protected from censorship or suppression by the First Amendment. Another important question is who gets to decide which is which.

Many state and federal courts have grappled with these questions, with dismal success. In 1964, Supreme Court Justice Potter Stewart recognized the futility of trying to circumscribe the precise parameters of obscenity. He wrote that he couldn't explain exactly how to define "hard-core pornography," which could be prohibited or criminalized, "and perhaps I could never succeed in intelligibly doing so. But," wrote Justice Stewart, "*I know it when I see it.*"

A law that limits a form of speech and expression and includes criminal penalties for its violation cannot, in practice, be based upon an "I know it when I see it" approach. Due process requires that you be given adequate notice that your conduct is criminal. Over the course of several decisions, the U.S. Supreme Court produced a test for defining "obscenity," but that test raised as many questions as it answered.

The test was set forth in *Miller v. California* (1973). It provided that if the following three elements were all met, a book, magazine, video, film, or other form of expression, could be subject to punishment:

1. Whether the average person, *applying contemporary community standards*, would find that the work, taken as a whole, *appeals to the prurient interest in sex*;

2. Whether the work depicts or describes, *in an offensive way*, sexual conduct or excretory functions, as specifically defined by applicable state law; and

3. Whether the work, *taken as a whole*, lacks serious *literary, artistic, political, or scientific value.*

Since *Miller* was decided almost fifty years ago, the courts have struggled with precisely defining the terms "prurient," and "offensive," and with determining what "serious literary, artistic, political, or scientific value" means in any given context. It's sort of like beauty being in the eye of the beholder.

But the "community standards" element of the *Miller* test is perhaps the most problematic. It means that the standard for what constitutes "obscenity" can be, and often is, different in different jurisdictions. For example, a work that is *not* considered obscene in Austin, Texas, under that city's "community standards" can be deemed obscene in rural Kentucky. This means that a mail-order distributer of X-rated movies could ship a video to someone in Austin without repercussion, but if the same video is instead shipped, for instance, to someone in Bowling Green, Kentucky, the distributor could be arrested and imprisoned, even if the purchaser intended to watch the video in the privacy of their own home.

The *Miller* test, practically speaking in a country as diverse as the United States, means it is literally impossible to know whether a particular book, image, or video is legally obscene until a jury, in whatever community a prosecution is initiated, determines that the material appeals to the then-existing "prurient interest in sex" (however that is defined) according to the "standards" (whatever that means) in that particular "community" (however that is defined). As Phil Harvey dryly observed, "The only way to find out [whether something is obscene] is to go on trial, which is a rather expensive way of obeying the law."

A critical distinction to make here is between what most people would call "pornography" and what the law deems to be "obscenity." Pornography, which is not illegal, is loosely defined as a depiction of sexuality or sexual acts for the purpose of sexual arousal; in other words, sexually explicit or sexually oriented material. "Obscenity," which *is* illegal, contains something beyond sexually explicit material that makes it appeal to a "prurient" interest in sex, which has been defined by the courts as "a morbid, degrading and unhealthy interest in sex, as distinguished from a mere candid interest in sex." All these definitions do is to add vagueness to what can be prosecuted.

In the 1980s, that vagueness was seized upon by Sam Currin and other zealots involved in the anti-pornography crusade, whose real goal was to eliminate the sale of *all* sexually explicit materials through the authority of state and federal obscenity laws. The prosecution of Adam & Eve was never truly about stamping out "obscenity." It was about ending the sale of all forms of sexual expression, just as Comstock had done a century before.

In light of Adam & Eve's indictment, Phil Harvey and several executives of the company in Alamance County, which at that time was a rural area of North Carolina, hired two of the preeminent criminal lawyers in North Carolina, Wade Smith and Joe Cheshire, along with one of the preeminent civil rights lawyers in the South, Adam Stein, to defend PHE, Phil, and the other individual defendants. I was then fortunate enough to be added to this all-star team.

The case went to trial in March 1987. Because the *Miller* test required the material on trial to be evaluated by the jury "as a whole," whatever material was alleged by the state to be "obscene" had to be shown to the jury from beginning to end, in its entirety. The state prosecutor, in a strategic blunder, had indicted four different videos of about sixty minutes each, so the jury had to endure *hours* of adult videos showing "sprees of anal and oral intercourse." The jury foreman described the videos as initially "tantalizing" but then almost immediately "boring." A large sexual device, bearing the unfortunate but accurate catalog description "footlong double dong," was entered into evidence and passed to the jury for handling and inspection. They appeared to be unimpressed.

Toward the end of the first day of watching the videos, the judge announced that there was one more left and asked the jury if they wanted to take a break and view the last one the next day. After conferring with one another for about thirty seconds, one of the jurors, a middle-aged man who had played minor-league baseball in Venezuela, stood up and announced simply, "Roll 'em." And the judge did.

Based on that comment, and our gut instinct that the jury was bored by the videos and offended that an SBI agent had ordered the videos to be delivered to their county (presumably because two-thirds of the people living in the county at the time defined themselves as "very religious" and attended church *at least* twice a week, according to our pretrial jury survey), we decided not to put on any evidence for the defense.

We argued to the jury that it was important to protect the First Amendment, even for material they didn't personally like, because "men and women have a right to receive materials in plain, brown wrappers in their post office boxes and to enjoy those materials in the privacy of their homes." I talked about Nazi Germany and Anne Frank (I can't remember how I made that relevant, but I did somehow), Joe Cheshire talked about his great-grandmother in Russia (who we assumed actually existed, though it didn't matter for argument's sake), and Wade Smith quoted Martin Niemöller about the need for ordinary people to speak out for others before there is no one left to speak out for them.

The jury was out for an hour before announcing its decision: PHE, Phil Harvey, and the other executives had been acquitted on all charges. Speaking to the newspapers following the verdict, the jury foreman, the Black man who had told the judge to "roll 'em," said they'd decided in just five minutes to acquit everyone but stayed in the jury room for an hour so as not to embarrass the prosecutors. The front-page banner headline in the Greensboro newspaper the next day said it all: "Adam & Eve Found Not Guilty!" It's still hanging in a frame on my office wall, yellowed with time but still inspiring.

The acquittal was significant, because it signaled—or should have signaled—that other prosecutions of Phil and PHE on the state and federal levels might be difficult. After all, Alamance County was pretty much rural, religious, and Republican. As one local editorial stated, "Alamance County is not exactly the Vegas of the Piedmont"—suggesting that the standards and tastes found in Alamance County, North Carolina, might be a bellwether for other counties and jurisdictions. It should have been the end of PHE's entanglement with the law.

Sam Currin and other true believers, however, were undeterred. On the day the not-guilty verdict was announced, Currin told the press that the federal investigation against Adam & Eve was still "full steam ahead." Behind the scenes, the Department of Justice was working hard to bring additional indictments against Phil and PHE in multiple different conservative federal jurisdictions. We would soon find out that the real trouble had not yet even begun. The federal government was at the brink of a years-long, coordinated campaign against PHE and other distributers of sexually explicit videos for the sole purpose of putting PHE and the others out of business. It would become a war of attrition.

In March 1987, the same month Adam & Eve, Phil, and his employees were acquitted, Attorney General Edwin Meese established the National Obscenity Enforcement Unit (NOEU) in the Department of Justice. Following the recommendations of the Attorney General's Commission on Pornography, the NOEU was designed to oversee "a major federal effort to crack down heavily on the producers, distributors, and retailers of obscene material."

Between 1987 and 1989, as part of an NOEU "multiple-prosecution" strategy that would soon become clear, federal prosecutors in Utah, perhaps the most religious and conservative state in the country at the time, used the threat of indictments against Phil as leverage in an attempt to secure PHE's agreement to *cease distribution throughout the United States* of *all* adult-oriented materials, including magazines, excepting only R-rated movies. The agreement proposed by the Utah prosecutors would have blocked PHE from distributing works that were clearly protected by the First Amendment, such as *Playboy* and *The Joy of Sex*. PHE had not sent any merchandise to Utah since the initial raid in 1986, but federal postal inspectors had ordered films from PHE in 1985, and Brent Ward, the U.S. Attorney in Utah, was adamant and unrelenting. When Phil rejected this proposed resolution, a federal grand jury was empaneled in Utah to bring charges against Phil, other employees, and PHE, which again carried the prospect of serious prison time for Phil and the other individuals, and bankruptcy for PHE.

Shortly thereafter, as we prepared for trial in Utah, another federal grand jury, this time in Kentucky, a jurisdiction well-known for its obscenity prosecutions, issued a subpoena to PHE to produce a broad range of sexually explicit materials. We were told that the assistant U.S. Attorney for the Middle District of Kentucky intended to obtain an indictment of PHE on federal obscenity charges in Kentucky in addition to the impending indictments in Utah.

By this point, we realized that the federal government was doing something unprecedented and truly astonishing: it was deliberately coordinating an attack on PHE in multiple pornography-intolerant jurisdictions at once—jurisdictions like Kentucky, Utah, and then Alabama, where the community standards would be more likely to result in a conviction. Simultaneous indictments and prosecutions in separate states would require Phil and PHE to defend themselves in several venues around the country at the same time, pitting them against a government with unlimited resources and making the contest one of attrition rather than due process. It was a deliberately unfair setup, and that was the basis of the government's strategy. It was an incredible abuse of the federal government's prosecutorial power, one that Phil Harvey wanted to fight as long as he had the resources—which might not have been that long, as things were going.

One afternoon, the attorneys were meeting with Phil in Wade Smith's office in Raleigh to discuss legal strategy. We knew that several similar companies had just folded up their shops and capitulated in the face of the government's multi-district onslaught, and Phil was giving serious consideration to doing the same thing. Martin Niemöller's famous statement rang in my ears, and I suddenly found myself lecturing Phil, who had thus far been stalwart in fighting the government's efforts but was obviously fatigued and discouraged. "Goddammit," I said, "we're talking about the First Amendment here! If *you* don't stop the government, who will? Every time we agree to a fine, they raise the ante. If we agree to these guilty pleas and escalating fines, there'll be no end to it. Someone's got to take a stand. If not PHE, who will?"* I didn't know it at the time, but I later learned from Phil's own book on the subject, *The Government vs. Erotica*, that this was a watershed moment for him. Inspired, he decided to continue the fight and never looked back.

Since the NOEU was targeting every distributor nationwide, my theory, for which I had absolutely no empirical evidence (but rather a strong gut instinct) was that the NOEU would end up prioritizing not the largest distributors, of which PHE was one, but those for which they could quickly show tangible results—namely putting them out of business—and thereby justify their existence to themselves and their supporters.

I therefore suggested what I described as the "we're not a tasty morsel" strategy. If the federal government was going to try to take a bite out of us, we were going to be extremely difficult to chew and very painful to swallow. We were going to be like a piece of spiny cactus. We'd make the NOEU prefer to focus on other distributors first—the so-called tasty morsels. We would vigorously contest every

---

* Emphasis added.

subpoena, every motion, and every act by the government in fur-
therance of its prosecution of Phil and PHE. Phil and PHE hired
multiple local attorneys to assist us in the jurisdictions where the
battles were being fought. The NOEU had to fight hard for anything
and everything they got.

On March 16, 1990, Phil and PHE carried the "we're not a tasty
morsel" strategy to its logical conclusion. PHE took the extraordinary step of suing the Department of Justice to stop the multiple
prosecution strategy, which was obviously designed to deny PHE
and Phil their First Amendment rights. Our expanding legal team,
which now included First Amendment expert Bruce Ennis of the
firm Jenner & Block in Washington, an extraordinary lawyer who
also represented *Playboy* magazine, filed a lawsuit in the District of
Columbia against the Department of Justice, the NOEU, and the
U.S. Attorney for the Middle District of Kentucky. We sought an
injunction against the federal government to block its multiple-
prosecution strategy on the grounds that it was an unconstitutional
attempt to prevent PHE from being able to defend its First Amendment rights and to put the company out of business altogether.
Bruce argued that "if the government can prosecute in two, ten, or
one hundred jurisdictions for the same alleged offense, the power to
indict will be the power to destroy."

We fortunately drew a federal judge who understood and agreed
with the argument. District Judge Joyce Hens Green, who had been
appointed to the federal bench by Jimmy Carter, entered a preliminary injunction against the Department of Justice, prohibiting it
from bringing multiple prosecutions against Phil and PHE. It was
an incredible moment for Bruce, the incredible team at Jenner &
Block, and the rest of us, but especially for Phil Harvey. The judge
wrote in her opinion: "The enormous disparity between plaintiffs'
resources and the resources of the government means, as a practical matter, that plaintiffs could be swiftly driven out of business
before they ever set foot inside a courtroom." She recognized that
the Department of Justice could "accomplish their purpose, i.e.,

obliteration of plaintiffs' business, without ever obtaining a valid conviction."

Notwithstanding the injunction against multiple prosecutions from the federal court in D.C., on September 19, 1990, Utah brazenly moved forward with criminal indictments against Phil, two employees, and PHE based on alleged mailings that PHE had previously sent to the state. The prosecutors claimed that unsolicited catalogs had been sent to two boys, one eight years old, the other sixteen, between February and May 1986, prior to the original raid on Adam & Eve. What they did not say was that there was no way for PHE to know the ages of the people whose names had been added to their catalog mailing list, generally as a result of someone using that name to receive sexually oriented materials from another seller, or that it was the boys' parents who had actually retrieved the catalogs when they arrived in their home mailboxes. There was no evidence that the boys had ever seen them. And although PHE informed those receiving the catalog that they would be removed from the mailing list upon request, no such request was ever sent before the indictments were brought.

It was disheartening to see Phil indicted in Utah, but it appeared we were slowly winning the war. Through the litigation in D.C., we had obtained internal Department of Justice memoranda regarding its multi-district prosecution policy. When the documents were turned over, we found one smoking gun after another.

One of the most damning pieces of evidence was a memorandum Currin sent to his staff on March 30, 1987, *one day* after Phil was acquitted in Alamance County. It read:

We must regain momentum after the Adam & Eve verdict *and come with as many indictments as possible.* . . . We also need to locate some other district attorneys who will prosecute Adam & Eve in their districts. . . . We need to get state indictments of Adam & Eve in some other districts.

Contact Utah and urge them to proceed with their indictments as soon as possible. Also discuss with [NOEU head] Rob [Showers] whether he wants the Middle District [of North Carolina] to do a RICO on Adam & Eve. If so, he needs to work the RICO case out of Washington. I doubt anyone in the Middle District has the sense to do it.[*]

As Currin had cynically said at the time regarding the National Obscenity Enforcement Unit, "Some of these stores will voluntarily close down rather than face prosecution. Either way, we win." Currin's memo put this statement into context.

Another incredibly damning document obtained through discovery was dated April 22, 1987, less than a month following Adam & Eve's state-court acquittal. It was a description of the government's so-called Project PostPorn, and it spelled out, in no uncertain terms, the Department of Justice's plan to run distributors like Adam & Eve out of business through sheer attrition. It read, in pertinent part:

> Project PostPorn is a national project consisting of multi-district, simultaneous prosecutions of major mail order obscenity distributors. . . .
>
> Objectives: 1. To have a significant impact on the mail order distribution market. 2. *To put major mail order obscenity distributors out of business.*
>
> Where to prosecute: . . . *Districts where predisposition can be shown.*
> All districts will:
>
> - make test purchases from the assigned target company
> - conduct grand jury investigation

---

[*] Emphasis added.

- indict
- plea or take to trial*

An additional DOJ PostPorn memo read:

A total of forty-six US Attorney districts have been selected to conduct *simultaneous, multi-district prosecutions against these targets.*[†]

Finally, there was Utah U.S. Attorney Brent Ward's letter to Attorney General Edwin Meese from September 1985. It was Ward who first proposed the multiple prosecution strategy. He wrote:

The heart of the strategy . . . calls for multiple prosecutions (either simultaneous or successive) in all levels of government in many locations. If thirty-five prosecutors comprise the strike force, theoretically thirty-five different criminal prosecutions could be instigated simultaneously against one or more of the major pornographers. . . . I believe that such a strategy would deal a serious blow to the pornography industry.

In a second letter, Ward wrote to Meese:

As profitable as these enterprises may be, there is a limit to the prison terms, fines, and forfeiture of assets to which obscenity distributors will subject themselves. Multiple, simultaneous prosecutions at both federal and local levels therefore carry the potential to undermine profitability to the point that the survival of obscenity enterprises will be threatened.

---

* Emphasis added.

† Emphasis added.

On the basis of the damning evidence we had accumulated, we filed a motion to dismiss the Utah indictments, claiming that the government's strategy of prosecuting PHE in multiple jurisdictions was unconstitutional. On May 26, 1992, the Tenth Circuit Court of Appeals agreed, citing "evidence of an extensive pattern of prosecutorial conduct dating back some five years that suggests a persistent and widespread campaign to coerce the appellants into surrendering their First Amendment rights." Another win for Phil and PHE! On November 2, 1992, Utah conceded defeat and dropped its case against Phil and PHE, and the U.S. Attorney's office dismissed the indictments. We hoped that would be the end. We were wrong.

Despite everything that had happened on this long journey since Phil was first indicted in 1986, including our victories in state court in North Carolina, in federal court in D.C., and again in federal court in Utah, the U.S. Attorney in Alabama decided he would join the fray. The apparent abuse of the Department of Justice's power by the zealots in charge was nothing short of astonishing.

On December 1, 1992, the offices of PHE were raided *again*. This time, thirty agents and postal inspectors arrived waving a search warrant and demanding customer records. They wanted to know the names and addresses of everyone in Alabama who had purchased merchandise from PHE. Because the raid lasted two entire days, the agents slept overnight in the PHE customer service area "to preserve the integrity of the operation." On May 14, 1993, the postal inspectors returned for a second raid on PHE.

Showing the incredible arrogance of power, on September 30, 1993, the Department of Justice filed a motion in our still-pending federal case in D.C. and asked the Court to modify the preliminary injunction to allow them to seek criminal indictments against PHE and Phil in Alabama. The Court denied the DOJ's motions, saying, "There exists doubt regarding the independence and good faith of the Alabama prosecutors." This held the government at bay to an extent, but it was obvious to us that the harassment against PHE would continue.

Our trial in the D.C. civil case was scheduled to start at the beginning of December 1993. By this point, PHE had spent more than $3 million on attorney fees and faced additional enormous expenditures related to the upcoming trial against the government.

With the trial just days away, we finally reached a global settlement with the Department of Justice that would end the harassment and multiple prosecutions, including the recent attacks from Alabama. Under the settlement, PHE, the corporation, agreed to plead guilty to a technical violation—sending a mailing to Alabama with the requisite "sexually explicit materials" warning on the package written *in the wrong-size font*. This was a minor concession that Phil was willing to make if it meant the years-long harassment by the federal government would end. After nearly eight years of litigation and no telling how many millions of dollars spent in multiple states, the federal government could say that they had caught Adam & Eve using the wrong font size on a warning on the outside packaging of a mailing to Alabama. Phil, on the other hand, could proudly say that he had fought back against the government's deliberate abuse of power and won. Despite all the bloodshed along the way, it was a good day for the First Amendment.

After he left the United States Attorney's Office, Sam Currin was appointed a North Carolina Superior Court judge. He served in that role for three years, from 1987 to 1990, and then went into private law practice. While in private practice, he also served as the chair of the North Carolina Republican Party for three years, from 1996 to 1999.

In 2006, a client came into my Charlotte office. He was under federal investigation for a massive fraud scheme involving the use of offshore shell companies in the Cayman Islands to launder the proceeds of the scheme. When I met with the prosecutors to discuss his case, they told me they were interested in what my client knew about one Samuel T. Currin, the attorney who had overseen the scheme to help my client launder the proceeds offshore using Currin's law firm trust account.

My client ended up being the primary witness against Currin, who ultimately pled guilty to various federal crimes, including money laundering and obstructing a federal grand jury investigation. In September 2007, Currin was sentenced to almost six years in federal prison. The judge who sentenced him was Judge Earl Britt, who had called Currin's bluff in the Wilbur Hobby case twenty-five years earlier. I have to admit to a touch of schadenfreude.

Part V

FIGHTING THE ABUSE OF POWER BY THE POLICE

16

A QUIET DEATH BY LETHAL INJECTION

An ever-increasing body of evidence has shown that, over the last three decades alone, thousands of innocent men and women in the United States have been wrongfully arrested, convicted, and incarcerated for crimes they didn't commit. For years, those of us who worked in the system had cases in which we knew, or at least reasonably believed, that an innocent person had been wrongfully charged and convicted, but our knowledge was anecdotal, and our claims were often received by the courts and the public with skepticism and outright disbelief. Then, in 1992, Barry Scheck, who I first met in 1975 when we worked together as public defenders in the South Bronx, founded the Innocence Project with Peter Neufeld, a fellow public defender. DNA was beginning to be used by police and prosecutors in solving crimes, but Barry and Peter decided to use DNA analysis not to prosecute the guilty but to free the innocent. And, as the old folk song goes, "the walls came a-tumbling down."

The first DNA exoneration, which occurred in 1989, was followed in subsequent years by scores of additional DNA exonerations from cases all over the United States. To date, there have been almost four hundred documented cases in which a defendant was convicted or pled guilty to a crime where DNA evidence later established conclusively that he or she was innocent. Many of these were serious crimes, often with the defendant's very life in jeopardy: more than a third were murder cases, and twenty-one defendants who were later exonerated on the basis of DNA technology served time on Death Row prior to winning their freedom. Imagine the plight of a single one of these innocent defendants—accused, perhaps, of taking the life of another human being. Imagine the terror and desperation they must have felt from the moment of their wrongful arrest, throughout their public trial and fruitless appeals, during all the bleak and desperate years of their incarceration, and during the endless, anxious hours awaiting execution—*for something they didn't do.* And we will never know how many of those who have been executed were in fact innocent.

DNA exonerations, while telling only part of the story, presage a much larger and more extensive problem. DNA evidence plays a role in a comparatively small percentage of cases, such as sexual assaults and other crimes in which a defendant has left biological evidence at the crime scene. In the majority of criminal prosecutions, DNA evidence is not relevant to the crime, and neither the state, nor the defendant, can rely on DNA to establish guilt or innocence. A defendant accused of committing a robbery at gun point, for example, on the strength of only an eyewitness account, cannot disprove the accusations by resorting to DNA evidence. The significant numbers of DNA exonerees, therefore, represent only a fraction of all persons wrongfully convicted of crimes. Emerging data on the total number of wrongful convictions over the past three decades confirms this.

The National Registry of Exonerations (NRE), which is maintained by the University of California Irvine Newkirk Center for Science & Society, the University of Michigan Law School, and the Michigan State University College of Law, tracks all known exonerations of innocent defendants in the United States. The stated mission of the NRE is "to provide comprehensive information on exonerations of innocent criminal defendants in order to prevent future false convictions by learning from past errors." Since 1989, the NRE has documented more than 2,800 exonerations of innocent defendants, with in excess of *twenty-five thousand years* of prison time served by those wrongfully accused of crimes. These are staggering statistics. Each exoneration reflects an innocent person whose journey through our system of criminal justice produced an erroneous and tragic result, often culminating in decades of confinement and deprivation of liberty. Each of these exonerees was utterly failed by a system that was designed, in theory, to err on the side of freeing the guilty lest the innocent be convicted, but which we now know is producing far different results.

And there's more. The alarming number of exonerations in the last thirty years is dwarfed by the likely number of wrongful convictions over the same time period. Exonerations are exceedingly rare, and this has more to do with the hostility of the criminal justice system to freeing someone convicted of a crime than to whether the person is actually innocent or guilty. The criminal justice system is loath to reverse jury verdicts and has long been reflexively resistant to efforts by prisoners to overturn their convictions. In our criminal justice system, the interest in finality, of "being done" with a case, generally overwhelms the interest in achieving justice.

A prisoner seeking to prove his or her innocence post-conviction faces any number of daunting obstacles, including, first and foremost, skeptical prosecutors and judges, who serve as the system's omnipresent gatekeepers to exoneration. Another challenge is the loss or degradation over time of physical evidence that might be used to establish the defendant's innocence. The rare successful exoneration often takes years upon years of diligent and tireless effort, usually by a team of unpaid volunteer lawyers and law students, and happens only when all the stars perfectly align. The nearly three thousand exonerations thus far represent only those very few fortunate souls who, against these odds, were able to establish their innocence and convince a court to restore their freedom. For every exonerated criminal defendant, there are undoubtedly countless others who remain behind bars, innocent but imprisoned.

Still, the foregoing doesn't tell the whole story. In addition to the problem of wrongful convictions in the United States, there is a related and even more widespread problem: *wrongful arrests and prosecutions that do not result in convictions.* Each year, significant numbers of innocent people are arrested and prosecuted for serious crimes in jurisdictions in every state. Innocent people who are wrongfully prosecuted can spend years in pretrial detention due to high bonds or preventive detention before they are ultimately set free. Although prosecutors are supposed to screen these cases to weed out those without merit, prosecutors are often as overworked as the public defenders, defer to the police on the merits of the evidence, and suffer from the same confirmation bias as jurors: too often, prosecutors believe that if someone was arrested by the police, they must be guilty.

A wrongful arrest and prosecution, even one that ends in a dismissal or a jury acquittal, can and often does devastate a person's life. Even worse, a false arrest too often leads to a false guilty plea—a problem that so far has not been extensively documented or written about. The trial penalty, described earlier, combined with high bonds for those accused of crimes, and the prevalence of plea bargains in which defendants are offered greatly reduced sentences if they plead guilty, leads many (and especially the poor) to enter guilty pleas to crimes they have not committed. Most people believe that an innocent person would never confess, let alone plead guilty, to a crime he didn't commit, but this is a serious and recurring problem. Senior U.S. District Court Judge Jed Rakoff cogently explained the prevalence of this phenomenon in an article for the *New York Review of Books* entitled "Why Innocent People Plead Guilty":

> *The few criminologists who have thus far investigated the phenomenon estimate that the overall rate [of false guilty pleas] for convicted felons as a whole is between 2 percent and 8 percent. The size of that range suggests the imperfection of the data; but let us suppose that it is even*

lower, say, no more than 1 percent. When you recall that, of the 2.2 million Americans in prison, over 2 million are there because of plea bargains, we are then talking about an estimated 20,000 persons, or more, who are in prison for crimes to which they pleaded guilty but did not in fact commit.

In light of what we now know regarding wrongful prosecution and conviction rates in this country, we must face the harsh reality that our criminal justice system is not just fallible. It suffers from systemic, inherent faults and abuses of power by police and prosecutors—abuses of power that routinely produce erroneous convictions of innocent people. Take the case of Henry Lee McCollum. As a young man with intellectual disabilities, he was sentenced to death for the brutal rape and slaying of a young girl in 1984. Henry's fifteen-year-old brother, Leon, who suffered from a similar but more pronounced disability, was also convicted and sentenced to die for the murder. Leon's sentence was subsequently reduced to life in prison, but Henry remained on Death Row. In 2005, Supreme Court Justice Antonin Scalia, in an opinion upholding the death penalty in a separate case, used Henry and Leon's case as an example of why the death penalty was not only constitutional, *but also an entirely appropriate form of punishment.* "For example," he wrote, "the case of the 11-year-old girl raped by four men and then killed by stuffing her panties down her throat. . . . How enviable a quiet death by lethal injection compared with that!" Yet not so enviable for an innocent defendant of limited cognitive ability who was coerced into a confession by the police, which a civil jury recently determined to be precisely what occurred. Scalia never took back his words, even after Henry and Leon were exonerated by DNA evidence in 2014 and the true culprit was identified. Henry spent almost three decades of his life on Death Row, saved only by the incredible happenstance of the real killer leaving a cigarette butt at the crime scene with sufficient DNA on the filter end to be tested thirty years after the fact. Henry

McCollum just barely managed to escape the fate that Justice Scalia had so self-righteously pronounced justified.* How many others have not?

The chapters that follow bring the systemic faults and abuses of power that are inherent to our system of criminal justice to light through an examination of shocking cases in which innocent people were accused of horrible crimes and faced the justice system's most severe penalties. Many occurred in North Carolina, where I have practiced criminal defense since 1982, but they are not outliers or exceptions to the rule. These cases graphically illustrate common, everyday abuses of power found in all parts of the country.

---

* McCollum and Brown were recently awarded $75 million in damages by a federal jury in North Carolina, reportedly the largest verdict ever in a wrongful conviction case.

17

SET UP TO BE GUILTY

Suggestive False Identifications

The eyewitness identification of Ray Finch by Lester Floyd Jones was the linchpin of Finch's 1976 conviction for the murder of Shadow Holloman. There were no other witnesses, and the only physical evidence was a shotgun shell of dubious origin and relevance, allegedly found in the back seat of Ray's car. Without Jones's testimony that he saw the man who shot Shadow, and that the man was Ray Finch, the state had no case.

As it turns out, Jones knew Finch. Wilson County was a small, mostly rural community, and everyone knew almost everyone else. But Jones's familiarity with Ray wasn't just passing. Ray had a charge account at Holloman's store and was living just a short distance from Holloman's Grocery at the time of the robbery and murder. Jones had seen Ray at the store often, and had put gas in Ray's car the Wednesday before the murder. Jones had also been there once when Shadow bought a car from Ray. But Jones didn't tell the state trooper who responded to the scene that the man who shot Shadow was Ray Finch. He didn't even tell the trooper the man looked familiar or that he might know who he was. He provided only the vaguest of descriptions. No height, no weight, no skin tone, no facial features. Only "3 Black Males," one with "a Stocking over his head," one wearing "a Black cap," and the other wearing "a Tobogen."

Even though there was no reason to believe that Ray had been involved in the robbery and murder, Chief Deputy Owens immediately put out an APB naming Finch as the suspected perpetrator and asking that he be arrested. Meanwhile, Owens had Jones come to the Wilson County Sheriff's Department so they could do a lineup. According to Owens, Jones told him at some point before the lineup that the gunman had been wearing a three-quarter-length black coat, although it was unclear whether that detail had been reported before or after Ray was arrested wearing that kind of coat. While at the jail, Jones heard on a police scanner that Ray Finch had been arrested for killing Shadow. As Jones waited for the lineup to occur, he saw Ray at the jail in handcuffs, also waiting for the lineup.

To fill out the lineup, Owens had five Black jail inmates brought up in street clothes to serve as stand-ins. They all had different physical characteristics—their height, weight, and skin tone all varied. None of them were wearing a coat. None seemed to bear any resemblance to the description of the perpetrators Jones gave to the police. And, of course, Jones had said that the man with the shotgun who had killed Shadow had a stocking over his head. If that was true, the only possible way to identify that man was by his clothing.

Then Owens put Ray in the lineup wearing the three-quarter-length black coat he had on when he was arrested. Jones promptly identified person #5, the man wearing the three-quarter-length black coat, as the man who had killed Shadow. Owens then repeated the lineup with the same men, only this time he put them in different positions in the lineup. For this second lineup, Ray was still wearing the same black coat, and nothing about his appearance or his attire had been changed from the first lineup. Predictably, Jones identified him again as the gunman, having just identified him moments before. Owens then conducted yet another lineup, with the men switching places yet again and this time putting a nonsensical-looking hat on Ray, who was still in his long black coat. Jones, of course, selected Ray yet again. Three lineups, all within the space of thirty minutes, all involving the same men, and all marking Ray for identification by having him wear the same three-quarter-length black coat in each lineup, while no other participants wore a coat of any kind.

Owens knew exactly what he was doing. Having Ray wear that coat, while all the other lineup participants were just wearing shirts, wasn't fair to Ray—it put a target on his back. And conducting three successive lineups only helped to solidify Jones's identification of Ray in Jones's mind. Regardless of how uncertain Jones's identification of the perpetrators might have been from the circumstances at the country store, where it was dark, the lights were off, and the shooter had a stocking on his head, once Jones identified Ray Finch in three lineups, his mind would not change. By the time of trial, Jones pointed to Ray in the courtroom and claimed he was absolutely certain that man had killed Shadow Holloman. Jones's testimony served as the primary basis for Ray's conviction and life sentence.

This type of unfair and suggestive lineup wasn't (and still isn't) a one-off, and it doesn't just happen to Black or Latino suspects. In the now-infamous Duke lacrosse case—when a Black student at North Carolina Central University accused three white Duke University lacrosse players of rape—police and prosecutors created a photo lineup with no wrong answers. It contained *only* photos of white lacrosse players who had attended the party where the rape had allegedly occurred. All the alleged victim had to do was pick any three of the photos, since anyone she picked out could theoretically have committed the rape. The three unfortunate players she selected were indicted, but the case disintegrated when the state's attorney general found that all three were innocent and that no rape had even occurred. But they had already been suspended by Duke, their reputations had been ruined, and they had to transfer to other schools.

Oftentimes the mistaken identification by a witness is simply an honest, though tragic, mistake. This problem is especially acute in cross-racial identifications where the suspect was not previously known to the witness. This isn't racism. Everyone has difficulty identifying people from a different race. It's based on the limits of human perception and memory.

But too often it is the result of police manipulation, done either intentionally, as happened in the Finch and the Duke lacrosse cases, or recklessly, as happens when the police believe they have identified the actual perpetrator, create a procedure that is unnecessarily suggestive for the witness, and then take the resulting identification as proof positive that their initial belief was correct. It's a vicious cycle that results in wrongful convictions that could and should have been avoided by more thorough investigation and a neutral identification procedure.

The prosecution and conviction of Marvin Anderson perfectly illustrates this point. Anderson, a Black man, lived in Virginia. When he was eighteen years old, his life turned completely upside down. Through happenstance, he became a suspect in a horrific sexual assault of a white woman. In fact, he became the sole focus of the police's investigation despite evidence pointing at another person—one who eventually confessed.

The police began their focus on Anderson based on comments the perpetrator made to the victim during the rape suggesting that he was in a relationship with a white woman. Anderson happened to be the only Black man dating a white woman known to the investigating officer, and that was all it took. Anderson had no criminal history of any kind, but he immediately became the investigator's sole suspect. Rather than that being the start of a fact-based investigation, it became the beginning of a suspect-based investigation designed to prove that Anderson was the perpetrator.

Since Anderson had never been arrested for anything before, the investigator didn't have a mug shot of Anderson to show the victim, so he obtained one from Anderson's employer. It was a color photo and had Anderson's Social Security number printed on it. When the investigator showed the victim a photo lineup that included Anderson's photograph, it was *the only color photo* in the lineup and *the only one that included a Social Security number*. This obviously made his photo distinctive, which the investigator should have known made it unnecessarily suggestive, in violation of Anderson's rights. He proceeded anyway, and the victim selected Anderson's photograph from the array even though there were notable differences between Anderson's appearance and the description first given by the victim to the police. The investigator appears to have just ignored those differences. He was a victim of confirmation bias and tunnel vision. Confirmation bias is a psychological tendency to seek only evidence that confirms your beliefs, while ignoring or discounting evidence that contradicts your beliefs. It is "the well-documented tendency, once one has made up one's mind, to search harder for evidence that confirms rather than contradicts one's initial judgment."* Tunnel vision goes hand in hand with confirmation bias. Tunnel vision occurs when we intently focus on a particular thing or idea, to the exclusion of other things and ideas. In the criminal context, this occurs when police or prosecutors narrow their focus to a particular suspect, usually based on incomplete evidence, while ignoring or overlooking other possible suspects or evidence that might implicate other suspects. The identification of Anderson by the victim confirmed the investigator's theory that Anderson was the culprit, so he focused on that and ignored the facts that undermined it. We all fall victim to these cognitive biases, but the consequences are especially egregious in the context of serious criminal charges.

Not even an hour after the victim selected Anderson from the photographic lineup, Anderson was brought in and placed in an in-person lineup before the victim. He was the only person from the photo lineup she'd just been shown to appear in the in-person lineup. Plainly, this too was suggestive, as the investigator surely

---

* Richard Posner, *How Judges Think*, p.111 (2008).

knew. Having just selected Anderson from his color photograph, the victim identified Anderson as the assailant in the in-person lineup. This served as a confirmation of her initial identification and ensured that *Anderson had now taken the place of the assailant* in the memory of the victim.

Despite testimony from a forensic expert that blood tests ruled out Anderson as the source of semen collected from the victim, and multiple alibi witnesses who testified to seeing Anderson elsewhere at the time of the attack, an all-white jury convicted Anderson and he was sentenced to 210 years in prison. The conviction was based principally on the eyewitness identification.

In 1988, six years after Anderson was convicted, John Otis Lincoln, who had been implicated in the crime but ignored by the investigator after he had focused on Anderson, confessed to committing the rape. In fact, he did so in court and under oath. However, the judge who had presided over Anderson's original trial refused to believe Lincoln's confession. Even though Lincoln, unlike Anderson, had a history of sexually assaulting women, the police, the prosecutors, and the judge continued to believe that Anderson was the perpetrator. It wasn't until 2001, thirteen years after Lincoln's in-court confession, that Anderson was finally exonerated on the basis of DNA evidence, with a pardon issued by the governor of Virginia the following year. That same DNA evidence, when run through the Combined DNA Index System (CODIS) database, matched two Virginia prison inmates. Although the names of the inmates were not disclosed, one of them appears to have been John Otis Lincoln, according to the Innocence Project, which represented Anderson in his bid for freedom post-conviction.

The Anderson case began with a mistaken identification based on a suggestive identification procedure, and the criminal process that kicked in afterward served only to solidify the manufactured identification. The trial judge likewise appears to have had his blinders so firmly in place that he could not be convinced, even in the face of a confession by the true perpetrator, that Anderson was not guilty. This illustrates another psychological phenomenon called belief persistence, also known as belief perseverance. It is a very real human tendency for a person to persist in one's initial beliefs and conclusions, even if those beliefs and conclusions are shown to be erroneous or misguided. The upshot is that once someone makes up his or her mind on any particular issue, they'll be resistant to change. It helps explain why eyewitnesses tend to become more positive of their identifications at trial than they were initially, and why police and prosecutors are so adamant about defending their arrests and convictions, even in the face of clear evidence of innocence.

PICKING COTTON

The case of Ronald Cotton is another tragic consequence of imperfect perception and memory contamination. In Burlington, North Carolina, in 1984, a young woman named Jennifer Thompson was raped by a Black man. Ms. Thompson has since courageously written and spoken publicly about her experience, including how it came to pass that she mistakenly identified Ronald Cotton as her attacker.

After the attack, she described her assailant to the police, and a composite sketch of him was prepared. The police later received a tip that the sketch resembled a man named Ronald Cotton. Thompson was shown a mug shot lineup that included a photograph of Cotton. After narrowing the choices down to two, she selected Cotton's photograph and said, "I *think* this is the guy." She was told by the officer administering the photo lineup that she did great, which increased her confidence in the identification.

Next came a live lineup. Cotton was brought before Thompson along with several other men who served as fillers in the lineup. None of the fillers had been in the photo array except for Cotton. Again, Thompson selected Cotton. She said that he *looked the most like* her attacker. She was then told by the detective that she had picked out the same person that she'd selected from the photo array, which further bolstered her confidence in the identification.

When the time for the trial came, Thompson took the witness stand and said she was "absolutely sure" that Cotton was the man who raped her. On the basis of her testimony, Cotton was convicted and sentenced to life in prison, plus an additional fifty-four years. He spent ten years in prison before being exonerated with DNA evidence. The true culprit was a man named Bobby Poole.

After the trial, at a post-conviction hearing, Thompson had the opportunity to see Poole in person to determine whether she could identify him as her attacker. She said, "I have never seen him in my life," and believed that with all her heart. This was because her memory of the original event had been changed. It had become contaminated by the police identification procedures and through the psychological necessity of having to come to sincerely believe that the man she had already condemned to a life in prison was truly her assailant. Ronald Cotton had become substituted in her memory for the man who assaulted her.

While the mistake may fairly be attributed to Thompson, the police officer or officers who were responsible for the mug shot lineup and the in-person lineup, and who ignored the uncertainty of her initial identifications, bear responsibility as well. Seeing Thompson's uncertainty in initially selecting Cotton and hearing her say that Cotton looked the most like her attacker from the array of suspects assembled by the police should have been serious red flags.

Thompson and Cotton have both spoken very publicly about this tragic case of mistaken identification, and remarkably, they have done so together. Thompson had the courage and wisdom to come to terms with the truth, and Cotton had the kindness and grace to forgive Thompson's error. Together, they have written a book called *Picking Cotton* that describes their mutual ordeal, and the lessons it teaches are profound.

18

JUSTICE FOR SALE

Purchasing False Testimony

[I]nformants granted immunity are by definition . . . cut from untrustworthy cloth. . . . Accordingly, we expect prosecutors and investigators to take all reasonable measures to safeguard the system against treachery.

—*Carriger v. Stewart*, U.S. Court of Appeals for
the Ninth Circuit (1997)

In an objective world where truth really mattered, it would be self-evident that the least reliable way to obtain truthful evidence would be to pay someone for providing it. Imagine, for example, if a defense lawyer offered to pay a defendant's friends to provide him with an alibi defense or to support a claim of self-defense. Providing an incentive for someone to testify for or against any party encourages, if not guarantees, perjury and obstruction of justice. No prosecutor would approve such conduct by a defense lawyer, yet prosecutors have no hesitation in using such testimony when it supports their case. Not surprisingly, incentivizing witnesses, whether jailhouse snitches, co-defendants, or citizens responding to so-called Crime Stopper rewards, is one of the prime factors leading to wrongful convictions. In the case of LaMonte Armstrong, it cost him seventeen years of his life.

LaMonte was charged with the murder of Ernestine Compton in 1994. Ernestine was a fifty-seven-year-old Black woman who lived alone in a small brick home at the quiet corner of Pichard Street and Ross Avenue in Greensboro, North Carolina. A whitewashed picket fence ran around her yard, and inside the yard she had a maple tree, a mimosa tree, and some lavender hydrangea. A mix of straggling flowers, baking in the summer heat, sprouted from an ornamental concrete planter on the front stoop, welcoming guests. Ernestine's house was one block away from an elementary school, which was visible down the wide street from her front yard, and nearby were several small churches. She enjoyed seeing children walking by her house on their way to school in the mornings. Ernestine had no reason to suspect that she'd be the victim of horrible violence.

A Philadelphia native, Ernestine moved to Greensboro to work at North Carolina A&T, one of North Carolina's historically Black universities, after receiving degrees from Temple University and Central State University in Ohio. She loved to teach and was once named North Carolina A&T's outstanding teacher of the year. She said, "I just think I'm never too busy to talk with students. They know that I'm always available."

Her generosity was not limited to her students. Ernestine had a big heart and did a lot for a lot of different people. Sometimes she lent small sums of money to her friends and neighbors—people in difficult financial straits who needed a little help. A list of names on her refrigerator reminded her to whom she had lent money and how much was still owed.

On Tuesday, July 12, 1988, a former student went to check on Ernestine after not hearing from her for a while and found her slumped in a chair in her living room. The room was a bloody mess, and Ernestine had been dead for days. The house had no air conditioning, and the room was stiflingly hot. Police had to wear oxygen masks just to enter the home, where they viewed a grisly scene. Ernestine had been viciously slain. She had been bound with telephone and electrical cords, the latter of which caused abrasions around her neck that left wounds resembling burn marks on her skin. Her chest showed multiple stab wounds. Her throat had been slit, and she was nearly decapitated.

The forensic evidence shed little light on what might have happened there or who might have done it. There were no signs of forced entry into the home, suggesting that Ernestine knew the killer or killers and willingly let them in. A partial knife blade was found beneath Ernestine's body. In a kitchen drawer beside the sink, investigators found a second knife, stained with blood, along with yet another knife, broken like the first one. A pillowcase from the master bedroom had stains that appeared to be blood, and a white-striped towel contained an unknown stain that couldn't be quickly identified by investigators. Finally, a bloody palm print appeared on the wall just above Ernestine's body.

In the midst of the horrific scene, and in an unlikely place, the police observed a critical clue. On the side of Ernestine's refrigerator, held there with a magnet, were a few small pieces of paper containing various names and numbers in Ernestine's handwriting. Nearby was a letter Ernestine had written, but not yet mailed, to someone Ernestine had lent money to, asking that he pay the $15 owed to her.

The two detectives assigned to the case, J. F. Whitt and David Spagnola, were employed by the City of Greensboro. With the notes from the refrigerator in hand, they quickly formed the theory that the crime was related in some way to the money lent by Ernestine. Perhaps someone came to her home wanting money and she refused. Perhaps she had called a debt due and someone didn't want to repay.

Newspaper accounts of the murder disclosed that Ernestine had been strangled, but did *not* also say that she had been stabbed or that her throat had been cut. The police deliberately withheld this information from the media and the public. Such facts held back by investigators in this way—sometimes referred to as "hold-back facts"—are facts that only the true perpetrator of the crime (or the police) would know. This is one way for the police to confirm the reliability of any statement or confession they might receive from a suspect.

Two weeks passed without an arrest. In aid of the ongoing investigation, a local newspaper ran a story about Ernestine's murder, and told of a $5,000 reward being offered by the governor of North Carolina to anyone with information about the crime. On top of that, the police offered a $500 reward, and Crime Stoppers contributed an additional $1,000, for a total of $6,500. The day after the rewards were announced, the Greensboro police received a tip through Crime Stoppers that pointed to a possible suspect. The tip came from Charles Blackwell, a street criminal who had been a Greensboro police informant for a number of years.

Every police department has informants—career criminals who work both sides of the fence. They commit crimes themselves and provide information to the police regarding other crimes in return for money or leniency or both. Blackwell was well-known to Detectives Whitt and Spagnola. Prior to Ernestine's murder, Blackwell had called Detective Spagnola frequently to offer information about criminal activity, and in return he usually asked for small sums of money.

In the two months immediately prior to Ernestine's murder, Blackwell had been charged with breaking and entering, as well as larceny, communicating threats, assaulting a female, possession of stolen goods, and possession of stolen checks—all occurring in June and July 1988. He was looking at considerable prison time and needed something to offer the police to keep himself out of prison. It was unlikely, in other words, that Blackwell was just acting out of a concern for public safety by providing a tip to the police.

Blackwell told Crime Stoppers that a man named LaMonte Armstrong was the person who had killed Ernestine. After some quick research, Whitt and Spagnola learned that LaMonte's family lived on the same street as Ernestine, and that LaMonte's mother and Ernestine were friends. LaMonte had even been a student of Ernestine's at North Carolina A&T. At one time, LaMonte had a job at the elementary school near Ernestine's house, but more recently he had fallen on hard times and was known to be using drugs. It all made perfect sense. Detectives Whitt and Spagnola made LaMonte their prime suspect.

Working closely with the detectives, Blackwell signed a sworn statement regarding what he claimed had happened on the night of the murder: LaMonte had been in search of cocaine, so the story went, but didn't have the money. According to Blackwell, LaMonte said he knew an old woman he could borrow money from. Blackwell drove LaMonte to a location near Ernestine's house, and forty-five minutes later, LaMonte returned with a "wad of money" and a lady's gold watch. Blackwell claimed in the statement that he had read about the murder in the paper the next morning, and that was why he contacted Crime Stoppers—except that the Crime Stoppers ad didn't run until two weeks later. This was a red flag, one of many, that Whitt and Spagnola seem to have missed.

With Blackwell's help, the police now had a statement linking LaMonte to the crime, but frustratingly, there was no physical evidence connecting LaMonte to Ernestine's murder. Nothing at the murder scene could be traced to LaMonte. The palm print found on the wall did not match LaMonte, and there were no fingerprints, no shoeprints, no articles of clothing, and no blood or DNA tying LaMonte to the scene. When it came down to it, all the police had on LaMonte was Blackwell's uncorroborated statement, which was weak and circumstantial and came from the mouth of a career criminal. It wouldn't be enough to convict, and they knew it. They held off on bringing charges against LaMonte as they continued their search for additional and better evidence.

A few months after the murder, Blackwell, who had been out on bond, found himself back in jail on other charges. Consistent with his practice, he called an investigator in the Rockingham County,

North Carolina, Sheriff's Office, where the new charges were pending, and offered to provide information about four breaking-and-
entering cases that occurred in that county in return for help getting
out of jail. He knew how the system worked and happily exploited it
for his own advantage whenever possible.

One month later, and prior to the time when any charges were
brought against LaMonte, Detective Spagnola visited Blackwell in
jail. They'd gotten nowhere in Ernestine's case and needed to make
something happen. Spagnola told Blackwell that he (Spagnola) *knew*
that Blackwell had driven LaMonte to Ernestine's house the night
of the murder and had waited right outside while LaMonte killed
her. He also told Blackwell he knew Blackwell had heard Ernestine screaming while the murder was taking place. Although none of
this was true, it immediately occurred to Blackwell, street-smart as
always, that he was being portrayed as an accessory to the murder,
which was an extremely bad turn of events. This signaled to Blackwell that he needed to up his cooperation game or things would end
badly for him.

Within a few hours, Blackwell's story had become remarkably
more specific. He was helpfully regurgitating Spagnola's version of
events back to Spagnola and Whitt—including that he had driven
LaMonte to Ernestine's house the night of the murder and waited
outside while LaMonte went in to ask for money. The detectives
recorded the interview. Blackwell claimed that he heard struggling
inside. He heard chairs hitting the walls, moaning and groaning, and
saw struggling in the shadows cast on the front windows—all very
imaginative details that were absent from his original sworn statement, but which matched the detectives' theory.

Despite Blackwell's new statements implicating LaMonte, the
police still made no arrests. There just wasn't enough credible evidence to proceed. For a time, Detectives Whitt and Spagnola turned
their attention to other more pressing cases. Ernestine's case lay dor-
mant for almost *six years*, with no new developments. It seemed that
the case might remain unsolved.

In March 1994, Detective Whitt decided to form a "cold case" squad for the Greensboro Police. He pulled detectives off active caseloads and assigned them to cases that had never been solved. It was a big deal for Whitt professionally, and he was proud to be responsible for starting it. Needless to say, it was important for the cold-case squad to have some successes early on to justify the police department resources dedicated to the effort. One of the first things Detective Whitt did with the cold-case unit was to reopen the investigation into Ernestine's murder. He started by going right back to Charles Blackwell.

Whitt located Blackwell and brought him to the police department to take a polygraph test regarding his involvement in the murder. Faced with the polygraph, Blackwell, to his credit, and perhaps realizing his prior mistake in providing false information, admitted that the statements he'd previously given the police regarding LaMonte had been fabricated. He said he'd needed money, hoped to get the reward, and was looking for help on his B&E charges from another county.

Whitt nevertheless made Blackwell sit for the polygraph, and afterward he informed him that he'd failed. Then, according to Blackwell, Whitt and Spagnola threatened to charge him with Ernestine's murder if he did not go to court and testify, with particularity, that LaMonte had killed Ernestine. As a result of this alleged threat, Blackwell reversed course and agreed that LaMonte had in fact killed Ernestine. He even went so far as to add new details to his statement. This time, he said he didn't try to stop LaMonte because LaMonte had been "speedballing" (combining heroin and cocaine), and Blackwell had been afraid that LaMonte might hurt him as well. With Blackwell back onboard, Detective Whitt finally obtained an arrest warrant for LaMonte for first-degree murder in the death of Ernestine Compton.

But without any forensic evidence to bolster the case, the police still needed something else to buttress Blackwell's self-serving story. To this end, they enthusiastically welcomed three more informants who claimed that LaMonte had indeed committed the murder, each one less credible than the last.

THE PILE-ON

The three men other than Blackwell who "volunteered" information implicating LaMonte were Timothy McCorkle, Dwight Blockem, and William Earl Davis.

At the time McCorkle gave his statement to Detective Whitt, he had just completed his first month of a twenty-five-year sentence for robbery with a dangerous weapon. In 1986, two years prior to Ernestine's murder, McCorkle had been convicted of robbery, largely on the testimony of one person—LaMonte's brother, Kermit. In an interview with Detective Whitt, McCorkle claimed he was painting a house on Ernestine's street and just happened to see LaMonte and Blackwell when they came out of Ernestine's home on the night of the murder. McCorkle said he saw Blackwell leave Ernestine's house that night and heard him say, "Damn, LaMonte."

The other two informants, Dwight Blockem and William Earl Davis, were classic jailhouse snitches. When Blockem reached out to the district attorney with his claim of information about LaMonte, he had just been convicted as a habitual felon and sentenced to fifteen years in prison. Blockem claimed that LaMonte told Blockem he was by himself when he murdered Ernestine, which of course was inconsistent with the stories told by Blackwell and McCorkle. Blockem had no new information about the crime, nor could he provide any details with any indicia of reliability, such as facts about the crime scene that only LaMonte might have known, or any of the "hold-back" facts known only to the police.

William Earl Davis, the third informant, had a long string of convictions, many of which involved fraud and dishonesty. He was a regular tipster for the Greensboro Police Department and had been so in 1988, when the murder occurred, but Davis only contacted Detective Whitt after being sentenced to twenty-two years for multiple offenses involving fraud. He claimed that while he and La-Monte were incarcerated together, LaMonte admitted committing the murder, saying that he and Blackwell had gone to Ernestine's house the afternoon of the murder with several other people and that LaMonte had killed Ernestine later that day. Once again, this story did not match up with what had been said by the other informants, but this did not deter Whitt, Spagnola, or the prosecutor from proceeding.

LaMonte's trial began on August 15, 1995, and lasted just four days, including jury selection and deliberations. The state's final witnesses were Blackwell, Davis, McCorkle, and Blockem. Each of them expected, and received, a personal benefit in exchange for their testimony.

For trial, Blackwell's testimony, now well-rehearsed, had been enlarged to include several new details, such as the claim that he accompanied LaMonte *into* Ernestine's home and sat on a couch while LaMonte and Ernestine argued about what LaMonte owed to Ernestine. He said that Ernestine took a list off the side of her refrigerator and said she wouldn't lend LaMonte any more money "until you pay that." Showing LaMonte the list, she said, "You already owe me this right here." Blackwell claimed that after LaMonte pushed Ernestine down and grabbed a rope from the top of the refrigerator, Blackwell left the home. Once outside, he saw Tim McCorkle on the street and said, "Damn, LaMonte."

McCorkle was the next witness called to the stand. Unsurprisingly, his testimony dovetailed perfectly with that of Blackwell's. By an unlikely coincidence, if his testimony was to be believed, he happened to be right in front of Ernestine's house at the precise moment that Blackwell walked out, and he was even close enough to hear Blackwell exclaim, "Damn, LaMonte." It was hard to imagine that someone had not coordinated their testimony. McCorkle testified that no one made him any promises in return for his testimony, but he ended up serving only seven years of his twenty-five-year prison sentence.

Blockem and Davis also got on the stand and told their stories, which in many important respects conflicted with the accounts offered by Blackwell and McCorkle, but they nevertheless pointed to LaMonte's culpability. When asked if anyone had made him any promises in exchange for his testimony, Blockem lied and said no, but in fact promises had been made to Blockem on the morning he testified. Detective Whitt had promised to get Blockem transferred to a prison in North Carolina from the prison in Tennessee to which he had been sent to serve out his sentence. Whitt delivered on this promise after the trial had concluded.

The state rested its case on the strength of these four dubious witnesses, having offered no physical evidence tying LaMonte to the murder or the scene of the crime.

What about the handwritten notes from Ernestine's refrigerator showing that LaMonte had borrowed money from her, the notes that Blackwell said Ernestine took down from the refrigerator and held in LaMonte's face, provoking his rage? The notes that, despite the violence in the kitchen, somehow made their way back to the side of the refrigerator and bore no traces of blood. The police didn't introduce these at trial. Detective Whitt, who testified for the state, suggested during his trial testimony that the notes from the refrigerator had not been collected by the police. He said he'd "have to look at my evidence list to be sure." He then read the jury an inventory list of property seized by the police from Ernestine's home, and the notes weren't on the list, leaving the impression that the notes from the refrigerator hadn't been taken.

LaMonte took the stand and testified in his own defense. He fervently denied killing Ernestine Compton, denied ever borrowing money from her, and denied making any inculpatory statements to William Earl Davis or Dwight Blockem. It wasn't enough. The jury convicted LaMonte on the basis of the informant testimony, and he was sentenced to life in prison.

LaMonte's arrest, trial, and conviction were an absolute travesty of justice. He was convicted almost entirely on the strength of incentivized testimony under circumstances that would have led any reasonable investigator to doubt the authenticity of the witness accounts. Even the witnesses who testified against LaMonte could see the injustice. Just six days after LaMonte's trial ended, Dwight Blockem wrote a letter to LaMonte's attorney admitting that his testimony was a fabrication. His letter read, in part: "I was dishonest at Mr. Armstrong's trial and a great deal of my testimony was Mr. Blackwell's idea to clear himself. . . ."

Tim McCorkle also wrote to LaMonte after his trial and offered something like an apology. He wrote that "things did not go the way it should have," and that when he was in the holding cell with Blockem and Davis, "I could hear a lot of bullshit lies. . . . I know they were lying."

What is extraordinary is that Blackwell himself had been conflicted by his role in implicating LaMonte and wrote to explain what Whitt had done to him. On May 17, 1994—*several months prior to LaMonte's arrest, and more than a year prior to LaMonte's trial*—Blackwell wrote a letter to LaMonte. It stated, "I don't know how this got so far out of hand, I told them I was just liaring [*sic*] to get money, but this detective Whitt wanted me to get on the witness stand and lie on you anyway. . . . I told them it was all a lie."

Blackwell didn't stop there. A few days after writing the letter to LaMonte, Blackwell wrote to Harold Murdock, the chair of the Criminal Justice Committee of the NAACP in Greensboro. He again said that Detective Whitt had told him that "if I didn't get on the witness stand and testify against LaMonte Armstrong, he would get LaMonte to testify against me and that would be the end of it. I would have a life sentence. . . . [H]e expects me to testify that LaMonte done it." The letter went on to say, "Back in 1988 when it happened I did tell a lie to get the reward money . . . but LaMonte is getting punished for a lie I told. . . . Could you please help me, guys over here in jail where I am at has already starting writing statements across the street trying to get less time." This letter was introduced into evidence at LaMonte's trial, but it did little to no good.

Blackwell just explained it away by saying he was trying to "protect his reputation in jail" and show that he wasn't a snitch for the state.

Years later, in 2010, while LaMonte remained in prison, Blackwell admitted to LaMonte's attorney, Henry Frye Jr., the son of the first Black chief justice of the North Carolina Supreme Court, that he had called Crime Stoppers in 1988 and implicated LaMonte for some "quick money." Blackwell told Frye that Detectives Whitt and Spagnola fed him information about the murder and the crime scene by asking him leading questions and supplying the answers. He said, "Everything, only thing I knew about the lady that got killed and LaMonte is what they told me." In response to questions about the testimony he provided in LaMonte's case, and his motivation for so doing, Blackwell said:

Q. How did you able [sic] to describe the inside [of Ernestine's house]?
A. They told me. They told me.
Q. How? Who told you?
A. Whitt and Spagnola.
Q. Did they describe how the house was or something?
A. They told me how the house was. They told me everything, they told me what I needed to know to say LaMonte done it.
Q. And you never went, you never went to the house?
A. No, don't even know where the house is. Right here to the day, I don't know where the house is.
Q. And the only reason you did it was to get the Crime Stopper money back then?
A. Crime Stopper money. It was a lie that started it, man. I never seen a lie spread like that, man. And you wouldn't expect for the police to be there with it. But I reckon they were putting so much heat on them to solve the case. That's what Whitt said.

When asked why he had testified against LaMonte after sending letters of recantation to LaMonte and Harold Murdock of the NAACP in Greensboro, Blackwell replied, "'Cause they told me I was gonna get a life sentence and they were gonna convict me of doing it. And I had no other choice, man. I had, like I said, you know, little kids, man. I couldn't do no life sentence."

The Duke Law School Wrongful Convictions Clinic came to LaMonte's aid after receiving a referral from the North Carolina Center on Actual Innocence, which believed that LaMonte's claim of innocence was "plausible and provable." Duke Law students and faculty worked tirelessly for years on LaMonte's case, uncovered critical new evidence, including the identity of the true perpetrator, and proved that LaMonte was innocent. He was exonerated in 2012 for the murder of Ernestine Compton after spending seventeen years in prison. He received a pardon from the governor the following year. While he was in prison, both his mother and father passed away, and he was not permitted to attend their funerals. He missed the entirety of his daughter's journey through elementary school, middle school, high school, college, and into the adult world. He suffered severe emotional distress. In the bottom righthand corner of his canteen card appeared the numbers "999," representing the number of months that the Department of Correction assigned to someone serving a life sentence. Once, he tried to sign up for a computer course offered by the prison but was told he didn't need to learn about computers because he would "never get out."

As for the handwritten notes from the refrigerator, attorneys for the Wrongful Convictions Clinic found them once they were given access to the police file pursuant to a new North Carolina law. They were in Detective Whitt's investigative file, the same one he had in his possession during LaMonte's trial when he suggested that the notes had not been picked up by the police. The reason the notes were not shown on the evidence inventory is because Whitt never turned them over to the police evidence custodian. And the reason he did not turn them over to the evidence custodian? Well, *LaMonte's name wasn't on any of the notes.*

As LaMonte testified, he hadn't borrowed money from Ernestine, and he didn't owe her any money. The notes from the refrigerator proved Blackwell's testimony was a lie, and they were in Detective

Whitt's file the whole time, so Whitt knew or should have known that Blackwell had lied. They were the essence of exculpatory evidence, as Whitt surely had to know. But they would not be discovered until many years after LaMonte's wrongful conviction.

LaMonte's case vividly demonstrates how and why wrongful convictions occur. It started with an assumption by the police about the motive for the murder. It was fueled by a false allegation from an informant trying to get reward money. The detectives became personally invested in proving LaMonte was the perpetrator, especially after Detective Whitt formed the cold-case squad. They developed tunnel vision as to LaMonte and ignored the dramatic inconsistencies in the informants' stories and their motives for lying. Finally, Whitt had not disclosed the exculpatory evidence that LaMonte's name was not on the notes as one of the people who owed Ernestine money, as turning those over would have completely undermined the case he had worked so hard to build. Whether he actually believed LaMonte was guilty by the time of the trial, or knew he was setting up an innocent man, is beside the point. In my opinion, Whitt plainly abused his power, Spagnola did nothing to stop him, and an innocent man went to prison for seventeen years.

WHO KILLED ERNESTINE COMPTON?

What is too often overlooked in cases of wrongful convictions is that for every innocent person who is wrongfully convicted, the victim and his or her family receives no real or lasting justice, and the actual perpetrator remains free to victimize others. In 2009, the Wrongful Convictions Clinic at Duke Law School contacted Michael Matthews, a homicide detective with the Greensboro Police Department, to ask his help in reviewing LaMonte's case. Matthews commendably agreed to take on this responsibility in addition to his existing caseload because, as he put it, "I felt like it was the right thing to do."

When several law students from Duke came to the police department to review the police investigative file related to LaMonte, Detective Matthews sat in a room with them from 8:30 in the morning until 4:30 that afternoon, answering questions and listening to their discussion and discoveries with interest. The students wanted to test the physical evidence in the case using improved technologies that were not available in the 1990s when the case had been tried.

Detective Matthews decided to run the bloody palm print found at the scene above Ernestine's body through a regional database of latent palm and fingerprints called SPEX. The database was so new that the Greensboro police had only entered historical prints for persons with last names beginning with the letters A through D. As soon as the palm print was entered into the database, it came back with a strong candidate for a match: Christopher Bernard Caviness.

On January 29, 1989, approximately six months *after* Ernestine was strangled and stabbed, Charles Caviness was robbed and murdered in his home, less than two miles away from Ernestine's house on Pichard Street. The cause of death was blunt-force trauma and incised wounds to the victim's neck. A broken knife was found at the scene, recalling the broken knife found in Ernestine's home after her murder.

The police arrested Mr. Caviness's son—Christopher Bernard Caviness—and charged him with the murder of his father. In June 1989, he pled guilty to second-degree murder and armed robbery in connection with his father's death. He was sentenced to fourteen years in prison, but was released after serving fewer than ten years.

Detective Whitt, while he was investigating the Compton murder, was also involved in the investigation of the Caviness murder. He knew from Ernestine's case that Charles Caviness; his wife, Dot; and their son Chris, *were all listed on the handwritten notes of debtors found on the side of the refrigerator* at Ernestine's house. He also knew that Ernestine had written, but not mailed, a letter to Chris asking him to pay the $15 that he owed her. Despite this, Detective Whitt never interviewed Chris Caviness about his possible involvement in Ernestine's murder, and never interviewed Ernestine's friends and family about any connection she might have had to Chris and the Caviness family. He also never had Chris's palm prints compared to the bloody palm print found at the scene.

Chris Caviness was never brought to justice for Ernestine's murder. He died in a car accident in 2010 while fleeing the police after committing another crime.

After LaMonte was exonerated, he went to work as a peer counselor for a Durham nonprofit. Along with David Pishko, I represented LaMonte in a civil lawsuit against Detectives Whitt and Spagnola for their role in LaMonte's wrongful conviction, and against the City of Greensboro for failing to adequately train and supervise Whitt and Spagnola. The City of Greensboro paid in excess of $6 million to settle the case, but no amount of money could compensate LaMonte for being sent to prison for most of his adult life for something he didn't do.

After receiving his settlement, LaMonte continued to work as a counselor, although he obviously didn't have to work at all. He also designed and began to build his "dream house." While it was still under construction, LaMonte learned he had cancer. He died in August 2019, without ever finishing his house.

19

HIDING THE TRUTH

Concealing Exculpatory Evidence

The number of cases in which a judge or jury may have convicted an innocent person, without becoming aware of all the favorable information actually in existence, remains unknown. One can fairly assume that for every wrongfully convicted individual who has been vindicated, there are countless others whose innocence remains invisible to the system.

—Excerpt, National Association of Criminal Defense Attorneys and Santa Clara Law School Study, 2014

The resources available to the state in investigating and prosecuting a criminal case dwarf what is available to any individual defendant, no matter how wealthy. In 1963, the U.S. Supreme Court, in *Brady v. Maryland*, attempted to level the playing field a little by requiring prosecutors to turn over to criminal defendants any evidence in the prosecutor's possession that might help the defendant fight the charges brought against him. Such evidence that is favorable to a defendant is called exculpatory evidence, and is often referred to as *Brady* material.

Brady material generally falls into one of three primary categories: (1) evidence that someone besides the defendant committed the crime, such as a statement by a third party admitting guilt; (2) evidence that the defendant did not or could not have committed the crime, such as the existence of alibi witnesses; and (3) impeachment evidence, which undermines the credibility of a critical prosecution witness, such as evidence that a confession was coerced, that a witness made a prior inconsistent statement, or that incentives given to the witness in return for her testimony.

Providing *Brady* material to the defendant is most important where the evidence of guilt is weakest and the odds that the defendant is actually innocent are therefore greatest. But that is precisely when police and prosecutors are most likely to violate the *Brady* rule. Particularly in those cases, police and prosecutors tend to believe that the *Brady* rule simply helps guilty defendants "get off." Sometimes, because they have become so convinced of the defendant's guilt, police and prosecutors actually fail to recognize the exculpatory value of the particular evidence they have. In other cases, they intentionally conceal the exculpatory evidence to increase the likelihood of a conviction.

In one extraordinary case involving a murder, a decomposing body, and fabricated statements by two teenage girls, the police covered up evidence showing that the victim was alive for days after his alleged murderer had been jailed on a separate charge, making it impossible for him to have committed the murder.

Allen Ray Jenkins was a fifty-seven-year-old truck driver who liked to party and do drugs with underage girls. On April 14, 1995, he was found dead of two shotgun blasts in his mobile home in the small town of Aulander in eastern North Carolina. From the looks of it, he might have been dead for days. Jenkins's body, which was crawling with maggots, was in a state of advanced decomposition, making it difficult to determine precisely when he had died. The local police chief, Gordon Godwin, called in the North Carolina

State Bureau of Investigation (SBI) to lead the investigation, and SBI Agent Dwight Ransome was assigned to the case.

Godwin and Agent Ransome, along with other law enforcement agents, promptly conducted interviews of anyone they could identify who knew Jenkins, looking for leads into the murder. What they learned about him was nothing short of disturbing. He had a prior conviction for molesting a thirteen-year-old girl, and witnesses who knew him reported that he was known to consort with juvenile girls, even paying them for sex. He also sold and abused Xanax, allowed the use of crack cocaine in his trailer, and reportedly had a recent conflict with a known crack dealer. He was not a model citizen, to say the least.

As part of their investigation, the police tried to pin down when the murder occurred. They went around asking friends and neighbors when they last saw Jenkins alive. Aulander, North Carolina, the town where all this happened, is about as small as you can get. It has a rescue squad, a "ladies' auxiliary," an ancient corner pharmacy, and a funeral home, but that's about it. The population there has hovered around a thousand people for years. If you live in Aulander, you probably know almost everyone else who lives there too.

As expected, Godwin and Ransome were able to find all sorts of people who knew Jenkins and had known him for a long time. They spoke to Jenkins's neighbor from across the street; they talked to his brother and other people in town who had crossed paths with him recently. Among the people interviewed by Godwin and Ransome, five of them saw Jenkins alive on April 7. Three others saw him on April 8. Two more saw him out and about on April 9, and seven people reported seeing Jenkins alive on April 10. It seemed probable, therefore, that the murder occurred sometime between April 10, when he was last seen alive, and April 14, when his body was found.

Inside the trailer, where Jenkins was discovered, the police found empty wine-cooler bottles and feminine hygiene products in the bathroom trash can. Suspicion soon fell on two fifteen-year-old girls,

Crystal Morris and Shanna Hall, who associated with Jenkins and hung out at his trailer, where he gave them alcohol and drugs. Initially, the girls denied knowing anything about Jenkins's murder, but over time a different picture emerged that placed the girls at the trailer on the day he was killed. Godwin and Ransome conducted additional interviews of the girls over a period of months, and their stories changed constantly, almost as if they were fishing to find a story that the police would find credible.

Facing the realization that their involvement in the crime could not be avoided altogether, both girls finally admitted they had been with Jenkins when he was shot—but they claimed someone else was the murderer. They alleged it was a young man named Alan Gell, who was well-known to the local police. In this latest iteration of the girls' evolving account, they claimed that Gell had killed Jenkins as part of a scheme, hatched in conspiracy with the two girls, to rob Jenkins and steal his money.

Gell lived about eight miles south of Aulander. He was twenty years old and was Shanna Hall's boyfriend. He had recently racked up some arrests for minor drug possession and for stealing a tractor, and he was going through a wild, lawless phase of his life. He partied hard with Shanna and Crystal, did some small-time drug dealing on the side, and was adept at finding new ways to get into trouble. It was not hard for the police to imagine that Gell had gotten himself caught up in some crazy plot that left a man dead.

Curiously, this new version of Crystal and Shanna's story naming Gell as the killer was inconsistent with the physical evidence found at the scene, including the position of Jenkins's body when it was found and the blood-spatter evidence. Even more curiously, Crystal was able to tell the police where to find certain items stolen from Jenkins's trailer during the crime, including the murder weapon, and none of these items bore any trace of Alan Gell.

Agent Ransome taped a call between Crystal and her boyfriend, Gary Scott, with the permission of the boyfriend. In the call, Crystal was highly distressed and anxious when talking about Jenkins. She admitted that she made up her story about Gell being the killer, and didn't answer when Gary Scott asked her if she had killed Jenkins. Later, Crystal and Shanna refused to take a polygraph examination about their involvement in Jenkins's death.

Notwithstanding these obvious warning signs, Godwin and Ransome targeted Gell as the killer. Immediately they encountered two significant obstacles. First, when Jenkins's body was discovered on April 14, Alan Gell was sitting in the Bertie County jail. He had been in the jail for more than a week, ever since April 6, when he'd been arrested for stealing a car. In fact, the only date in the first two weeks of April on which Gell could have committed the murder was *April 3*. The day before that, he'd stolen the tractor mentioned previously and had been locked up in the county jail for a day. On April 4 and 5, Gell was traveling outside the state on an errand to purchase drugs, and the timing of this trip had been well documented. Unless Jenkins had died on April 3, Gell couldn't have been the killer.

The second obstacle for Godwin and Ransome, directly related to the first, was that no fewer than *seventeen* of the witnesses they interviewed in the two days immediately following the discovery of Jenkins's body reported that they had seen Jenkins in and around Aulander *after* Gell had been detained in the Bertie County jail for car theft on April 6. None of these witnesses knew Alan Gell, but all of them had known Allen Ray Jenkins for years, including his own brother. None had any reason to lie. If any of the seventeen statements were accurate, Gell had to be innocent.

Statements by witnesses in criminal cases that prove the defendant could not have committed the crime most often involve "alibi" witnesses. Alibi witnesses usually testify that they were with the defendant in another location at the time the crime was committed, making it impossible that the defendant committed the crime elsewhere. Gell's case was unusual, in that the witnesses proved the *victim* was alive at a particular time—days after Gell had been locked up for stealing a car.

Agent Ransome, realizing these witness statements doomed Gell's prosecution, went back to the witnesses *three months later*, when their recollections were more malleable, to tell them that Jenkins had in fact been killed on April 3. This meant, he told them, they must have been mistaken when they claimed to have seen Jenkins alive on April 7 and in the days following. Ransome succeeded in getting some, but not all, of the witnesses to recant their statements regarding when they had last seen Jenkins alive, and he prepared new statements for the witnesses who agreed to revise their accounts.

Crystal and Shanna, meanwhile, were offered and accepted a deal in which they pled guilty to second-degree murder and armed robbery, and the state agreed to juvenile sentences of ten years in exchange for their testimony naming Gell as the murderer. With the plea deal for Crystal and Shanna in place, and the revised witness statements in hand, the state charged Gell with the death of Allen Ray Jenkins. There was, however, no physical evidence connecting him to the crime. His arrest and indictment were based solely on the statements of the two fifteen-year-old girls.

THE DATE OF DEATH

Up until three weeks before the trial was to begin, no forensic determination of the date of Jenkins's death had been requested by the prosecution. At that time, the two prosecutors assigned to Gell's trial, as well as Godwin and Ransome, met with a forensic pathologist to discuss Jenkins's date of death. The pathologist told the prosecution team that "the last confirmable time a person was seen alive is critical to the process of determining the time of death and is information that is routinely and reasonably relied upon by experts in the field of forensic pathology." She had seen a note in the initial autopsy report indicating that Jenkins "was last seen on April 8, 1995 by his neighbor," and specifically asked about this. She was told that the statement was mistaken, had been retracted by the witness, and that no one had seen Jenkins alive after April 3, 1995.

Based on this false information, the forensic pathologist testified at Gell's trial that Jenkins had been killed on or before April 3, the one day on which Gell might have committed the murder. This perfectly tracked testimony from Crystal Morris and Shanna Hall, who claimed Gell had shot and killed Jenkins *on* April 3. It all fit together quite convincingly.

Gell was represented at trial by two overworked and underpaid public defenders, who had no real answer to this testimony and had not retained a competing medical expert regarding Jenkins's probable date of death. Gell maintained throughout his trial that he was innocent, even one time shouting from the defense table that he denied the charges, but to no avail. The jury returned a guilty verdict in just over an hour. All that remained was the determination of Gell's sentence: life in prison, or death at the hands of the state. During the sentencing phase of the trial, the prosecutor, in oratory more fitting for a church than a courtroom, passionately urged the jury to sentence Alan Gell to death for killing Allen Ray Jenkins:

> *From the Old Testament and the Book of Numbers, anyone who kills a person is to be put to death as a murderer upon the testimony of witnesses. You've heard the testimony of witnesses. . . . Now, they might argue to you the New Testament changes all that. No, it doesn't. Jesus didn't come to destroy the law or the prophecies of the Old Testament. He came to fulfill them.*
>
> *Listen to this in Deuteronomy. "Cursed is the man who kills his neighbor secretly and all the people shall say amen. Cursed is the man who kills an innocent person for money, and all the people shall say amen." It's time to sentence this man, a murderer, to die, and let the people of Bertie County say amen.*

This was enough to persuade the jury, and Gell was sentenced to die. He was transported to Death Row at Central Prison in Raleigh.

Four years later, as Gell spent his days and nights under a death warrant, an attorney named Mary Pollard was asked to volunteer her services to try to prevent Gell's impending execution. Her first step was to review the prosecution file. In the file, she came across a witness's statement saying that the witness had seen Jenkins alive during the time that Gell was in the Bertie County jail—after April 6. Then she saw another, and then another, and started making a list. "I just couldn't believe what I was seeing," she recalled. "It took my breath away."

As difficult as it was to imagine, she learned that not a single one of the seventeen witness statements indicating that Jenkins was seen alive after April 6 had been turned over to the defense prior to or during Gell's trial. If these witnesses were correct, and it was hard to believe they had all been mistaken, it meant Gell was innocent, even though at that moment he was sitting on Death Row, waiting for his execution date to be set.

Agent Ransome, or the prosecutors, or both, had deliberately concealed the witness statements, which were clearly exculpatory and favorable to Gell. With the help of one of her law partners, Jim Cooney, Mary succeeded in overturning Gell's conviction based on the *Brady* evidence that had been withheld from Gell's defense team at his trial. The state elected to retry him for his life, claiming that the witnesses must have been "mistaken" when they told Ransome they had seen Jenkins alive in the days after Gell was already in jail. A number of these witnesses testified at the retrial, and Gell was acquitted in 2004. He had spent nine years in prison, half of that time on Death Row, facing execution.

I was asked by Gell's attorneys to help Gell bring a civil action against the prosecutors, Agent Ransome, and Godwin. Predictably, Agents Ransome and Godwin denied any wrongdoing. I was joined in the case by Barry Scheck, one of the founders of the Innocence Project, with whom I have been close friends since we were "baby lawyers" working as public defenders in the South Bronx. Barry was already experienced in litigating civil rights cases arising from wrongful convictions and provided the legal backup. I was in charge of developing the facts that showed that the violation of Gell's constitutional right to a fair trial had been intentional and not the result of mere mistake or negligence, as the defendants all claimed.

A judge ruled that even if the prosecutors had knowingly and intentionally concealed the reports from the defense in order to put Gell on Death Row, they were entitled to "absolute immunity" and could not be sued for their misconduct. The police did not have such immunity, however, and the defendants ultimately settled the case for $3.9 million. Agent Ransome, who received a commendation, a promotion, and a raise after Gell was first convicted, was never disciplined, or even demoted, after Gell was exonerated.

20

THE USUAL SUSPECT

Just before ten o'clock on the night of July 27, 1990, Dr. Edward Friedland, a respected nephrologist in Charlotte, North Carolina, drove home to his wife, Kim, and their adopted infant son, Elliot, after a long day of making rounds at three local hospitals.

As he drove up the driveway, he noticed the lighting inside the house seemed different than it usually appeared when he came home in the evenings. When Ed entered the house from the front door, the lights in the hallway were off. He could hear the baby crying in the bedroom, but neither Kim nor the family dog came to the door. Ed called out, but there was no response. When he reached the foot of the stairs leading to the living room, something out of place caught his eye. There was something, or someone, on the far side of the dining room table. When he looked more closely, he could see that the rug under the table was soaked with blood.

Ed's wife, Kim Thomas, was born in 1958. She was, from a very early age, a vibrant and dynamic person of many interests and talents. Happy to march to her own drum—indeed, determined to do so— she pursued a variety of important callings with energy and enthusiasm. She was well-respected, loved, and known by those who came in contact with her to be a compassionate and kind human being.

She met her future husband, Ed Friedland, in 1979, when she was in college in New York. He was in medical school at the time, at the University of Rochester School of Medicine, which was followed by a residency at Mount Sinai Hospital in New York City. They were married in 1984 and moved to Charlotte in 1986. By that time, Kim had a master's degree in music, and Ed was board-certified in internal medicine, nephrology, and critical care. They had their whole lives ahead of them.

In Charlotte, Kim soon became a vocal and effective voice for women's rights. She was a leader in Charlotte's National Organization for Women, and the co-chair of Southern Piedmont Adoptive Families of America. She also counseled victims of domestic violence and was an advocate for women in abusive relationships. Meanwhile, Ed had established a dialysis practice that would quickly begin to grow and thrive.

Kim and Ed adopted an infant son, Elliot, in 1989. He was their only child. They lived in a home on Churchill Drive in Charlotte, a well-to-do pocket of secluded homes close to uptown. It was within close walking distance, across a busy avenue, of a ramshackle neighborhood known as Grier Heights, an area known at that time for significant crime and prolific drug use. Because of the proximity of Grier Heights to Churchill Drive, break-ins and burglaries were not uncommon in their neighborhood.

On the morning of July 27, 1990, at about 7:45, Ed left home for work, arriving at Presbyterian Hospital at approximately 8:00 a.m. He asked his assistant to push back his first appointment for the day. Kim and Elliot, who was then ten months old, were at home. Kim had her own appointments scheduled for the morning, including a Gymboree class for Elliot and a hair appointment at 11:45 a.m., but she did not arrive for either one. A babysitter who was supposed to watch Elliot during the hair appointment called Kim as early as 8:45 a.m. to confirm, but Kim didn't answer the phone. Kim and Ed had an answering machine, but it was not turned on that day.

Ed returned home that night after a difficult day of work. What he found when he got home was almost indescribable. Still in her nightgown from the previous night, Kim was nearly decapitated on the dining room floor. She was lying on her stomach, close to the wall, with metal handcuffs binding her hands behind her back. Her nightgown, saturated with blood, was bunched up around her waist, and her legs were spread apart. She had been dead for several hours, and dried blood surrounded her body and darkened the rug on which she lay. Elliot was in his crib in the nursery, unharmed but completely soiled after being left unattended for so long. The family dog was in the bedroom, and the door to the bedroom was closed. Ed called 911 at 9:58 p.m.

He did not rush to Kim's body when he discovered her. He did not go to her or touch her in any way. He told investigators he could tell from the foot of the steps leading into that part of the house—several feet away—that she was dead. He said it looked like "someone blew her brains out."

Crime-scene forensics painted a grim picture of what had occurred there, although every new fact discovered seemed to raise more questions than it answered. Kim was found to still have an earplug in one ear (used for sleeping); the other fell to the ground when her body was moved for the first time. According to entries in her diary, it was not unusual for her to put in earplugs and go back to bed after Ed left for work in the morning. There were large spots of blood found on the bedclothes in the master bedroom. Bare footprints (hers) tinged with blood went from the master bedroom, down the hall, and into the dining room, signaling that the initial attack may have occurred in the master bedroom. Shoe prints, presumably those of her attacker, paralleled Kim's footprints through the house. More blood on the floor—possibly marks made by Kim's bare heels—gave the appearance that she had been fleeing and was caught by her assailant near the kitchen and dragged into the dining room. There were several blunt-trauma injuries to her head, trunk, and arms, with dramatic bruising on her arms near her elbows. Her wrists showed abrasions under the handcuffs, meaning that she was alive when the handcuffs were put on. She had been cut, slashed, and stabbed repeatedly, showing as many as twenty-six separate knife wounds. Most of the wounds were to the back of her neck and her throat. The medical examiner soon determined that the official cause of death was blood loss from the incised and stab wounds to her neck.

The only item of value taken from the home was Kim's wedding band, which she was likely wearing at the time of the murder. Other jewelry, including a diamond necklace and gold bracelet that she had on, were left behind. Her purse, hanging from her office door, was undisturbed. The day's *Charlotte Observer*, a local newspaper, was lying on a table in the bedroom.

There were no indications that the killer had forced his way into the home. No windows or doors were broken or pried open. Slight smudges of blood appeared on papers at Kim's desk, on a stack of raffle tickets, as if the killer, wearing bloody gloves, picked them up briefly to examine them. Some of the desk drawers had been opened and closed. More traces of blood were found in Dr. Friedland's closet, on the light switch in the master bedroom, and on a pair of hospital scrubs. The top sheet of the bed in the master bedroom was missing. Blood was observed on both an inner and outer door leading from the kitchen to an outside deck. The deck led to a trail that ran through the woods to a neighboring road. There was a pedestrian tunnel that ran under the road to the Grier Heights neighborhood.

Crime-scene technicians found several shoe prints of dried blood in the dining room, near Kim's body. There were two distinct sole patterns in the blood, made by two different shoes. One of them was a docksider or deck shoe of some description, with a pattern of wavy lines on the bottom. The other had a contrasting pattern of uniformly spaced parallel bars. The shoe prints were a critical piece of evidence, because they very likely belonged to the killer or killers, or belonged to someone who was in the house after the murder had occurred. Investigators determined that the shoe prints did not match any of the shoes owned by Ed.

There was no indication that the house or crime scene had been cleaned up or manipulated by the killer (or killers). There was no evidence that bloody rags or towels had been washed or that bloody hands had been rinsed in the sink. The trap from the sink in the bathroom contained no evidence of blood. Forensic tests for blood revealed no evidence of blood in the shower.

The hiked-up nightgown and splaying of Kim's legs looked at first like a sexual assault, but a postmortem medical examination revealed that, in fact, there was no clear evidence that a sexual assault had taken place. No traces of semen were found. Why, then, was the nightgown raised in this way, and why was Kim's body positioned as it was?

As I found out later, the police were stumped at first. The evidence just didn't add up to a coherent, predictable, familiar narrative. The motive did not seem to be a burglary; nothing appeared to have been removed from the home except Kim's wedding band. The blood smudges on drawer handles in the home office and the papers that had been riffled through didn't contribute to the analysis in terms of determining motive. Rape was also ruled out as a motive because there was no evidence of sexual assault.

Police investigators briefly focused on a Black man named Marion Anthony Gales, a handyman of sorts who lived nearby in Grier Heights with his family. Gales was no stranger to the police. He had a long rap sheet of arrests, mostly for larceny and for his history of drug use. He lived just a short walk away from where Kim and Ed lived. He'd been seen in the neighborhood on the day of the murder, and it was easy to think that he might have been involved.

But everything changed when the police received a call to their tip line alleging that Ed was having an affair with a nurse at one of the local hospitals. This shifted the focus of the entire investigation, and the police quickly lost interest in Gales. Ed became the prime suspect, even though he had been at three different hospitals surrounded by witnesses from 8:00 a.m. until he left from work to go home around 9:45 p.m.

Investigators interviewed the nurse who had been involved with Ed, and she told them the affair had been going on for a few years. What really got their attention was when she said Ed had recently talked with a divorce attorney and decided it wasn't worth it when he learned how much a divorce and the ensuing alimony would cost. The police seized on this as a compelling motive. Now it all made sense. As they saw the case, Ed killed Kim to get out of an unhappy marriage, while also protecting his growing assets.

The problem the police had was that there was no physical evidence of any kind connecting Ed to the murder. The case was entirely circumstantial. There were no eyewitnesses, and the forensic evidence was inconclusive at best, allowing for countless explanations. Despite the messy crime scene and significant blood spatter, police had uncovered no actual evidence—no blood, fingerprints, hair, DNA, or anything else—that tied Ed to the murder. There was no murder weapon. No bloody clothes were found in the trunk of his car or in a nearby dumpster, and there was no indication that he had hauled away evidence from the house. His fingerprints and DNA did not appear on the handcuffs used to bind Kim's hands behind her back. His skin cells were not found under Kim's fingernails. A stain in Ed's car was too small to be tested for blood and could have been anything. A cigarette butt found outside and bagged by investigators couldn't be tested for DNA because there wasn't enough saliva. And, of course, there were two different sets of bloody shoe prints in the house that appeared to belong to other people. That had to be figured into the analysis somewhere.

For four years the police struggled to put together a case against Ed, convinced he was guilty, and for four years he lived under a terrible cloud of suspicion. Kim had been a well-known and very popular figure in the women's movement in Charlotte, and there was great public interest in the case. Exploiting this, the police leaked details to the press that made it seem like Ed had brutally murdered Kim, and this further heightened the tension. Many of the couple's close friends believed Ed was innocent, but acquaintances and others in the community, including his patients, felt uncomfortable around him. Even if they didn't see him as a killer, they now knew he had been unfaithful to his son's murdered mother based on accounts that appeared in the newspaper. Either way, he wasn't winning any popularity contests, and his medical practice was ruined because his partners as well as his patients didn't know what to think or whom to believe. The nightmare was ongoing and seemed to have no end in sight. Ed was living in purgatory.

During this time, the police weren't inclined to follow up on anything that could prove to be exculpatory to Ed because, as one year ended and the next began without an indictment, they were coming under increasing pressure from the public, their superiors, and Kim's family to solve the case. The outpouring of concern and outrage over her death was immense and growing. The community held candlelight vigils, and the media continued to closely follow the case and report on every new finding.

Details about the couple's infidelity, both his and hers, were reported, along with rumors that Ed and Kim used cocaine. Lou Thomas, Kim's father, upon learning about Ed's long-standing affair with the nurse, became wholly convinced that his son-in-law was the murderer. He urged police and the prosecutor's office to charge Ed early on, and he didn't let up. As the investigation dragged on, Kim's family understandably became more and more agitated by the lack of progress in the case.

In Charlotte, then and now, the police could not arrest someone for a crime as serious as murder without the approval of the district attorney. Despite all the pressure to solve the case, the police just couldn't gather enough evidence to persuade the district attorney's office to seek an indictment.

With no tangible evidence tying Ed to the murder, police began focusing on Kim's time of death. Given that Ed was at work from 8:00 a.m. until approximately 9:30 p.m. on the day of the murder, during which time he'd seen thirty patients throughout the day, the only way to show that Ed committed the crime would have been to prove that Kim's death occurred before he left for work that morn-ing. However, the state and the county medical examiners who performed the autopsy concluded it was not possible, based on the evidence, to determine her time of death. There was no scientific or medical way to prove that Kim had been killed before Ed left for work.

This didn't dissuade investigators from pushing ahead. They had all made up their minds that Ed was guilty, and they were bound and determined to prove it and get a conviction. In 1994, the police, still under enormous pressure from Kim's family, finally found a forensic expert—Dr. Michael Baden, the former chief medical examiner for the City of New York—who agreed to render an opinion that the medical examiners in North Carolina were not willing to provide: that Kim Thomas had likely died before 7:30 a.m., before Ed left for work. It was what they'd been waiting for. Prosecutors finally agreed to take the case to a grand jury, and the news broke far and wide: Dr. Ed Friedland had been indicted by the grand jury for the mur-der of his wife, Kim Thomas.

The police arrested Ed outside his medical offices, within sight of his patients, his staff, and his partners. Prior to the arrest, the police ensured that the news media was contacted in order to maximize the publicity of his arrest. As a result, his arrest for murder was filmed by all the local television stations. Video of him being handcuffed outside his medical offices and put into a police car was broadcast extensively. If convicted of the murder, he would face the death pen-alty for a particularly vicious and brutal crime.

The case didn't receive as much coverage in the Triangle area of North Carolina, where I lived at the time. I first became aware of it when Ed called me at my law office in Chapel Hill. Almost choking on his words, he said, "I didn't do this, and I need help." Defense lawyers regularly talk to people who are experiencing the most des-perate moments in their life. Ed's desperation in that moment was as extreme as I had ever heard. There was a frightened urgency in his voice. In the background, I heard noises that sounded like traffic. He was calling from a pay phone, probably just outside the courthouse where, he explained, he had just pled not guilty to his wife's murder. Ed had gotten my name from his lawyer, who had determined he had a conflict and could not continue to represent Ed, and from the lawyer's investigator, Ron Guerette, who I would go on to work with on a number of difficult and high-profile cases. I told Ed I would talk to his former lawyer and his investigator and then meet with him.

His lawyer told me the police didn't much care for Ed from the start. They said he wasn't "acting right" on the night he discovered Kim's body. He wasn't "emotional enough," they felt. He was "conducting business" on his phone the night of the murder, according to one source. They found it telling that he hadn't rushed to her body upon discovering her dead on the dining room floor, as surely anyone would have done, as everyone does in the movies. The police saw him as an outsider, and not someone they could relate to. He came across to them as an elite East Coast type, an aloof and somewhat arrogant Jewish Yankee who hadn't taken to the ways of the South. It was true that Ed didn't suffer fools and could be sarcastic. It wasn't a good combination for an outsider in his situation.

As an outsider myself, I could identify. I was also a Yankee who had invaded their turf. I thought the Civil War was history, but here in the South it was still a reality. Some native southerners still didn't like, understand, or trust northerners. Police, like many others, often treat people differently whom they perceive as outsiders, whether it's a Jew from New York, or a person of color, or a Muslim, or someone in the LGBTQ community. Even when the treatment does not rise to the level of physical brutality or some other form of abuse or blatant discrimination, it has a corrosive effect on the rule of law. It also greatly exacerbates another common problem in police investigations.

As we saw in the Marvin Anderson case discussed earlier, investigators and prosecutors, once they decide on a particular theory and suspect, often fall prey to confirmation bias and tunnel vision, causing them to focus only on a single suspect and overlook or dismiss exculpatory explanations or evidence. Law enforcement decides who they "like" for a crime; generally, one of the "usual suspects," such as the spouse in a murder case. They did this in the Michael Peterson case, chronicled in the Netflix series *The Staircase*. They did it in the Sam Sheppard case, which served as the inspiration for the TV series and movie *The Fugitive*. Sometimes this is supported by sound evidence and reasoning, but sometimes it is based on stereotypes, hunches, or intuition.

In the latter cases, hubris takes control. The detective, who has "solved" hundreds or maybe thousands of cases, becomes convinced he is right. He just has to prove his intuition correct. The investigation becomes suspect-based rather than fact-based, and investigators work to rule a particular suspect *in*. Rather than trying to determine objectively from the facts what happened, the goal becomes developing evidence to prove that a particular suspect or suspects committed the crime. Confirmation bias brings about tunnel vision, which in turn causes the detective to ignore evidence that is inconsistent with his theory and leads him to focus on and inflate the importance of evidence that seems consistent with his theory.

These psychological phenomena are often at the root of what goes wrong in an investigation, because when the evidence necessary to prove the preferred theory isn't readily available, the police, whether consciously or unconsciously, may manipulate the evidence or decide to fabricate it. The means by which this occurs includes subjective forensic methods that don't meet scientific standards, coerced and fabricated confessions, and even the planting of false evidence. Alternatively, investigators may decide to conceal evidence, as we believed had occurred in the case of Alan Gell. To those police officers who cover up or withhold exculpatory evidence, proving the guilt of the killer, by whatever means necessary, is justified. It has come to be known as "noble-cause corruption," otherwise described as "the ends justifying the means," and it goes hand in hand with confirmation bias.

In the Peterson case, it was Michael's bisexuality and the death of a family friend in Germany. In the Friedland case, it was Ed's affair, his demeanor, and the fact that he didn't act how police thought he should have acted in the minutes and hours after discovering his wife's body. All these things added up to a hunch that Ed was the killer, and after that mental switch had been flipped, evidence gathered by the police was either viewed as consistent with that hypothesis or was otherwise rejected and ignored.

In Ed's case, for example, the police said that the number of stab wounds on Kim's body was evidence of "overkill" and showed that the murder was clearly a crime of passion, such as might be inflicted by an enraged, out-of-control husband. Perhaps Kim found out Ed was having an affair, the police suggested. Simultaneously, the police argued that the murder had been methodically staged, with Ed carefully planning the killing so as not to leave a trace of evidence implicating himself. The killer, they argued, was wearing gloves. This was proof of a high level of planning. The killer left no fingerprints on the blood-soaked handcuffs. More careful planning. The killer left bloody glove prints in tantalizing places to mislead investigators. Truly diabolical. So was the killer enraged and out of control or devious and calculating? Every detail and every clue was massaged, manipulated, and artificially forced to fit into the investigators' theory, no matter how nonsensical or unscientific, and even when conflicting with other parts of the police's theory.

Another example can be found in the investigators' interpretation of the blood evidence found at the scene. Special Agent P. Duane Deaver of the North Carolina State Bureau of Investigation, who I would encounter again in the Peterson case, and who we demonstrated in that case was willing to say almost anything to help the state, was called in to examine the blood patterns and traces left around the home. His opinion was that the "blood stains in the office looked unusual. . . . It looked contrived to me. . . . [B]ased on my experience, like an individual tried to make it look like they were rummaging through effects to find something . . . instead of actually going through them." In fact, he had no "experience" to support this conclusion, and no basis for making such suppositions, other than that they happened to conform with the police's working hypothesis showing Ed as the killer.

Take the positioning of the nightgown and Kim's legs as another example. Investigators argued that the killer must have lifted Kim's nightgown and spread her legs after her death, and that this was done to mislead investigators and make them think the motive for the crime was a sexual assault. This could only have been done by someone as deliberate and calculating as Dr. Friedland, so it was posited.

However, Dr. Friedland, as a physician, would surely know that Kim's body would be immediately examined for evidence of sexual assault. He would likewise know that staging the body to appear as if a rape had occurred would be a pointless exercise; such a ruse would take almost no time to disprove. Nevertheless, every bit of evidence was read as inculpatory.

After his arrest, Ed was released on a $300,000 bond that he had to secure by taking out a second mortgage on his house. Then his situation quickly moved from bad to worse. When the indictment was announced, his partners insisted that he leave the medical practice, which meant he had no source of income and was living off his savings. He had broken off his relationship with the nurse soon after Kim was murdered. In the ensuing four years, he had met another woman and remarried. They had two very young children of their own, and with Elliot, Ed's adopted son, and a child from his new wife's previous relationship, they had four children to support. He wanted to move his new family out of the area, but he couldn't get a job as a doctor or go anywhere until his name was cleared. The toll this was taking on him, emotionally and financially, was staggering.

I met with Ed and agreed to represent him. To me, there was no evidence of his guilt, no motive for him to have murdered Kim, and no indication that he was the kind of person who would commit a murder as vicious, bloody, and personal as this, no matter his motive.

There was zero violence or abuse in his background. He seemed altogether incapable of such a horrific crime. I could see a gunshot, maybe, though he didn't own any guns. But a knife attack that virtually decapitated his wife, no way.

I began working on Ed's case as much as I possibly could. I had a lot to catch up on in a short time. Ron Guerette, the retired Charlotte homicide detective who had been working the case for Ed's previous attorney, stayed on as the investigator and helped me build a solid defense. It would be the beginning of an exceptional professional and personal relationship that lasted until Ron's death in June 2018. His investigative expertise was critical to the cases we put together for Ed's defense; for the defense of Rae Carruth, an NFL player who was indicted for capital murder in 1999 for allegedly hiring a hit man to kill his pregnant girlfriend; and for Michael Peterson's defense in 2002, among many others. Dogged, gritty, and sharp, Ron was the best investigator I have ever worked with.

Ron unearthed a key piece of evidence in the police call logs, which showed that police had received several complaints about suspicious activity involving the original suspect, Marion Anthony Gales, just before and during the time of Kim Thomas's murder. But there was no mention of Gales in the discovery materials that the district attorney had provided us, and that office had a well-earned reputation for providing the defense with all the exculpatory evidence (*Brady* evidence) in their possession. We therefore filed a motion asking that the Charlotte police be ordered to produce any reports in its possession regarding Marion Gales, and sought a hearing to determine whether the police had any other *Brady* evidence that should be turned over to us. We also subpoenaed the four police officers who had been involved in the investigation, as well as their supervisor, requiring them to bring to the hearing all of their reports related to Gales. We wanted to know what the police knew about him and when they had known it.

At the hearing, Richard Gordon, the prosecutor, asked that the reports brought by the investigators first be turned over to the judge for review so the judge could determine if the reports were exculpatory. If so, the records would be turned over to us. The judge agreed, and he and Gordon went back to his chambers to review the reports. After an hour, Gordon appeared with a stunned and shaken look on his face.

"You're not going to believe this," he said, handing me a stack of police reports. "This is the first time I have seen any of this. I had no idea."

21

THE OBVIOUS SUSPECT

I started reading the police reports related to Marion Gales and was astounded by the amount of evidence the police had that pointed to Gales as the killer—evidence that had been discounted or dismissed by the investigators once they had begun focusing on Ed as their primary suspect. Gales was the person the Charlotte police had first identified as a suspect in the murder of Kim Thomas, but they had long since turned their attention to Ed.

Gales's first contact with law enforcement occurred in 1979, when he was still a teenager. On March 8, 1979, he entered an unlocked door at 3909 Churchill Drive—*only about two hundred feet from where Kim and Ed lived in 1990*—with the intent to steal the homeowner's purse. When the homeowner came downstairs and surprised Gales, he shot her with a handgun. He then fled to his mother's house in Grier Heights, across the street, and attempted to hide his involvement by changing his clothes. A witness informed police that Gales had also attempted to enter her home, also located on Churchill Drive, and when confronted, he had claimed he was only looking for work. He was convicted of burglary and assault with a deadly weapon inflicting serious injury. He was sentenced to ten years in prison as a youthful offender but served little of the time.

In 1981, he was convicted of "assault on a female" (as the crime is called in North Carolina). In May 1985, he was arrested for a burglary occurring at 4:40 a.m. (the charge was dismissed). In September 1985, he was again convicted of assault on a female. In December 1985, he was alleged to have raped his former girlfriend, Brenda Moore, after getting into her house without permission. When police officers responded to the call, Gales ran from the police. He twice pointed a gun at the pursuing officer, who then shot Gales in the jaw. He was arrested for assaulting a police officer with a deadly weapon and was sentenced to ten years in prison, but he was released in 1989.

In or around December 1989, Gales was alleged to have assaulted his girlfriend, Bernice Robinson, breaking several of her ribs and injuring her badly enough to require hospitalization. He was alleged to be high on cocaine at the time and was known to drink heavily. On December 13, 1989, Gales was arrested for assault with a knife in a case where he struck the victim in the face with pliers hard enough to knock out two of his teeth, and then cut the victim's head with a knife. According to Gales's girlfriend, it was his habit to carry a six- to eight-inch knife.

In February 1990, Gales continued to drink heavily and had allegedly become addicted to cocaine, and he was routinely breaking into houses and selling stolen property, including jewelry, to buy the drugs necessary to support his addiction. His sister told the police that his cocaine habit had become severe. His addiction would only get worse in the coming months. During this time, Gales was living on Billingsley Road in Grier Heights, which was within easy walking distance of Churchill Road through a small drainage tunnel under the road separating Grier Heights from where Kim and Ed lived.

On June 18, 1990—a little more than a month before the murder—Kim Thomas was at home, visiting with one of her close friends, Jan

Ellen Brown. Without warning, Gales appeared out of the woods near the back of the home, surprising Kim's friend and making her uneasy. Gales walked around to the front door, and Kim opened the door to greet him. He asked her for work, and Kim agreed. She had him clean the moss off the flagstone walkway, paying him with cash. Kim's friend was highly distressed by this whole interaction and told Kim to stay inside the house and turn on the alarm. Two days after the murder, the friend informed the police she believed that it was this man who had likely killed Kim, though she didn't know his name at the time.

On June 24, 1990, Gales committed a burglary of a residence and set the house on fire. He was subsequently arrested (after Kim's murder), convicted, and sentenced to fourteen years in prison for this crime. A week after this burglary, Betty Jones, who lived just down the road from Kim Thomas, noticed a man matching Gales's description stalking the neighborhood for about two weeks.

Eight days before the murder, Gales again came out of the woods behind Kim's house while Kim was there visiting with another friend, Nancy Verruto. The friend later gave the police this chilling account of the incident:

> *And he came out of the woods. He actually shocked us. We were in the kitchen. . . . And the first I saw of him was in her kitchen. She's got a window looking at the driveway . . . and I saw him. I saw him come like this way, and I went, "Kim, who's this guy?" And she said, "Oh, him."* *And she looked at me in the living room; she told me who he was. He does odd jobs* and she said I'm thinking about putting my alarm on during the day when I'm home. . . . *She went and she just—door was wide open, and in retrospect I look back at that now and I could look through the dining room and see him standing there on that side of the doorway through the dining room windows, see outside and I could look through the hallway, see Kim up there and now when I think of it, I think, Oh God, it just seemed very bizarre to me that Kim, just little*

Kim, opened this door and there's this strange Black man that came out of the woods, and sure enough she put him to work.

Again, Kim paid Gales in cash. When Kim was murdered, the friend immediately believed that this person, who she later identified from a photograph as Marion Gales, killed Kim, and she said this to the police on the night of Kim's murder.

During this same week, Gales told his brother-in-law, James Roseboro, that he stole some jewelry out of a lady's house while she was in the backyard. Robert and Betty McCorkle, who lived on the same driveway off Churchill Road as the Thomas house, saw a man matching Gales's description asking for yard work in the area.

Meanwhile, Gales seemed to be accelerating downward, fueled by the need to feed his drug addiction, with endless collateral damage. On July 23, Gales allegedly assaulted his sister Annie Roseboro by striking her on the face and back and grabbing her around the neck. On July 24, Gales committed a burglary at his other sister's house. He was arrested later (again, after Kim Thomas was murdered) and convicted.

And all that, all of which was known to the police before Ed was arrested, just brings us up to July 26, 1990, the night before the murder.

At approximately 10:30 p.m. that night, Gales broke into a residence located at 3715 Ellington Street and stole some jewelry. Ellington Street intersects Billingsley Road and is within walking distance of the house where Kim and Ed lived. After this burglary, Gales made his way, slowly but surely, toward Kim and Ed's house on Churchill Road.

At about 4:00 on the morning of the murder, Gales was seen and confronted by some young men who were outside winding down a party on Ellsworth Road, just around the corner from Churchill Road. Gales appeared to be high on drugs. He lied and told the young men that he did work for the homeowner next door but could not give the homeowner's name. He also claimed he had run out of gas and offered a ring (apparently stolen from the house on Ellington) as security for a $20 cash loan. The police were called, but Gales was not found when police arrived at the scene. Gales's attempt to get even $20 in cash—probably to be used to buy cocaine—gives some measure of Gales's desperate state of mind.

At 5:30 a.m., Gales was still prowling about and was now on Churchill Road. Gales appeared at the door of David Moore, a resident of Churchill Road near Kim and Ed's house, and attempted to impersonate a police officer. He told Moore through the door that Moore's car had been broken into, and that he should come outside with his wallet and keys. Moore wisely called the police and made a report, noting that the man had something unusual about his jaw—consistent with the injury Gales had suffered when he was shot in the face running from the police in 1985.

After Gales's interaction with David Moore at 5:30 a.m., there are no further witness accounts of Gales being seen anywhere until that night. When later questioned by the police, he could not account for and substantiate his whereabouts on the day of the murder, and he had no alibis. He tellingly claimed not to know Kim Thomas, said he had never been to Churchill Road, and denied ever having been to Kim's house, all of which was demonstrably untrue.

On the evening of July 27, hours after Kim had been murdered, Gales showed up at the back door of the residence of his sister and brother-in-law, Annie and James Roseboro. According to James Roseboro, Gales was wearing docksider shoes (as found in the bloody footprints by investigators). Roseboro said Gales was acting strange, not like he usually did. Gales had blood on his shirt, and took a shirt and pants from the Roseboros' clothesline to replace his own.

On July 28, the day after the murder, James Roseboro called the police and told them that he and his wife believed that Gales might have killed Kim Thomas. In a second interview with the police on August 1, Roseboro told police that Gales didn't want to stay on Billingsley Road, near Kim and Ed's house, so he had gone to stay elsewhere. Roseboro also told the police that he once drove Gales to Churchill Road so Gales could do some work there, near Kim and Ed's house. In one of the most intriguing clues in the case, Ed identified Roseboro, from a photograph shown by police, as someone who had previously done yard work at the house. This same identification was made independently by a housekeeper for Kim and Ed. When asked about this by the police, Roseboro said, "I ain't never been there. I ain't never been there in my whole life."

The police administered a polygraph to Roseboro on August 1 regarding whether he was lying to investigators. The report indicated Roseboro "answered questions incorrectly, asked a number of times for questions to be repeated, hesitated on practically every question before responding, and at times was unable to be still." Roseboro did not pass the polygraph; the results were inconclusive. The police did not check to see whether Roseboro owned shoes that matched either of the bloody shoe prints found at the scene, nor did they ever see if Gales's Docksiders matched the prints.

Three weeks later, Gales himself called the police department and spoke to a detective. He volunteered that he "didn't kill that woman." When the detective asked him "what woman," Gales said, "That white woman" who got murdered. He agreed to come to the police station to talk but never showed up.

The police interviewed Gales's sister. She told them Gales had "never been this bad before" and said he "needs to be off the street." They learned that Gales, since the murder, had been staying with his girlfriend, Bernice Robinson, in a different neighborhood and was no longer living in Grier Heights. The same day, police received information that Bernice had said that Gales had done "something real bad" on Wendover Road (which backs up to Churchill Road).

The next day, the police interviewed Bernice. She said Gales admitted to her that he knew Kim Thomas. She also said Gales had been "doing crazy things" on cocaine and that he beat her "real bad" once while high. She believed that Gales killed Thomas.

Gales later admitted to an investigator that he had purchased a pair of metal handcuffs from the Army-Navy Store on Trade Street in Charlotte and once tried to put the handcuffs on Bernice while she resisted just to see if he could do it. The handcuffs sold by the Army-Navy Store prior to 1990 were identical to the handcuffs found on Kim Thomas. Gales's mother also admitted, in a tape-recorded statement, that Gales owned handcuffs and that Gales had told her he no longer had them, that he had left them at his girlfriend's house.

The police attempted to arrest Gales on August 24, but he fled. Eventually, he was caught and taken into custody. While they had Gales in custody, the police took hair and saliva samples from him, but those samples were never analyzed or compared against hairs collected by investigators from the scene. They simply decided that the murder did not match Gales's modus operandi and released him, turning their attention instead to Ed Friedland, based on the newly discovered information about his affair. One police investigator later admitted that the decision not to pursue Gales as a suspect in Kim's murder was not based upon any fact, but rather was based on his "intuition."

After deciding not to pursue Gales as a suspect, the police failed to investigate him any further, allowing for the destruction of evidence that might have connected Gales to the crime scene. For example, the police did little to find the clothes worn by Gales on July 27, despite having a specific description of the items he wore. They did not search the homes of Gales's mother, his girlfriend, the Roseboros, or any other known associates of Gales, in an effort to find incriminating evidence. Police effectively ceased all investigation of Gales after August 28, 1990.

Let's step back for a moment and consider just a few of the pieces of evidence connecting Marion Gales to Kim Thomas. We know Gales, a violent felon with a history of drug use, had been to Kim's house at least twice, and likely more than twice, in the weeks leading up to the murder. Then, on the day of the murder, Gales was seen in her neighborhood, and then *on her street*, by multiple people—first, by the late-night partiers; and second, by David Moore, who Gales tried to lure out of his home at 5:30 a.m., in close proximity to Kim and Ed's house, in order to commit an offense that would necessarily have involved a violent confrontation, if Moore had been foolish enough to open the front door. But in this attempt, Gales was not successful, leaving some goal unfulfilled. Some need unmet. That need was cash with which to buy drugs. Where did he know he could get cash? Did he see Ed come out that morning and retrieve the day's newspaper, only to leave home a few minutes later? What truly are the chances that a serial violent offender who had been to Kim Thomas's house, and who was *on her street* looking for money that morning within mere hours of her death, had nothing whatsoever to do with her murder? It seemed pretty clear to me that this was no mere coincidence.

Notwithstanding Gales's history of reckless, depraved, and escalating criminal behavior, not to mention his presence on Churchill Drive on the morning of the murder, the police believed it was more likely that Ed Friedland, a physician who had no history of criminal activity, no history of domestic violence, and no physical evidence connecting him to the crime, had killed his wife to avoid alimony and a division of marital assets. If you wanted to give an example of how confirmation bias and tunnel vision lead to wrongful arrests and convictions, you would be hard-pressed to come up with a more vivid and compelling example.

And precisely because the police had zeroed in on Ed, against whom they had no evidence, they wrongfully concealed and withheld *all* of the evidence pertaining to Marion Gales from the prosecutors. Every bit of it. The Charlotte police hid the evidence regarding Gales from the district attorney because they knew that evidence would dissuade the district attorney from indicting Ed. Then, once Ed was indicted, the police continued to conceal the Gales evidence because they knew the district attorney, an ethical prosecutor, would have provided the evidence to the defense as he was constitutionally obligated to do. In their minds, Ed was guilty, and they figured Ed would walk if the district attorney knew about this evidence and disclosed it to Ed's defense attorney—so they concealed it. And they surely would have continued to conceal it at Ed's trial and while he awaited execution if Ron Guerette hadn't examined the call logs, and if we hadn't subpoenaed the Gales evidence the police had accumulated.

Regardless of what you might believe with respect to who killed Kim Thomas, it is beyond dispute that the evidence against Marion Gales is seriously damning, and it is equally beyond dispute that the police had a constitutional obligation not to conceal this evidence from prosecutors and from Ed. It was an inexcusable and profound abuse of power in a death-penalty case.

THE TIME OF DEATH

Incredibly, the Gales evidence wasn't all that the police hid from the prosecutor. It was critical to the state's case against Ed to show that Kim had died before he left for work that morning. The police sought this opinion from the medical examiners for Charlotte and the state, but both said it was not medically possible to rule out that Kim had died after 8:00 a.m. So the police did something unprecedented: they looked outside North Carolina for a forensic expert who would give them the testimony they needed. They found their guy in Dr. Michael Baden, a controversial former chief medical examiner for New York City, who would go on to serve on O. J. Simpson's defense team and become known for television appearances, high-profile cases, and contrary medical opinions.

The detective assigned to the case called Dr. Baden and told him that the police felt it was vital to show that Kim Thomas died prior to Ed leaving the house in the morning. Dr. Baden eventually gave a written opinion to the detective that Kim had likely died before 8:00 a.m., before Ed had left for the hospital, and it was this key piece of evidence that had finally persuaded the district attorney to indict Ed.

If the North Carolina medical examiners could not determine the time of Kim's death during the autopsy, how could Dr. Baden manage such a feat so long after the death occurred? He claimed he could do this based on the level of potassium in the vitreous humor of Kim's eye. I'd never heard of such a thing. I began to research the science behind Dr. Baden's claim and quickly learned that Dr. John Coe, the first medical examiner in Minnesota, was the expert who pioneered that technique. I called Dr. Coe, and he informed me that it was only accurate to plus or minus *six hours*. In other words, no one could tell from this test if Kim had died before 8:00 a.m., between 8:00 a.m. and 9:00 a.m., or sometime after.

It was infuriating to me that someone could seemingly be so loose with an expert opinion in a capital case where a man's life was at stake. This was not a game. It was the first time I had come up against what I considered to be "fake science"—in a death-penalty case, no less—and I promptly filed a motion to exclude Dr. Baden's testimony from being heard at trial. In the meantime, I read every scientific study Dr. Coe sent me on determining the time of death using the level of potassium in the vitreous humor of the eye at the time of the autopsy.

While preparing for the hearing on my motion to exclude Dr. Baden's testimony, I received an unexpected but very welcome surprise. Susan Weigand, an assistant public defender who was not involved in the Friedland case, called me out of the blue and said, "David, I think you're going to want to hear this tape I just got from the Charlotte police." That turned out to be the understatement of the century.

I came to learn that the police detective who called Dr. Baden and sought his testimony against Ed had recorded the call onto a cassette tape. He used the same audio tape to provide a copy of a 911 call to the assistant public defender, but the 911 call was short and took up only a small part of the tape. The remainder still contained much of the detective's telephone call with Dr. Baden. Once the assistant public defender realized what it was, she called me. Ron picked up the tape from the public defender's office.

As I listened to the call, I heard the police detective tell Baden that he was "convinced" Ed "did it." Baden then asked, "Everybody knows he did it?" and the detective answered, "Yeah, everybody pretty much thinks so." The call continued, and I listened to the detective tell Baden, in essence, what the police wanted and needed Baden to conclude regarding Kim's time of death—namely, that she died before Ed left for work.

No ethical detective would have done this, in my opinion. Psychological biases can affect experts just as they do detectives and everyone else. Telling an expert the desired outcome has the tendency to influence the expert, and the expert may then unconsciously but inaccurately interpret his or her own data trying to reach a particular result. In order to avoid this, scientific and forensic tests and examinations must and should be performed independently of any desired outcome.

Despite the obvious pressure from the detective, Baden initially responded that the science wasn't that precise, and he couldn't say, with a reasonable degree of medical certainty, the time of Kim's death. I listened in amazement as he admitted that the science "can't distinguish plus or minus an hour. Say he leaves at 7:45 in the morning—the body would look the same if she were dead at 6:45 or she were dead at 8:45. It can't rule out dying at between 7:45 and 8:30."

I was amazed because I had received the opinion letter that Dr. Baden had subsequently provided to the Charlotte police. In the letter, Baden stated he *could* testify under oath that it was "much more likely" that Kim had died before 8:00 a.m. It was this letter that the police relied on to convince the district attorney to finally indict Ed. Naturally, the police did not tell the district attorney's office what Baden had conceded about the technique's limitations in the phone call, and they didn't turn over the audiotape of the call to the district attorney either.

With Dr. Coe's help in researching scientific articles, and with the audiotape in my back pocket, I was able to discredit Baden's opinion at the hearing on the admissibility of his testimony at Ed's trial. On the stand, he couldn't explain the limitations of the vitreous potassium formulas that were described in the articles, finally saying, "I can't tell you how a watch works, but I can look at it and tell you what time it is." The judge was not impressed with Baden's analogy. He ruled Baden could not testify and excluded his time-of-death evidence.

After learning of the Gales evidence and that Dr. Baden had told the detective he could not say precisely when Kim Thomas's death had occurred, both of which had been concealed from the prosecutor by the police, the district attorney dismissed the charges against Ed, and that part of the case was over.

THE AFTERMATH

In August 1995, after the charges against Ed Friedland were dismissed, the police subjected Marion Gales to a polygraph test. The test showed that Gales was lying when he denied that he cut Kim Thomas's throat. No tape recording, transcript, or report was made of the police's interview of Gales following the polygraph. No further investigation was done. That would have proved that by not focusing on Gales in the summer of 1990, the Charlotte police had indeed done immeasurable harm to Kim Thomas, to her family and loved ones, and to Ed Friedland. Better to let that alone.

In order to restore Ed's name and professional reputation so he could start over in another place, we sued Marion Gales so that we could present the evidence the police had concealed to a jury and to the public. The jury unanimously found Gales responsible for Kim's death and returned a completely symbolic verdict of $5 million in punitive damages. We never tried to collect a penny, but Ed was able to begin his life again in another city.

We also sued the police officers responsible for concealing the Gales evidence and the Baden tape from the prosecutors, but the Court ruled that they had not violated Ed's constitutional rights, holding that the exculpatory evidence did not have to be turned over to the prosecutors *until the time of trial.* Since we had gotten the case dismissed prior to trial, the Court held the concealment did not constitute a constitutional violation by the police, notwithstanding the damage done to Ed by the wrongful arrest and prosecution themselves.

Marion Gales was never prosecuted for Kim Thomas's death. In 2008, after spending time in prison for other offenses, Gales was charged with the murder of twenty-seven-year-old Lacoya Martin, a mother of four who was sixteen weeks pregnant at the time of her death. Gales admitted that he knew the victim and had shared drugs with her, but he denied killing her. He eventually pled guilty to manslaughter and is still in prison for her death.

And to this day, Kim's family has never received any closure. More than thirty years after the fact, Kim's case remains unsolved. As described by the *Charlotte Observer*, it is the city's "most impenetrable murder mystery."

The Ed Friedland case was, unfortunately, not an anomaly. It was not an isolated case where the police accidentally withheld exculpatory evidence from the prosecution, including compelling evidence of a third party's guilt, and evidence that forensic testimony was not based on true science. The same police department did the same thing to another criminal defendant, Timothy Bridges, the very same year! Such conduct deprives the defendant not only of the evidence he or she needs to establish reasonable doubt, if not outright innocence, but also of constitutionally required protections. This phenomenon of the police (and some prosecutors) withholding, concealing, or flat-out ignoring evidence favorable to the defense is all too common. It has happened in every state in the country. It happens to poor defendants, it can and did happen to a well-to-do doctor in Charlotte, and it can and did happen to a U.S. Senator, Ted Stevens, in a federal prosecution in Washington, D.C.

Studies of exonerations that have occurred in the past thirty years show that *almost half* (44 percent) of those wrongful convictions involved prosecutors or police, or both, hiding or withholding exculpatory evidence. And these are just the cases we know about. A study by the National Association of Criminal Defense Attorneys (NACDL) and Santa Clara Law School in 2014 highlights the true scope of the problem:

> *The question of how often prosecutors violate* Brady v. Maryland *is impossible to answer because, by its very nature, the withholding of* Brady *material [exculpatory evidence] is hidden, and withheld information may never surface. The number of cases in which a judge or jury may have convicted an innocent person, without becoming aware of all the favorable information actually in existence, remains unknown. One can fairly assume that for every wrongfully convicted individual who has been vindicated, there are countless others whose innocence remains invisible to the system.*

In the Friedland case, Ed was fortunate that the evidence pointing to another suspect was discovered prior to trial. He was equally fortunate that the state was not allowed to put on unscientific evidence related to Kim's time of death, and this came about partly because of the fortuitous discovery of an audiotape that the police *accidentally* turned over to a public defender in a completely separate case—an audiotape that I otherwise would never have heard.

Ed endured the loss of his wife, the loss of his job, years of probing suspicion by the police, a humiliating public arrest, and an even more public prosecution for a murder he didn't commit, along with years of opprobrium and shame from the community. And it really came down to almost chance that he wasn't convicted and sentenced to death. Countless others have not been as fortunate. We will never know their number. In many cases, the police and prosecutorial misconduct is not discovered until years after the defendant has been convicted, sentenced to prison, or even executed. In most such cases, it is never discovered at all.

22

A THOUSAND TO ONE

Twenty years after the Friedland case was dismissed, I discovered that in 1990, the same supervisors involved in the Friedland matter that very year had permitted detectives investigating yet another brutal crime to conceal evidence from prosecutors, much the same as they did in the Friedland case. This time, the concealed evidence included, among other things, an actual confession from another suspect. The police also utilized "fake science," an alleged forensic expert in the field of microscopic hair analysis and comparison who provided critical testimony that was not based on valid scientific principles, and which ensured the defendant's conviction. This time, they got away with it for twenty-five years.

In the early months of 1989, the City of Charlotte reeled from a series of horrific sexual assaults on elderly women in the eastern part of the city. When the first one occurred, the police assumed it was a singular, isolated incident—and then it happened again: another elderly woman was raped in her home. And then yet again. The city was on edge as the police scrambled to solve the crimes and find the attacker.

One of the victims was Modine Wise, who was eighty-three years old. She lived alone and was confined to a wheelchair. She lived on one side of a single-story duplex a few miles from downtown. Her home was modest but practical. A small but tidy living room, a kitchen, a bathroom, and two narrow bedrooms made up the whole living space.

Modine was a religious person, and religious imagery was found throughout her home. Next to a small television in the corner of the living room was a Holy Bible, white and gold, and visibly well-read. On the wall above was a painting of Jesus, in a gilded frame, leading a flock of sheep. Beside a small electric clock, its cord running down the wall to the outlet below, hung a solitary wooden cross.

The hall from the living room to the back of the house was dark and narrow, and the walls showed countless marks at knee-level above the floor where Modine's wheelchair had passed back and forth down the hall, day in and day out. At the end of the hall were two bedrooms, and in the larger bedroom there was a twin bed that took up most of the room. A shopping cart Modine got from somewhere, which helped her move things around the house more easily, was at the foot of the bed, and next to it was a metal ironing board that Modine put up once and never took back down. The ironing board was covered with an old quilt, and Modine used this as a makeshift shelf for odds and ends. It was here, in this room, that Modine was viciously raped on Mother's Day in 1989. The wanton cruelty exhibited by Modine's attacker was beyond imagining.

Modine's sister-in-law, Virginia, found her the day after the attack occurred. Modine was barely alive. She was half-dressed and moving in and out of consciousness. She had been brutally beaten about the face, chest, and arms. The swelling on her face had closed both her eyes, and her face and hair were pink with blood. She would recover in time, albeit slowly.

The motive for the attack was not robbery, for nothing of value had been taken from the house. A purse containing money was still pinned to Modine's torn and bloody dress. As incomprehensible as it was to imagine, the attack appeared to have had one motive, and that was sexual assault.

Modine gave the police a description of her attacker: he was a young white male with long curly hair that was either blond, blondish brown, or brown. She told the police that she could identify her attacker if shown a photograph, but no one ever showed her a photograph of any potential suspects, even after the police had later narrowed their focus to one man.

Inside the house, the police found a wealth of clues. The attacker had been incredibly careless. He had left behind a stain-covered jacket on the bed, from which it would later be possible to extract the rapist's nuclear DNA. In the bathroom, on the floor beside the toilet, was a pair of dirty white tube socks belonging to the attacker. On the quilt-covered ironing board at the foot of Modine's bed, the police found an open pack of Salem Lights (Modine did not smoke) and a pair of black eyeglasses that did not belong to her.

Blood was found throughout the house. A spray of blood appeared low on the bedroom wall, near where the attack occurred, and the mattress and bedclothes were soaked with blood. Most critically, on the wall next to the light switch in the bedroom, right above where Modine had been raped, there was a single bloody palm print—one showing a lot of detail. Modine was quickly ruled out as the source of the print, so the police reasonably concluded it belonged to the rapist.

Using the description given by Modine, the police focused on virtually every young male with long, light-colored hair who was known to frequent the area, which turned out to be quite a few. Recognizing that the palm print left at the scene was the key piece of evidence, the police rounded up and took palm-print impressions of approximately fifty young males, including a young man named Tim Bridges.

The police knew Tim because he had previously been caught using drugs, and he sometimes resorted to male prostitution to pay for the drugs he was taking. He had recently gotten out of rehab and was back on the street, and he had been seen in the vicinity of Modine's neighborhood. The police took Tim's prints and sent them to the crime lab for analysis, but his prints did not match the palm print found on the wall. Tim was ruled out as the source of the bloody palm print on Modine's wall.

One right after the other, persons of interest brought in by the police were excluded on the basis of the palm print. Given that several sexual assaults of elderly women had happened in that part of the city, pressure in the community for police to solve the crimes was mounting. In June 1989, the police ran a piece in a local newspaper asking for the public's help with respect to Modine's case in particular.

The Charlotte police officers who had regular informants in the area turned up the heat on their informants to try to get information. One of the informants was Matt Donaldson, who was sixteen years old. Despite his age, he was known to work as a prostitute and had a cocaine habit. He was arrested twice in July 1989 for loitering for the purpose of committing a crime against nature. He had been observed walking the streets near Modine's house and had been considered a suspect for several break-ins in that area. He also fit the description provided by Modine.

On the night of August 2, 1989, with all the rape cases unsolved and the public frightened and searching for answers, Matt Donaldson's father called the officer for whom Matt served as an informant. He said that Matt, while high on drugs, had told him Tim Bridges was the person who had raped Modine. Two days later, the Charlotte police officer assigned as the lead investigator on the case, Cheryl Horner, interviewed Matt, who was facing charges from his recent July arrests. He told her he had heard on the street that Tim Bridges had committed the rape. Following the interview, Horner was suspicious of Matt's story and even had Matt's palm prints checked against the palm print found at the scene. They came back negative.

Matt's statement, despite lacking any indicia of reliability, was eventually accepted by Detective Horner as being true. This was the first faltering step in the investigation. Although he had been ruled out as the source of the telltale palm print in Modine's bedroom, and therefore eliminated as a suspect, Tim fit the description given by Modine. Donaldson's self-serving statement somehow flipped a mental switch for Horner. Her fact investigation, for all practical purposes, came to a halt at that point. Henceforth, Horner's efforts seemed to be aimed exclusively at proving Tim, and Tim alone, was the rapist. All evidence contrary to this hypothesis would be ignored.

As of late August 1989, three months after the incident, no arrests had been made. The police were getting desperate to make some progress in the case, and they needed more than just Matt's statement that he had "heard" Tim was the culprit. To this end, Detective Horner advised Charlotte police officers who had seen Matt and another police informant "trolling" for homosexual males to stop them and threaten to "lock them up" in order to "give us some leeway [i.e., leverage] with them. . . ." She suggested the officers say something like, "You talk to us *about Tim* and we won't charge you with loitering." She also told another detective, "You and I need to reinterview [Matt] Donaldson. After tonight, he may break."

Before long, the police had lined up two other longtime police informants who had stories to tell that were similar to Matt's: they too claimed to have *heard* that Tim was Modine's attacker. The new statements initially seemed to back up Matt's account, but they hardly withstood scrutiny. On September 13, 1989, Clarence Neal Williams, who also fit the description of the suspect in Modine's case, was arrested for "crimes against nature." He told the arresting officer that a week earlier, Tim had just casually volunteered to him, while walking down the street, that he (Tim) had committed the rape.

The other informant, a woman named Vicky Jones, who the police knew struggled with a drug addiction, claimed that while she was driving a car by a street corner in Charlotte in September, she had heard Tim Bridges say to someone else (who she could not identify), "Yeah, man, that was me," and that Tim subsequently got into the car she was driving and admitted to raping Modine.

To experienced defense lawyers, it is not surprising that these two informants had begun to echo the statement made by Matt

Donaldson in August. It was exactly the corroboration that Detective Horner was looking for. It suggests only that these two informants were sufficiently streetwise to recognize who Horner's prime suspect was. You didn't have to be Sherlock Holmes to figure this out from the questions the police were asking. When a street-savvy informant hears investigators asking a lot of questions about a particular suspect, it's pretty easy to figure out who the police believe committed the crime. Over time, an informant will gradually revise and refine their story to give the answers that the police want to hear. A corollary to this is that the police will then usually accept such answers as true, because those answers are what they want to believe to be true. It's a dangerous feedback loop.

Clarence Williams and Vicky Jones had both claimed Tim had admitted raping Modine Wise *to them*, but Matt was still claiming only to have "heard" that Tim had committed this crime. Then, on January 8, 1990, Matt was convicted for prostitution and possession of drug paraphernalia and was sentenced to probation. Now the police had additional leverage over Matt. His probation could be revoked if he didn't cooperate. Two weeks later, the police interviewed Matt yet again about Modine's case. For the first time, he claimed in this interview that he had personally heard Tim Bridges say that he had raped Modine Wise.

Now Detective Horner had three unreliable witnesses rather than two. That was enough to get the district attorney's office, which had previously refused to approve Tim's prosecution based just on the statements from Clarence Williams and Vicky Jones, to approve Tim's arrest.

THE ARREST OF TIM BRIDGES

On March 27, 1990, ten months after the incident, Tim Bridges was arrested for the rape of Modine Wise. He was indicted for first-degree rape, breaking and entering, and assault with a deadly weapon with intent to kill inflicting serious injury on a handicapped person. There was no physical evidence placing Tim at the crime scene, and there was plenty of reason to believe he didn't do it. He didn't wear glasses, such as the ones found at the scene, and did not smoke Salem Light cigarettes. He didn't have a coat like the one left by the attacker on Modine's bed, which was two sizes too big for him anyway. And of course there was the issue of the bloody palm print. All that tied Tim to the rape were the statements of the three police informants who claimed, in one conflicting form or another, to have heard Tim confess. None of the informants could provide police with other corroborating information they claimed that Tim had given them, such as a detail regarding the crime that only the perpetrator might know.

From the beginning, Tim adamantly denied any involvement. After his arrest, he waived his rights and agreed to be interviewed by the police. He offered to take a polygraph, which the police never gave him; voluntarily provided saliva for DNA analysis; and voluntarily gave head hair, pubic hair, facial hair, arm hair, and leg hair to be used by investigators in a comparison with hairs found at the crime scene. He told investigators, "I'm going to do everything I can to prove my innocence."

The day after Tim's arrest, Detective Horner prepared a media briefing sheet to alert the media of Tim's arrest. At the end of the briefing sheet, Horner wrote (in all capital letters), "THIS CASE IS NOT RELATED TO THE CURRENT RAPES OF ELDERLY WOMEN ON THE EAST SIDE OF CHARLOTTE." Detective Horner had found no evidence that this sexual assault of an elderly woman in that part of the city was related to the other sexual assaults of elderly women in that part of the city. Those assaults continued after Tim's arrest.

THE HAIR MATCH

The prosecutor was justifiably skeptical of Detective Horner's witnesses, and Horner wanted more than just the statements provided by the informants. She wanted something to actually put Tim inside Modine's house. She had come up short on all the other forensic evidence. She needed the police hair examiner to make a match to solidify her case.

A few months before the trial, Detective Horner met with the police hair examiner, Elinos "Linus" Whitlock, to go over the facts of the case. Whitlock had been the hair examiner in the Kim Thomas case, as well as several others, and had received training from the FBI on hair examination. It was going to be his job to compare, first with the naked eye, and then with a stereo microscope, hairs found at Modine's house with those provided by Tim Bridges. He had to know that having a hair match was important, if not essential, for the state's case against Tim.

Days and weeks passed while Detective Horner waited for Whitlock to complete his analysis. She began to get anxious and called the prosecutor's office to say that Whitlock had not completed the hair comparison. The assistant prosecutor agreed to call him. She told Detective Horner if the hairs matched, "the defense attorney might plead Tim guilty."

Another two weeks passed without a word from Whitlock. Detective Horner again called the assistant prosecutor to say that Whitlock had not yet finished the hair comparison. The assistant prosecutor, in turn, called Whitlock again to check on the status of the hair comparison. These repeated calls were no doubt a further indication to Whitlock that the hair analysis was important to the police and the prosecution.

Finally, on June 25, 1990, Whitlock completed his microscopic comparison of Tim's hair to the hairs collected at the scene, and he called Detective Horner to tell her the results. Two of the head hairs recovered from the crime scene, he had concluded, "matched" Tim's hair. Horner was over the moon. In her notes, she excitedly wrote, "Linus! Dictated today: (2) head hairs—defendant's!!!" She immediately called the prosecutor's office with the good news.

At last, the prosecutor had the evidence she needed to put Tim at the scene of the crime. But what about the bloody palm print? That was still a big unanswered question. If it didn't come from Modine, and it didn't come from Tim, who made the print? The police's original, logical theory, was that it had been left by the perpetrator. So they did two more comparisons against Tim's prints to see if they could get a match, but they simply couldn't. Since Tim had been excluded as the source, and the defense would obviously be arguing that the print was made by the real perpetrator, the police changed course on the print.

Instead of exploring the possibility that Tim was actually innocent, Detective Horner abandoned her initial belief that the perpetrator had left the print and instead adopted the theory that someone unconnected to the crime must have left the print (even though the blood at the scene had long since dried by the time Modine was found the next day). Detective Horner speculated that the print must have been left by the person who first found Modine after the incident—Modine's sister-in-law, Virginia.

The problem was that Virginia had passed away. Detective Horner decided the only thing to do was to have Virginia's body exhumed so her palm-print impression could be taken and compared to the bloody print at the scene. And as extreme as it sounds, that is exactly what she did. On a sunny day in November 1990, Virginia's coffin was pulled up out of the ground, and a Charlotte police crime-scene technician with years of experience taking and processing prints reached into the coffin, extended Virginia's hands, and took impressions of her palms.

Virginia's palm prints were then sent to the police crime lab to be compared with the palm print on the wall. Kathleen Ramseur was the supervisor of the crime lab. She had twenty-five years of experience in comparing latent prints with known prints to determine whether the comparison was positive (a match) or negative (not a match). Prior to receiving Virginia's palm prints, she had compared the palm prints of approximately fifty suspects to the bloody palm print found at the scene. For each, she had filed a report stating that the latent print (i.e., the bloody palm print) had been compared to the print of the suspect "with negative results." On November 6, 1990, Ramseur signed a report stating that the comparison of Virginia's palm prints to the palm print left at the scene was also "with negative results." So the problem remained.

How could the prosecutor take the case to trial when no one knew who made the bloody palm print, and it didn't come from Tim Bridges? Detective Horner came up with yet another idea to explain it away. She asked all the EMT and law-enforcement personnel who'd responded to the crime scene to go to the crime lab to give their own palm-print impressions. In a memo explaining her request, she wrote, "[A]s you probably could imagine, the defense is making a big deal of the unknown print, as it does not belong to the man we have in jail, Timothy Bridges."

Following Horner's request, all the police officers and EMTs who responded to the crime scene gave comparison prints. All were negative. Despite the fact that the source of the bloody palm print had not been determined, other than that it did not belong to Tim Bridges, the case proceeded to trial.

The jury first heard testimony from the three incentivized witnesses, Matt Donaldson, Clarence Williams, and Vicky Jones, who each claimed to have heard Tim Bridges confess. Then came the scientific testimony from the state. The police hair examiner, Linus Whitlock, took the stand and was sworn in. He testified that two hairs found at the crime scene matched hairs provided from Tim's body. He told the jury that, based on his training and experience, the chances that these two hairs belonged to anyone but Tim Bridges was *a thousand to one*. This testimony was devastating and seemed irrefutable. It was, after all, testimony from an FBI-trained scientific expert who had done the hair comparisons with a high-powered microscope.

Tim's lawyers were two excellent attorneys from the Mecklenburg County Public Defender's Office. Despite the unfortunate way the trial had unfolded thus far, they believed the mysterious bloody palm print would create a reasonable doubt. The prosecution would have to admit it was put on Modine's wall by someone other than Tim—someone with blood on their hands.

The state put Kathleen Ramseur, the supervisor of the crime lab, on the stand. After going through her qualifications, the prosecutor asked Ramseur about her comparison of Virginia Wise's palm print, taken from Virginia postmortem, with the print from the scene. Ramseur had previously written a report stating that she had compared Virginia's palm prints to the palm print found at the scene "with negative results." She had told the defense attorneys a few weeks before that she had excluded Virginia as the source of the bloody print. Now, in a surprise reversal, she testified she could *not* exclude Virginia Wise as the source of the palm print. She claimed that Virginia's palm print didn't have sufficient detail to exclude her as the source of the print.

The prosecutor, in closing arguments to the jury, said, "And as Ms. Ramseur said on the stand, there wasn't enough of a print, palm print there to compare. So I submit that it's still possible that it's Virginia's print. . . . I submit that it's Virginia Wise's print, but we just can't prove that." This satisfied the jury.

On February 2, 1991, Tim was found guilty and was sentenced to life in prison. In his jail cell following his trial, he cried uncontrollably. He was put on suicide watch and left in a cell with no clothes on and with only a thin mattress on the floor on which to sleep. His mother and grandmother visited him at the jail and told him they knew he was innocent. The next day, he was transferred to the maximum-security prison in Raleigh, one hundred fifty miles from his family. He was only twenty-three at the time. He would not see the outside world as a free man again for twenty-five years.

23

JUSTICE DELAYED

Throughout his twenty-five years in prison, Tim continued to assert his innocence. When he became eligible to enter the Sexual Offender Accountability and Responsibility (SOAR) program offered by the North Carolina Department of Correction, he refused to apply, even though completing the program would have resulted in an earlier parole from his sentence. As part of the program, the offender had to admit his guilt. That was something Tim was simply not willing to do, even if it meant spending the rest of his life in prison.

In October 2007, Tim wrote to the North Carolina Center on Actual Innocence (NCCAI) and requested help establishing his innocence. After investigating the case, the NCCAI sent an urgent request to the Charlotte police to determine if there was any evidence retained by the police that could be tested for DNA. After a search, the Charlotte police responded in writing that all the physical evidence collected at the scene—the men's coat, the tube socks, the pack of cigarettes, the bloody fabrics—had been destroyed. As a result, the NCCAI informed Tim regretfully in 2010 that it could not help him prove that he had been wrongfully convicted.

In the face of what were obviously extremely long odds, Tim

refused to give up. He next contacted North Carolina Prisoner Legal Services (NCPLS), a nonprofit agency based in Raleigh dedicated to representing inmates in the state prisons in a variety of matters, including challenging their convictions. By this time, Mary Pollard, who had been instrumental in obtaining Alan Gell's new trial and eventual release, was the head of NCPLS. They agreed to take Tim's case.

In 2014, Lauren Miller, an attorney at NCPLS, with the help of two attorneys with the Innocence Project in New York, filed a motion asserting that Linus Whitlock's testimony regarding the statistical probability of a hair match between Tim's hair and the hairs found at the scene exceeded the limits of science. The basis of the argument was that the "science" of microscopic hair comparison was not sufficiently precise to allow for the level of statistical precision testified to by Whitlock. NCPLS also filed a motion to require the state to locate and preserve evidence related to Tim's case. The state, echoing what the police department had previously told the NCCAI, responded that *none* of the items of evidence in Tim's case, including the hair samples, still existed.

But on September 18, 2015, *five years* after the Charlotte police told the NCCAI that no evidence remained that could be tested for DNA, the county clerk's office discovered that, in fact, some of the evidence from the 1991 trial was still in the county's possession. One piece of evidence was the men's coat left by the attacker on Modine's bed.

On October 1, 2015, the judge agreed with NCPLS that Linus Whitlock's testimony regarding the hair "match" entitled Tim to a new trial. The Court further entered an order requiring that the police department preserve any items of evidence it still had and directing the police crime lab to conduct expedited DNA testing on any evidence that was suitable for testing. The same day, the district attorney's office consented to a motion for relief filed by NCPLS that sought to vacate Tim's conviction, and Tim was released on an unsecured bond of $10,000.

Four days later, the Charlotte police crime lab issued a report regarding the DNA analysis it had performed on the items of evidence found at the clerk's office. Semen was detected on the exterior right arm of the coat, and male DNA was found in a stain on the interior lining of the coat. Also, a partial male DNA profile was obtained from a cigarette butt found in the pocket of the coat. None of it came from Tim. The DNA test conclusively excluded him as a contributor.

Finally, on February 16, 2016, the district attorney agreed to dismiss the charges against Tim with prejudice. Tim was officially free—although his life had been damaged beyond repair.

THE AFTERMATH

Tim's time in prison had been a nightmare. He went into prison in 1991 as a young man and emerged in 2015 as a middle-aged man of forty-eight. What he endured in prison was horrific. He was physically assaulted. His personal possessions were stolen. He suffered injuries and was hospitalized. Every day of his waking and sleeping life was spent behind bars, often in solitary, based on rules infractions he intentionally committed to get away from the other inmates to stay safe. He was told when to wake up, when to eat, when to exercise, when he could take a shower, and when he had to go to sleep. He knew he was innocent, but no one would listen.

During Tim's time in prison, he lost his uncle, his paternal and maternal grandmothers, his father, and his mother, to whom he was especially close. When Tim's mother was dying, Tim was allowed to visit her in the hospital one time. Two days before she died, even though her condition had rendered her almost completely incapable of speech, she found a way to say, "I love you, Timmy." Tim cries every time he talks about his "momma."

For Tim, it didn't have to be this way. His wrongful conviction could have been avoided. All the signs were there, but they were obscured by the tunnel vision of the police, who had so made up their minds that Tim was guilty that they not only concealed the prior inconsistent statements made by Matt Donaldson, Clarence Williams, and Vicky Jones from the prosecutor's office, but also ignored and concealed evidence pointing to other suspects. And there was another prime suspect.

THE CASE AGAINST RONALD KIRKLAND

Ronald Eugene Kirkland lived in an adjacent county, but in May 1989 he had been working as a painter in Charlotte. On June 7, 1989, he was arrested in the neighboring county for the rape of *three elderly women in their homes that occurred in May 1989—the same month that the assault against Modine had occurred.* He had also been charged with kidnapping and assault with a deadly weapon with intent to inflict serious injury.

On June 21, 1989, the Charlotte police were quoted in an article in a local newspaper titled "Police Ask for Help on Assault." The article noted that the police had been "stymied" in their investigation into Modine's case, and asked for the public's assistance in finding the person responsible for the attack. In the article, the perpetrator was described as "a slender white male, 15–18 years of age, 5 feet 6 to 5 feet 8, with shoulder length blond hair."

The article caught the eye of a police detective with the Gaston County Sheriff's Office, which was responsible for the neighboring county. He called the Charlotte police department and spoke to an investigator assisting Detective Horner. He told the investigator about Ronald Kirkland, and said that Kirkland had "done three old women" in Gaston County, and that Kirkland was in Charlotte in May working as a painter when Modine's assault occurred. He described Kirkland as five feet seven inches tall, with a thin build and sandy hair down to his shoulders—which matched the description given by Modine. He also smoked menthol cigarettes, like those found at the scene. Most tellingly, on May 23, just nine days after Modine had been assaulted, the Gaston County police searched

Kirkland's room and found a T-shirt, blue jeans, a blue baseball cap, and white Adidas tennis shoes, all with blood on them.

The investigator from Charlotte traveled to Gaston County to talk to the detective about Kirkland as a possible suspect in Modine's attack. He took with him an eight-by-ten photograph of the palm print in dried blood. When he showed it to the Gaston County detective, the detective said he believed, just eyeballing it, that the palm print in the photo didn't correspond to the dimensions of Kirkland's hand. And that was all it took. The investigator did not go to the Gaston County jail to interview Kirkland, and he did not bother to take Kirkland's booking palm print back to Charlotte to be examined by an expert.

Although the investigator prepared a report about Kirkland that was put into the investigative file, Detective Horner didn't try to interview Kirkland either. She did not have the blood found on his clothing compared to Modine's blood. She didn't have Modine view a lineup containing a photograph of Kirkland. Most irresponsibly, she failed to take a palm print from Kirkland to compare against the palm print found at the scene. Instead, two months later, Detective Horner zeroed in on Tim Bridges.

Kirkland's name resurfaced in October 1989. That month, Detective Horner was informed that Kirkland had bragged in the Gaston County jail about committing the Modine Wise rape. She wrote this on a Post-it note and put it in her file. By this point, though, the decision had been made that Tim was the perpetrator, and the police had invested time and effort into securing statements from their informants incriminating Tim. Because the informants were saying it was Tim Bridges, the police department wouldn't change course. If they charged Kirkland, those statements claiming Tim had confessed would be exculpatory evidence for Kirkland, and how would Horner explain how she had gotten Matt Donaldson, Clarence Williams, and Vicky Jones to falsely implicate Bridges? So even this astonishing admission from Kirkland did not prompt the Charlotte police to do something as simple as get a palm-print impression from Kirkland or test the bloody clothes found in Kirkland's room just days after Modine was attacked. The die had been cast, and Tim was the perp.

This is a tragic illustration of the danger of using unreliable informants, who were rewarded for giving Horner what she wanted at the time: alleged confessions by Tim. It's hard to understand how any reasonable investigator would have simply ignored Ronald Kirkland as a suspect in the case after hearing he had confessed, but that is exactly what Horner did. She was locked in by the false evidence she had secured from Donaldson, Williams, and Jones. Any evidence inconsistent with their statements claiming Tim had confessed was ignored by Horner.

The case against Tim went to trial despite the fact that there was another more likely suspect who had apparently confessed in a neighboring county jail, as well as evidence that might have exonerated Tim if tested. Tim and his attorneys had no idea about any of this.

But Horner appears to have done more than just ignore the evidence against Kirkland. In the weeks immediately prior to Tim's trial, Tim's defense attorneys filed a motion to compel any exculpatory information held by the state to be turned over to the defense. This included "any evidence pointing to the guilt of [any other] suspects," as well as any evidence regarding similar crimes committed by someone other than Tim. This would include the information Detective Horner had learned about Ronald Kirkland. In response to the motion, the prosecution had an affirmative constitutional duty to provide any such information to Tim and his attorney.

In court on this motion, the judge asked the prosecutor directly, with Horner sitting right next to her at the prosecution table, if there was any evidence pointing to the guilt of other suspects. The prosecutor replied, "I don't have any evidence pointing to the guilt of any other suspects." Later in the hearing, the judge asked again whether the prosecutor was in possession of any evidence of third-party guilt and ordered, "[I]f you have any evidence of third-party guilt, please produce it." Finally, the judge ordered the state to "produce any evidence you have tending to show that . . . the crimes charged and similar offenses were committed by a person not the defendant." Detective Horner sat on her hands and said nothing, even after the prosecutor asked Horner to go back through her police file to make sure there wasn't any such evidence.

It was discovered years later why the prosecutor had told the judge she didn't have any evidence pointing to the guilt of any third party: *she, the prosecutor,* didn't. Detective Horner had apparently concealed the information regarding Ronald Kirkland's possible guilt from the prosecutor's office, and then still failed to divulge the information despite the judge's order and the prosecutor's request that Horner examine her file for any such evidence. Because the evidence pointing to Kirkland was not turned over to the prosecutor, it was never provided to Tim's attorney and was never heard by the jury. It went undiscovered for years as Tim languished in prison. It was found only when I compared the police file with the district attorney's file in preparing Tim's civil suit.

My wife and law partner, Sonya Pfeiffer, and I represented Tim after the charges against him were dismissed and he was released from his twenty-five-year wrongful incarceration. In comparing the district attorney's file with the police file, we also found that Detective Horner had also apparently concealed evidence from the prosecutor that showed the three witnesses for the state—Matt Donaldson, Vicky Jones, and Clarence Neal Williams—had at first provided inconsistent statements to the police that undermined their reliability. The inconsistent statements made by the witnesses were in the police file but were not given by the police to the prosecution. One of the notes found in the police file years later stated that before implicating Tim in 1989, Vicky Jones had been "maintaining she does not know" who attacked Modine.

What we found regarding the exculpatory information that was concealed from the prosecutor, and therefore from Tim's defense attorneys, was not surprising to me, given what had happened in Ed Friedland's case around the same time and including the same official supervising the investigations. But it was profoundly tragic, because it showed how easily Tim's wrongful conviction, and the years he lost in prison, could have been avoided. Instead, the police violated Tim's constitutional rights, and he was deprived of his freedom and his very life for twenty-five years.

Sonya and I filed a lawsuit against the persons responsible for Tim's wrongful arrest and conviction. In sworn testimony in that case, the assistant district attorney who prosecuted Tim said she never would have indicted him if she had known about Ronald Kirkland's confession and the impeachment evidence regarding the three informants.

The City of Charlotte agreed to pay $9.5 million to settle Tim's claim. It was the largest settlement for police misconduct in the city's history, although the police, of course, denied any wrongdoing. And despite the wrongs that were committed and the unthinkable harm done to Tim and his entire family, no one from the City of Charlotte or the Charlotte police department apologized to Tim or acknowledged their misdeeds.

Tim did get an apology from the Republican governor of North Carolina, Pat McCrory, in connection with his application for a "pardon of innocence." Interestingly, the governor asked to meet with Tim and me before he made a decision on the pardon. During the meeting, the governor apologized to Tim for the wrong the state had done to him and gave him a hug. Tim still can't talk about this without crying. The governor's acknowledgment and apology meant more to him than all the money the City of Charlotte paid him to settle the case.

Tim Bridges, Alan Gell, and LaMonte Armstrong all received financial compensation for the years they lost as a result of the concealment of exculpatory evidence, which compensation helped them rebuild their lives, but they are the exceptions. For most of those wrongfully convicted, there is no monetary compensation. Ed Friedland's suit against the Charlotte police was dismissed because the judge ruled that the police were not under any legal obligation to inform the prosecutor about exculpatory evidence before trial even when the prosecutor was making the decision to indict Ed—and even for a crime carrying the death penalty. The judge ruled that the police were only obligated to provide the prosecutor with exculpatory evidence *at the time of Ed's trial.* It still makes no sense to me; prosecutors should have all the evidence when deciding whether to indict someone, but I am not aware of any case that has extended the *Brady* rule that far.

Financial compensation can hardly make up for the trauma and tragedy of a wrongful conviction that could have been avoided had the exculpatory evidence been disclosed. Tim Bridges lost both his parents while he was in prison and never had children of his own—a loss that he feels deeply. Ed Friedland's medical practice was destroyed, and he had to move to another state to rebuild his reputation, career, and life. Alan Gell was traumatized every time someone on Death Row was executed. He never knew when his name would be called next.

Damage awards may serve as a deterrent against misconduct by police and as an incentive for better training. Those of us who represent people who have been wrongfully convicted certainly hope they achieve these ends, but so far, the damages awarded don't seem to have had that effect. The refusal of most police departments to admit their failures and officer misconduct, combined with the doctrine of qualified immunity, which protects police negligence, no matter how egregious or devastating the results, serves to perpetuate similar conduct by others. So too does the doctrine of absolute immunity for prosecutors, regardless of how intentional and malicious their conduct may have been. The Supreme Court decided it didn't want prosecutors "looking over their shoulders" when making decisions, so corrupt and overzealous prosecutors are given a pass for any "prosecutorial decision" they make, including what evidence to turn over to defendants. They incur no financial penalty, are only rarely held to account by ethics proceedings, and are virtually never prosecuted criminally for even intentional misconduct that results in a wrongful conviction.

Ed Friedland. Alan Gell. Tim Bridges. LaMonte Armstrong. Four different people, each with their own story. Each was the victim of the police or prosecutors concealing different exculpatory evidence. What they share is that each ultimately secured their freedom from a corrupted criminal justice system. Their experiences were incredibly traumatizing, but they are among the fortunate ones, relatively speaking. They fought for and won their freedom. Thousands of others like them remain imprisoned despite their innocence.

24

COERCING FALSE CONFESSIONS AND GUILTY PLEAS

We have learned the lesson of history, ancient and modern, that a system of criminal law enforcement which comes to depend on the "confession" will, in the long run, be less reliable and more subject to abuses than a system which depends on extrinsic evidence independently secured through skillful investigation.

—*Escobedo v. Illinois* (1964)

There's a special power that comes with a confession. To the human mind, to our ears, it seems superior to every other kind of evidence. We're predisposed to believe in the veracity of confessions. While we reflexively question denials made by an accused—because we know from experience that denials are self-serving—we readily accept confessions. Confessions are often made against one's self-interest and are therefore deemed more credible. All of us who represent defendants in criminal trials involving confessions have to answer the critical question every juror has: Why would she confess if she was innocent? Every juror believes absolutely, "*I would never confess to something I didn't do.*" Every judge deciding a post-conviction challenge to a guilty plea starts with the presumption that no one would plead guilty to something they didn't do, especially a serious crime. The truth is, however, that suspects falsely confess every day in the United States. And even more people plead guilty to crimes they didn't commit, because the option of waiting months, or even years, to go to trial, and the consequences of losing that trial, are overwhelming.

Thankfully, the era of extracting confessions by physical torture has passed in the United States—except for alleged terrorists who were waterboarded after 9/11—but we're not far past it.

In Kemper County, Mississippi, north of Meridian but south of Tupelo, and not far from the Alabama state line, a white farmer named Raymond Stuart was murdered on March 30, 1934. He'd been killed with an axe, and his body had been hidden behind a shed, according to one account, while another account reported that his neighbors found him murdered in his home when he didn't show up for work. Three Black men—Ed Brown, Arthur Ellington, and Henry Shields—were promptly arrested for his murder. Their trial, "speedy" by even the most rigorous standards, began six days later. There was no evidence that the men had killed Stuart except for their confessions. The all-male, all-white jury found them guilty, and the three men were sentenced to death.

A harrowing, deeply upsetting record of how their confessions were obtained was part of the court record in the U.S. Supreme Court case of *Brown v. Mississippi*:

The crime with which these defendants, all ignorant negroes, are charged, was discovered about 1 o'clock p.m. on Friday, March 30, 1934. On that night one Dial, a deputy sheriff, accompanied by others, came to the home of Ellington, one of the defendants, and requested him to accompany them to the house of the deceased, and there a number of white men were gathered, who began to accuse the defendant of the crime. Upon his denial they seized him, and with the participation of the deputy they hanged him by a rope to the limb of a tree, and, having

let him down, they hung him again, and when he was let down the sec-
ond time, and he still protested his innocence, he was tied to a tree and
whipped, and, still declining to accede to the demands that he confess, he
was finally released, and he returned with some difficulty to his home,
suffering intense pain and agony. The record of the testimony shows
that the signs of the rope on his neck were plainly visible during the
so-called trial. A day or two thereafter the said deputy, accompanied by
another, returned to the home of the said defendant and arrested him,
and departed with the prisoner towards the jail in an adjoining county,
but went by a route which led into the state of Alabama; and while on
the way, in that state, the deputy stopped and again severely whipped
the defendant, declaring that he would continue the whipping until he
confessed, and the defendant then agreed to confess to such a statement
as the deputy would dictate, and he did so, after which he was delivered
to jail.

The other two defendants, Ed Brown and Henry Shields, were also
arrested and taken to the same jail. On Sunday night, April 1, 1934, the
same deputy, accompanied by a number of white men, one of whom was
also an officer, and by the jailer, came to the jail, and the two last named
defendants were made to strip and they were laid over chairs and their
backs were cut to pieces with a leather strap with buckles on it, and they
were likewise made by the said deputy definitely to understand that the
whipping would be continued unless and until they confessed, and not
only confessed, but confessed in every matter of detail as demanded by
those present; and in this manner the defendants confessed the crime,
and, as the whippings progressed and were repeated, they changed or
adjusted their confession in all particulars of detail so as to conform to
the demands of their torturers. When the confessions had been obtained
in the exact form and contents as desired by the mob, they left with the
parting admonition and warning that, if the defendants changed their
story at any time in any respect from that last stated, the perpetrators of
the outrage would administer the same or equally effective treatment. . . .

The sheriff of the county of the crime admitted that he had heard of
the whipping, but averred that he had no personal knowledge of it. He

admitted that one of the defendants, when brought before him to confess,
was limping and did not sit down, and that this particular defendant
then and there stated that he had been strapped so severely that he could
not sit down, and, as already stated, the signs of the rope on the neck of
another of the defendants were plainly visible to all.

On the basis of the forced confessions, a grand jury was hastily empaneled and, before the end of the day, returned indictments against
the men. The defendants were then summoned into court, as an extra
detail of police officers with "machine guns, sawed-off shotguns, and
tear gas bombs" stood guard outside the courthouse. Inside, the judge
asked if the defendants had counsel representing them. The men replied "that they had none, and did not suppose that counsel could be
of any assistance to them." The judge set the trial to begin the following morning.

At the farce of a trial, the defendants were able to argue that their
confessions were not made voluntarily, and the state freely, perhaps
proudly, admitted that the defendants were whipped and beaten to
procure their confessions. One deputy who participated in the beatings was put on the stand, and when asked how badly he had beaten
Arthur Ellington, he stated, "Not too much for a negro. Not as much
as I would have done if it were left to me."

With full knowledge that the three defendants had been whipped
and tortured to bring about their confessions, the all-white jury voted
to convict, and the men were sentenced to die "on the gallows." Their
death sentences were to be carried out just more than a month after
their conviction. On appeal, the state Supreme Court of Mississippi,
despite having an accurate account of how the confessions were coerced, did nothing to call out the travesty that occurred in the trial
court and summarily upheld the convictions of the three men.

At last, the case reached the U.S. Supreme Court. The Supreme
Court reversed the convictions and sent a scathing rebuke to the
courts below. Justice Charles Evans Hughes, who authored the opinion, wrote, "[I]n pertinent respects the transcript reads more like

pages torn from some medieval account than a record made within the confines of a modern civilization which aspires to an enlightened constitutional government." Justice Hughes continued, "It would be difficult to conceive of methods more revolting to the sense of justice than those taken to procure the confessions of these petitioners, and the use of the confessions thus obtained as the basis for conviction and sentence was a clear denial of due process."

After the Supreme Court's decision in *Brown v. Mississippi*, which made it unconstitutional for the police to procure confessions by force, the prevalence of physical beatings and torture as a method for extracting confessions dropped out of favor, and trenchant psychological pressures brought to bear by the police, in lieu of physical beatings, took their place. We now know, from abundant evidence, that such psychological pressures and other questionable interrogation tactics used by the police can be just as effective in bringing about false confessions. We saw this in the case of the Central Park Five, perhaps the most famous false-confession case, in which five young men all falsely confessed to raping a jogger in Central Park. As extraordinary as it sounds, this was not a onetime phenomenon.

"SAVE YOURSELF"

> He said, "Well, the early bird gets the worm." He said, "Somebody going to death row."
>
> —Teddy Isbell, murder suspect

Monday Night Football was on. The Redskins were playing the Cowboys, but Walter Bowman didn't care much for football. He told everyone goodnight and went to bed. It was September 18, 2000, the last night of Walter Bowman's life.

His stepdaughter, Wanda Holloway, got up off the couch to let the dogs out. One of them barked more than usual and ran straight back to the house. As she stood in the doorway, Walter's adult son, Shaun, told her to shut the dogs up in a bedroom for the night. Wanda closed the door but left it unlocked, and returned to the couch to finish watching the game. It was 11:34 p.m.

The Cowboys kicked a field goal. Another minute passed. The doorknob turned on the front door, and three men brandishing firearms loped into the room. They were wearing gloves and had bandanas covering their faces. Wanda tried to escape into the kitchen but was caught and dragged back into the room by her hair. One of the men cornered Shaun and put a gun to his head. Shaun was the reason they were there. The intruders had heard a rumor that he was holding $108,000 in cash as part of a drug deal, and they were there to take the money.

Walter Bowman opened his bedroom door, saw what was happening, and slammed it closed again. A man holding a pistol-grip shotgun pivoted in Walter's direction and fired waist-high through the door. He then kicked the door open and found Walter lying on the bed, bleeding from his abdomen. The man yelled, "I shot him, I shot him!" The three intruders then ran from the house and sped away in their car, taking nothing.

In the hectic few minutes that followed, Wanda and Shaun tried to figure out what to do. Walter was dying, and someone needed to call for an ambulance, but Shaun was wanted by the police. He couldn't be there when the police arrived. Finally, they decided that Shaun would leave, and Wanda wouldn't tell the police he had even been there that night.

She called 911 at 11:55 p.m. Walter died on the way to the hospital.

After the emergency call came in, Buncombe County officers and detectives traveled to the scene to begin the investigation. Wanda told them that three men burst through the door and yelled, "Get down!" In the commotion, she heard a gunshot. When she looked up, terrified, she saw the men running out of the house. The bandanas and hats they wore made it impossible to identify them.

All of this happened just off Graveyard Road, in a small and insular, mostly Black, community outside of Asheville, in western

North Carolina. Although Asheville and the surrounding area in Buncombe County are now best known for the artisans who make up much of the local population and the gourmet restaurants lining the streets around Pack Square, to which hundreds of thousands of tourists flock each year, that was not the case in 2000. Asheville was just emerging from its historical roots as a community that was physically segregated and bitterly divided racially.

Buncombe County sheriff's detectives George Sprinkle and Michael Murphy were assigned as the lead investigators. They had good reason to believe that the murder was drug-related. Walter Bowman had prior felonies for drug possession and attempted distribution, and Walter's son, Shaun, also had a number of run-ins with the police involving drugs. In the home, the detectives found pills and drug paraphernalia.

The next morning, a U.S. Postal Service carrier saw what appeared to be bandanas and gloves on the side of the road not far from the Bowman home. Not knowing anything about the crime, she had the presence of mind to call 911 to inform the police about the items. A crime-scene technician and other law enforcement officers, responding to this call, found three bandanas and four gloves along a stretch of road near the Bowman house. The bandanas and gloves were on each side of the narrow road, spaced out, as if they had been thrown from a moving car. The items looked new and appeared as if they had recently been discarded. The crime-scene technician placed all of these gloves and bandanas into evidence envelopes and logged them on a property-control sheet. DNA evidence on the bandanas and the masks was preserved.

There was an Amoco gas station and convenience store not far from the Bowman house. The gas station used time-lapse video surveillance and maintained the surveillance videos on VHS tapes in the back of the store. Detective John Elkins went to the Amoco and obtained the VHS tape from the previous evening. The video showed three Black men arriving in a car and walking into the store at 11:19 p.m. The car left the station at 11:32 p.m., leaving it enough time to reach the Bowman house before the murder happened. Taking the tape into evidence, Elkins wrote, "Possible Evidence in Homicide" on a property-control sheet and delivered the tape to Detective Sprinkle.

Witnesses from the gas station that night reported seeing the three men shown on the video. One of the witnesses, Jason Cope, relayed that three Black men pulled up to the station, got out of a car, and were "acting strange." He indicated that the car was an older model, possibly a Buick or an Oldsmobile, with a light vinyl top. Jack Holland, who was with Jason Cope at the Amoco on the night of the murder, also described the car as "old" and having a light vinyl top.

Two days after the murder, the sheriff's office received a Crime Stoppers tip relating to the crime. The caller claimed that the three men who committed the Bowman invasion and homicide were Lacy "J.J." Pickens, Robert Earl "Tricky" Rutherford, and Bradford Summey. The caller also provided information on where the police could find Rutherford. All of these men were known to the police as being involved in drug distribution in Buncombe County.

Lacy Pickens owned a 1971 Oldsmobile Cutlass with a light vinyl top, similar to the one described by witnesses at the Amoco station. Buncombe County deputies knew this, as they had given Pickens at least two traffic citations while he was driving his car that summer. Even though the Crime Stoppers tip specifically mentioned Pickens's name, and Pickens drove a car similar to the one described by witnesses at the gas station, and also that the murder appeared to be drug-related, Detectives Sprinkle and Murphy did not question Pickens about the Bowman murder. Someone at the sheriff's office mistakenly thought, without confirming it, that Pickens had been in jail on the night of the murder. Therefore, Detectives Sprinkle and Murphy discounted the tip entirely, never returned to it, and never gave it any credibility. Because of this, the detectives failed to show the two witnesses, Cope and Holland, any lineups containing photos of Pickens, Rutherford, or Summey, or of Pickens's car. They also made no effort to use the information provided in the Crime

Stoppers tip to find and interview Rutherford, nor did they attempt to find or interview Summey, or any known associates.

Pickens had not, in fact, been in jail on the night of the murder. But he would never be charged with Walter Bowman's murder. Instead, the police doggedly pursued and obtained guilty pleas from five other young men, four of whom confessed, for the crime actually committed by Pickens, Rutherford, and Summey. It was the Central Park case redux, this time in rural North Carolina rather than Manhattan.

Four days after the murder, Robert "Detroit" Wilcoxson, a twenty-three-year-old who had recently moved to Asheville from Michigan, and Larry Williams, a sixteen-year-old with a history of mental-health problems, were involved in a car chase with the police. Wilcoxson was driving. While fleeing from the police, he wrecked the van he was driving, and he and Williams escaped on foot. The police took custody of the van and connected it to Wilcoxson. The police knew Wilcoxson from his recent arrest over the summer for possession of a stolen handgun and a small amount of crack cocaine, which were still pending charges. News of the dramatic car chase and the fugitives' escape spread through the community, and people wondered whether it was related to the Bowman murder.

In the days that followed, the police received several more tips from the public regarding the murder, fed in part by media accounts. News stories of the Bowman murder appeared in the local papers. The *Asheville Citizen-Times* headline declared, "3 Suspects Sought in Fairview Slaying," and touted a $3,000 reward.

Once word of an unsolved crime reaches the community at large and people begin to see news coverage of it, rumors and disinformation begin to surface. Jailhouse informants see unsolved crimes as an opportunity to trade alleged jailhouse confessions and other information for favorable treatment from the state. It's not uncommon for the rumors and disinformation to proliferate like the children's game of Telephone, where words and ideas mutate as they pass from person to person until such time that they no longer bear any resemblance to the original. What transpired in Buncombe County regarding the Walter Bowman murder was akin to this, in that the names of several young Black men known to the police department, such as Robert "Detroit" Wilcoxson and Larry Williams, became associated with the crime, and before long the unfounded rumors entirely replaced the truth. Much of this was caused by the police.

It began with the second Crime Stoppers tip, which came about five days after the murder. The tipster, who wished to remain anonymous, claimed that the three men responsible for the murder of Walter Bowman were Kenny Kagonyera, Aaron Brewton, and Larry Williams. This tip seemed to do more to capture the interest of law enforcement than the first one. It was more consistent with what they had come to believe to be true. Kagonyera, Brewton, and Williams were all well-known to the local police. Kagonyera, for example, was wanted for questioning regarding a shooting that had taken place months before, and Brewton was wanted on a common-law robbery charge.

Investigator Sam Constance tracked down Kenny Kagonyera and questioned him about Bowman's murder. Kagonyera had long Black hair in dreadlocks that hung down past his shoulders. His arrest record included convictions for cruelty to animals, possession of marijuana, and a recent assault with a deadly weapon with the intent to kill. He denied being at the Bowman residence or having any information about the shooting. Meanwhile, Detectives Sprinkle and Murphy found and interviewed Aaron Brewton. He also denied having anything to do with the Bowman murder.

The next day, Detective Murphy, along with a detective from the Asheville Police Department, interviewed Larry Williams, the sixteen-year-old who had fled from police in the van with Robert Wilcoxson. He too denied any involvement in or knowledge of the homicide. Other than the Crime Stoppers tip, the police had nothing that connected Kagonyera, Brewton, or Williams to the Bowman homicide. It seemed like a dead end.

Then along came Teddy Isbell. One morning several days after the murder, a wild-eyed and threadbare Isbell showed up on the doorstep of Life on Life's Terms, a local drug-rehabilitation center where he was a perennial client. Isbell had lived thirty-five hard years and wasn't making things any easier on himself. He'd been on a sustained crack binge for three consecutive weeks, during which time he hadn't even bathed or brushed his teeth. He asked his counselor for money for a motel so that he could rest and take a shower, saying that he hadn't slept for days. Knowing that Isbell sometimes hung out with drug dealers, his counselor, who worked frequently with the police, asked Isbell if he knew anything about Walter Bowman's murder. Isbell deflected, but his counselor must have believed Isbell knew something, because he called the police and Investigator Constance came straight down to talk.

We don't know what Constance said to Isbell during the interview, only what Isbell allegedly said to Constance. All we know is that the police were looking for information that Wilcoxson, Kagonyera, Brewton, and/or Williams were in some way responsible for the Bowman murder, and Teddy Isbell gave them precisely that. According to police records, Isbell claimed he had overheard Kenny Kagonyera at a dice game saying he (Kagonyera) was involved in the Bowman murder, and that Wilcoxson was the shooter. After this first interview, Constance then took Isbell to the Interstate Motel, where he paid for Isbell's room.

Later that same day, Constance picked up Isbell from the motel and brought him to the Buncombe County Sheriff's Office for further questioning, where he was still "visibly high." This time, the district attorney, Ron Moore (a former student in my clinical program at UNC law school, and the only one, to my knowledge, to go on to be an elected D.A.), and the sheriff of Buncombe County, Bobby

---

* In fact, Lacy "J.J." Pickens, one of the people named in the first Crime Stoppers tip, was a drug dealer who supplied Isbell with drugs, and Isbell thought of him like a brother. He therefore had a motive to protect Pickens in connection with the Bowman murder investigation.

Medford, lent their weight to the interview. According to Moore, he said nothing to Isbell other than to encourage him to be honest with investigators. Isbell, however, remembered it differently.

Isbell recalled his conversation with the district attorney in this way: "He said, 'Well, the early bird gets the worm.' He said, 'Somebody going to death row.'" Isbell knew what this meant. Confess first and save your own skin. And it was this very idea, well-known to law enforcement, defense attorneys, and seasoned defendants alike, that precipitated a cascading series of incriminating statements by one suspect against another.

Over the course of the day's interrogations, still reeling from a drug-induced delirium, Isbell tried to give the investigators what they wanted. In between streams of rambling nonsense, he spun additional tales about Walter Bowman's murder, each of which was different from the previous one. He first stated he was involved in planning the Bowman robbery but denied being present during the murder. He then claimed, after a time, that Larry Williams had told Isbell that he (Williams) was present during the murder. Isbell next claimed he had been in Robert Wilcoxson's van with Kagonyera and Williams on the night of the murder but said he had gotten out of the van earlier that evening, hours before the murder was committed.

The accounts offered by Isbell were, when viewed together, implausible and clearly inconsistent with one another. Isbell also gave details that the police knew were at odds in some instances with the physical evidence from the scene. This didn't seem to trouble the investigators, who decided, based on Isbell's statements, that Robert Wilcoxson, Kenny Kagonyera, Larry Williams, Aaron Brewton, and Teddy Isbell were responsible for Walter's death.

On September 26, Detective Murphy caught up with Wilcoxson and interviewed him regarding the murder. Wilcoxson denied any involvement and claimed to have been with his girlfriend, Dea Johnson, at her house in Asheville at the time the murder occurred. Wilcoxson's girlfriend confirmed his alibi.

That same afternoon, Investigator Constance went back to Larry

Williams for another interview. It was the third such interview of Williams, and thus far, he'd admitted nothing. The police knew that Williams was the most malleable of the suspects given his age and fragile mental health. It was their strategy going in to get Williams to put the murder on the others. Williams, however, remained steadfast and vehemently denied having anything to do with the crime—at least up until the sheriff arrived to take over the interrogation.

Bobby Medford had developed quite a reputation after being elected the sheriff of Buncombe County in 1994—both within the sheriff's office and in the community at large, especially the Black community. It had been alleged that he would personally inject himself into witness and suspect interviews, lie to suspects, bully witnesses, coerce them into making false statements, and provide them with the non-public details of crimes to incorporate into their false statements to make them appear credible.

Sheriff Medford took Williams into the interrogation room alone and told Constance to wait outside. In the interrogation room, Medford lied to Williams and told him the police had proof he was involved in the murder. This was perfectly acceptable in the criminal justice system, according to the U.S. Supreme Court. When this produced no results, Medford shouted at Williams and threatened him with the prospect of life in prison if he did not implicate himself and others in the murder. Medford then asked Williams a series of leading questions about the Bowman murder, giving him the names and details necessary to "confess."

After some time, Medford walked out of the interrogation room and told Investigator Constance that Williams had confessed. Williams, in turn, gave a statement to Constance, saying he was present in Robert Wilcoxson's van outside the Bowman house when the murder occurred, and that Wilcoxson entered the house with a shotgun. He then heard a shot, and Wilcoxson ran back to the van and drove back to Asheville.

After giving his statement, Williams asked to speak privately with a detective who was employed by the City of Asheville, not the Buncombe County Sheriff's Office, and who was Black. He immediately told the detective that the statement he had just given was a lie. When Investigator Constance reentered the room, Williams said again that he'd made up the statement to appease Medford, who'd frightened him. He said he wasn't actually there during the shooting of Walter Bowman and had not been with Wilcoxson during any homicide. Two days later, when the detectives returned to interview Williams for a fourth time, Williams again said that the statement he'd given after speaking with Sheriff Medford was made out of fear and was not true. He became emotional and insisted that neither he nor Wilcoxson had anything to do with the Bowman murder.

While all this was going on, the police learned from a jailhouse snitch—one of several who predictably came forward with the hope of receiving some benefit—that another young Black male, Damian Mills, said he had something to do with the Walter Bowman murder. When questioned by police, Mills denied being involved.

At this point in the process, the police had six men in their sights as possible culprits in the Walter Bowman homicide: Robert Wilcoxson, Kenny Kagonyera, Aaron Brewton, Larry Williams, Damian Mills, and Teddy Isbell. In October, all six men were charged with first-degree murder. Except for Williams, who was a juvenile, each man faced the death penalty and could be executed if convicted. The jury would likely be all or almost all white.

With this extraordinary leverage in place, and the suspects facing the harsh reality of a criminal justice system that they justifiably believed would probably not treat them fairly, the police began to play the men against one another. It became a race to the bottom. They all knew how the game was played. As Teddy had been told, the early bird got the worm; a holdout might get the death penalty.

Two days after he was arrested, Damian Mills was interviewed again, this time for five hours. He was told the police believed he was the trigger man and therefore the most likely to get the death penalty, but they would help him if he confessed and implicated the others. Mills succumbed to the pressure and told the police that he, Wilcoxson, Kagonyera, Williams, and Brewton were all involved in the murder of Walter Bowman. He cut a deal with prosecutors and agreed to plead guilty.

Faced with Mills's statement, Williams and Isbell then also made deals and furnished the police with statements implicating Kenny Kagonyera. Kagonyera maintained his innocence for over a year and refused to make a deal. His attorney told him that Williams, Isbell, and Mills would all testify against him at trial, that they would "have their stories straight," and that it would be hard to show they were lying, particularly since Mills was Kagonyera's cousin. His mother, aunt, and grandmother all pleaded with Kagonyera to enter into a plea bargain, because they feared he would be convicted at trial and would either get the death penalty or spend the rest of his life in prison.

Kagonyera finally relented, entered into a plea agreement with the district attorney's office, and made a statement implicating Robert Wilcoxson, who was still maintaining his innocence. Wilcoxson and Brewton remained in jail, awaiting trial.

By August 2002, Wilcoxson had been in jail for almost two years, and no trial had been scheduled. In North Carolina, it's the district attorney who controls when cases get set for trial, and there was no telling when Ron Moore would get around to scheduling Wilcoxson's trial. Four of his co-defendants had pled guilty to second-degree murder and made statements implicating Wilcoxson. He was told that all four would testify against him and would allege that he had fired the fatal shot. He was a young Black man from Detroit who had dealt drugs in Asheville. He was told by his attorney that he would likely be sentenced to death if he went to trial and was convicted, or, at best, he would spend the rest of his life in prison.

Despite the confessions from the other defendants implicating Wilcoxson and Brewton, there were problems with the prosecution's case. When the bandanas and gloves found by the side of the road the morning after the murder were tested for DNA by the State

Bureau of Investigation, Wilcoxson and all five of his co-defendants were excluded as the source of the DNA found on the bandanas— *but this was not made known to Wilcoxson or any of his co-defendants.*

Also, a portion of the videotape obtained from the Amoco station had mysteriously been taped over. Detective Sprinkle, who denied having anything to do with it appears to have held the tape for a month instead of turning it in to the evidence custodian for safe-keeping, which would have been the proper course of action. He didn't surrender the video to the evidence custodian until October 23, 2000. Four minutes of the video—the portion showing the car with the light vinyl top, and the three Black men walking up toward the front doors and entering the convenience store—had been taped over with a scene from a television soap opera. The soap opera was *Guiding Light,* and the episode on the tape was broadcast only one time—*on October 23, the same day Detective Sprinkle turned in the tape.* The destruction of this portion of the videotape suggested that as early as a month into the investigation, the police knew that Wilcoxson, Kagonyera, Williams, Isbell, and Brewton were not involved in Walter Bowman's murder, and that the evidence from the gas station, which showed the true culprits, had to be concealed or destroyed. It was the very next day, October 24, that the police charged Wilcoxson, Kagonyera, Williams, Isbell, and Brewton with first-degree murder.

In light of these evidentiary problems, the district attorney's office offered to allow Wilcoxson to plead guilty to second-degree murder. Because he had no record of criminal convictions, and with credit for the twenty-two months he had already served, he was told that by pleading guilty to second-degree murder, he could be released in 2008. His attorney urged him to take the plea, and he decided to accept the deal. He had become a father just before entering jail, and he thought of his new daughter in agreeing to plead guilty. If he was tried and convicted, "She wouldn't have a father for the rest of her life.... So, it was either go with the flow and get as less time as I can or still remain and claim my innocence...."

He refused, however, to make any statement confessing to the crime or implicating anyone else. Despite what he'd been told regarding his probable term of confinement, he was sentenced to 150 to 189 months in prison. The earliest he could be released from prison would be 2013.

And that was how it came about that the state secured guilty pleas from *five* men, based on four confessions, and sent those five men to prison, for a crime committed by *three* different men altogether.

ROBERT EARL "TRICKY" RUTHERFORD CONFESSES

Just six months after Wilcoxson was sentenced, Robert Rutherford, who was then serving a federal sentence for drug trafficking in the western district of North Carolina, called DEA Special Agent Barnabas Whiteis. Agent Whiteis had been on the drug task force team that investigated and helped prosecute Rutherford and others for drug offenses in federal court in Asheville in 2001.

During that phone call, Rutherford told Agent Whiteis that he had information about a drug-related robbery in Buncombe County that had gone wrong and resulted in a killing. Over two phone calls on March 27 and 28, 2003, Rutherford told Agent Whiteis that he, Bradford Summey, and Lacy "J.J." Pickens—the three men named in the first Crime Stoppers tip—planned the attempted robbery of Shaun and Walter Bowman, who they believed had a significant stash of drugs and money located at their home in Fairview, just outside Asheville.

Rutherford confessed to Agent Whiteis that he and Summey were driven to the Bowman residence in Pickens's "1970s model blue Olds Cutlass sedan, stopping at a store prior to the shooting near Reynolds High School." This was consistent with the statements given by witnesses Jason Cope and Jack Holland, and with the videotape seized from the Amoco station near Reynolds High School before it was erased by Detective Sprinkle or some other officer in the sheriff's office.

Rutherford further told Agent Whiteis that he, Summey, and

Pickens had initially hidden in the bushes by the house. He said all three men entered the Bowman house with bandanas over their faces, that Pickens and Summey had gloves on, and that they had a handgun and a pistol-grip shotgun. This was consistent with what the police had been told by Wanda Holloway, Walter's stepdaughter, shortly after the murder, and with the bandanas and gloves found near the scene the next day. Rutherford gave other details of the attempted robbery and homicide that closely matched the initial recounting of events given to the police on the night of the murder by Wanda. For example, Rutherford accurately described Wanda running into the kitchen when they first entered the house, he accurately described the locations of the two bedrooms in the house, he accurately described the shotgun used, and he accurately identified the room in which Walter Bowman was shot. He even told Agent Whiteis how he had learned there was a substantial quantity of drugs and cash at the house—from a girl named DeWanna Bowen. Bowen had dated Rutherford, was close to Shaun Bowman's sister, and had been to the house where the murder occurred several times before September 18, 2000. She was supposed to be there that night but had canceled at the last minute.

Rutherford's statement to Whiteis should have set off alarm bells and flashing lights for the men responsible for putting Wilcoxson and the other defendants in prison for their alleged roles in the crime, particularly in light of the fact that the DNA on the bandanas and gloves tested by the SBI in 2001 didn't match any of the men who pled guilty. But the police and the district attorney managed to sit on this information, ignored it, concealed it, and otherwise swept it under the rug for *eight more years*.

Agent Whiteis called the Buncombe County Sheriff's Office and informed a detective there of the substance of Rutherford's confession. Detective Sprinkle was told of this confession, and on March 31, 2003, two days after Rutherford confessed to Agent Whiteis, Sprinkle ran a record check of Rutherford.

Two weeks later, Agent Whiteis faxed his three-page report of

Rutherford's confession to Captain Farnsworth of the Buncombe County Sheriff's Office. On the fax cover page, Whiteis included his personal telephone number in case the detectives there had any questions. Whiteis never heard back from anyone.

After learning about Rutherford's confession, Detective Sprinkle told the Buncombe County district attorney's office that Rutherford's confession was not reliable because Pickens had been in jail on Monday, September 18, 2000, the night of the murder. This was not true. Pickens was serving a sentence that only required him to be incarcerated during weekends; he was not in jail that Monday night. Based on Sprinkle's false representations about Pickens, without doing any further checking on Rutherford's story, and ignoring all the corroboration Rutherford had provided, District Attorney Moore concluded that Rutherford's confession should be ignored, and that neither Wilcoxson nor his attorney even needed to be notified of its existence. Wilcoxson and his four co-defendants, completely unaware of Rutherford's confession, remained in prison.

Four years later, in 2007, the North Carolina SBI received a notice that the national DNA database known as CODIS had just gotten a hit on a DNA profile related to the Bowman murder. The DNA taken from saliva found on the bandanas and epithelial cells in the gloves had been entered into the national database in 2001. Now, a new DNA profile that was recently entered in the system triggered a match with the DNA profile from one of the bandanas. The person from whom the new DNA sample had been taken was Bradford Summey, one of the three men named in the original Crime Stoppers tip, and one of the accomplices in the Bowman robbery attempt and murder as described in Robert Rutherford's confession.

The match was checked and confirmed by the SBI lab. The odds that someone other than Summey was the contributor of the DNA on the bandana were calculated by the SBI as more than *one trillion* to one. There could be no dispute that Bradford Summey had worn the bandana that was used in the Bowman homicide.

On June 25, 2007, SBI Agent Tim Baize called the Buncombe

County Sheriff's Office to inform them of the DNA match and asked for Detective Sprinkle. When he was informed that Sprinkle no longer worked there, Baize left a message. Detective Elkins called Agent Baize back the next day, and Baize informed Elkins of the CODIS hit on Bradford Summey in the Bowman homicide. Elkins told Baize "he would talk to the D.A. and call [Baize] back."

At this time, Elkins was the person in charge of the Criminal Investigations Division at the sheriff's office. He had been intimately involved in the Bowman murder investigation and had access to the investigative file. Incredibly, Baize never received a phone call back from Elkins.

Months later, after hearing nothing from Elkins, Agent Baize sent the sheriff's office a report showing the CODIS hit matching Summey to the DNA on the bandana. Again, he received no response. Elkins did nothing to further investigate Summey's involvement in the Bowman murder and did not inform the district attorney's office of the information linking Summey to the murder. Wilcoxson and his four co-defendants remained in prison.

What makes this so profoundly inexcusable beyond the obvious injustice is that all of this occurred against the backdrop of repeated, highly visible attempts by Kenny Kagonyera to obtain the original DNA results performed by the SBI in 2001, which had not been provided to the co-defendants, and to have additional DNA testing done to prove his innocence.

In the spring of 2003, Kagonyera requested the 2001 DNA results from the clerk's office. His request was denied. In June 2003, he filed a pro se motion for DNA testing. Also denied. In June 2005, he again requested the results of the 2001 DNA tests. There is no record of any response from the district attorney's office to this request. In July 2005, Kagonyera repeated the request. No response. In August 2005, another request. No response. In April 2006, Kagonyera filed an affidavit asking for the results of the 2001 DNA tests. In September 2006, he filed a motion to compel the district attorney to release the results of the 2001 DNA tests. In July 2008, the district attorney's office wrote in response that the prior DNA testing was "either negative or inconclusive," which was false. The next day, a judge ordered DNA testing of Robert Rutherford to occur by August 15, 2008. For this purpose, Rutherford was transferred from federal prison to a Buncombe County jail so that law enforcement could obtain a DNA sample. Seven months later, he was returned to federal custody without anyone from the sheriff's office, which ran the jail, having obtained a DNA sample from him. The apparent obstruction by the district attorney's office and law enforcement with respect to the efforts of Kagonyera and the other co-defendants to obtain exculpatory evidence was breathtaking.

From the date of his arrest, and throughout his incarceration, Robert Wilcoxson maintained his innocence. In 2010, he was finally successful in getting his case accepted for review by the North Carolina Innocence Inquiry Commission (NCIIC). The NCIIC is an agency created by statute in North Carolina in 2006 to evaluate claims of innocence by incarcerated persons in the state. It was the first of its kind in any state, and has the statutory authority to determine a defendant's actual innocence post-conviction.

In January 2010, the NCIIC obtained DNA samples from Pickens, Summey, and Rutherford. An independent forensic laboratory, LabCorp, was hired to conduct full DNA testing of all six of the original suspects, Wilcoxson, Kagonyera, Williams, Mills, Brewton, and Isbell; the three new suspects, Summey, Pickens, and Rutherford; and the bandanas and gloves found near the scene of the murder the day after the crime.

The DNA analysis confirmed the results of the 2001 DNA tests run by the SBI—that Robert Wilcoxson and all of his co-defendants were definitively excluded from contributing to the DNA profiles found on any of the gloves or the bandanas.

The tests also determined that Lacy Pickens's DNA profile contained a rare allele that was found on two gloves collected on the side of the road near the murder scene. Finally, the tests determined that Rutherford's DNA was likely contained in a DNA mixture found on one of the bandanas. Specifically, the "probability of randomly selecting an unrelated individual with a DNA profile that would be included in the mixture of DNA obtained from" the bandana was approximately 1 in 6,060 for the Black population. A new DNA analysis performed by the SBI in July 2010 again confirmed the 2007 SBI analysis matching Bradford Summey to one of the bandanas.

Despite this compelling evidence of innocence for Wilcoxson and the other defendants, District Attorney Ron Moore clung fast to the confessions of Wilcoxson's four co-defendants and the guilty pleas by each, including Wilcoxson, and refused to acknowledge that the pleas were obtained wrongfully or erroneously.

Steve Drizin, a professor at the Northwestern School of Law in Chicago and a nationally recognized expert on false confessions, was hired by the NCIIC as an independent expert to evaluate the confessions of Isbell, Williams, Mills, and Kagonyera. Drizin's report noted that:

> *The defendants' confessions, like those of the Central Park Jogger defendants, differ with respect to specific details of virtually every major aspect of the crime—who planned the attack, who carried what weapons, what the perpetrators were wearing, the number and type of cars driven to the crime scene, who entered the home, who was the lookout, who fired the fatal shots, where the defendants went after the attack, what was done with the clothing and the guns, etc.*[*]

Professor Drizin concluded that the statements of Isbell, Williams, Mills, and Kagonyera were "highly unreliable" and that:

---

[*] Affidavit & Report of Steven A. Drizin, p. 40.

*The statements are internally inconsistent, inconsistent with one an-
other, and uncorroborated. DNA evidence obtained from items recovered
from the scene excludes all of the defendants.*[*]

Professor Drizin also pointed out that there was "evidence of
contamination in this case—the police reports indicate that Larry
Williams claimed that Sheriff Medford had given him details of the
crime. . . ."[†] Moreover, "[n]one of the defendants were able to lead
the police to any evidence corroborating their confessions. The defendants did not provide the police with a single verifiable fact that
the police did not already know about."[‡]

After the case was initially evaluated by the NCIIC, it was referred to a special panel of judges for an evidentiary hearing. My
law partner at that time, Chris Fialko, was appointed to represent
Robert Wilcoxson at the hearing. On September 22, 2011, after a
full evidentiary hearing before a panel consisting of three Superior Court judges, the Hon. W. Erwin Spainhour, the Hon. Patrice
A. Hinnant, and the Hon. Bradley B. Letts, Robert Wilcoxson *was
unanimously found to be innocent* of the murder of Walter Bowman.
He had pled guilty and served eleven years in prison for a crime
he did not commit.

Chris and I then filed a civil action against the Buncombe County
Sheriff's Office, Sheriff Medford, and the individual officers who
we alleged had coerced the false confessions from Wilcoxson's co-
defendants, which in turn had forced him to enter a false guilty plea
to avoid a possible death sentence if convicted after trial. We also
sued the officers who we alleged covered up Rutherford's confession
and the CODIS hit on Summey's DNA. The district attorney, despite

---

* Ibid, p. 42.

† Ibid, p. 41.

‡ Ibid, p. 40.

what we believed he and his office had done to keep Wilcoxson in prison after Rutherford's confession and the DNA corroboration, was absolutely immune from civil damages. All the defendants in the case denied wrongdoing and responsibility for what had occurred. After fighting the lawsuit for almost two years, Buncombe County finally agreed to pay Wilcoxson $5.1 million to settle his claims—but this was not accompanied by an apology or statement of regret.

Kenneth Kagonyera, like Robert Wilcoxson, was exonerated in 2011 by the North Carolina Innocence Inquiry Commission.

The charges against Larry Williams, Damian Mills, and Teddy Isbell related to the Walter Bowman murder were dismissed by the district attorney in 2015, but only after they had each served their respective sentences. They received "pardons of innocence" by the governor of North Carolina on December 17, 2020.

The charges against Aaron Brewton were dismissed without explanation by the district attorney prior to Brewton's trial.

Lacy "J.J." Pickens was fatally shot by police in 2006 in the parking lot of a Cracker Barrel restaurant in Asheville, North Carolina.

Sheriff Bobby Medford was indicted in 2007 on federal corruption, extortion, and money laundering charges relating to his conduct as the sheriff of Buncombe County. He was convicted by a jury and sentenced to fifteen years in prison. He died of Covid-19 in federal custody at Federal Correctional Institution Butner near Durham, North Carolina, on June 3, 2020.

When the innocent are convicted, the guilty go free. Robert Rutherford and Bradford Summey were never prosecuted for the murder of Walter Bowman. Bowman's family, the other victims of the abuse of power by law enforcement in Buncombe County, is still waiting for justice.

25

FABRICATING CONFESSIONS

Robert Wilcoxson was a rational and intelligent twenty-three-year-old man when he agreed to plead guilty to a crime he had not committed. And there was a logic to his decision. It was a strict cost-benefit analysis, which many defendants who are offered an attractive plea bargain while facing a trial at an uncertain time with an uncertain but potentially drastic result engage in every day. Imagine an indigent defendant, locked up and unable to make bond for a relatively minor offense, who is offered a plea to a misdemeanor and a sentence of "time served," immediate release, versus staying in jail to fight the charges. We can say we would never plead guilty to something we didn't do, but we are not sitting in a bleak jail cell being offered immediate freedom if we just say the word "guilty."

The problem of false confessions and false guilty pleas is even more widespread for juveniles like Larry Williams, drug addicts like Teddy Isbell, and especially those suffering from intellectual disabilities. I've represented three individuals with severe intellectual disabilities over the past decade—Floyd Lee Brown, Edward McInnis, and James Blackmon—all of whom were ultimately exonerated. Yet before they were exonerated, they had served fourteen years, twenty-seven years, and thirty-seven years, respectively, for crimes they did not commit. All three had falsely confessed. James Blackmon had entered an Alford plea, and Edward McInnis had entered a false guilty plea, while Floyd Lee Brown had been found incompetent to stand trial and as a result was incarcerated in a prison mental hospital without ever even being tried.

EDWARD MCINNIS

Edward McInnis had an IQ of 76. On three separate occasions, he had either broken into the homes of, or approached, older women and asked for sex or exposed his genitals. For one of these incidents, he was convicted of indecent exposure. So when someone climbed through the bedroom window of the home of an eighty-one-year-old woman and raped her, Edward was considered by the police to be a likely suspect. The attacker stabbed the victim with a letter opener, which broke off in the victim's shoulder, and took money from her purse. The victim survived but did not get a good look at her attacker. She described him as being a Black male in his late teens or early twenties, and said he was very articulate and that he spoke clearly during the attack.

No physical evidence or eyewitness testimony linked Edward to the rape. Contrary to what the victim reported, he had a speech impediment, which made it very difficult to understand him. When Edward was arrested, he denied having anything to do with the crime over the course of two interrogations, and his alibi witnesses all confirmed that he was at his niece's house at the time of the assault. He remained in jail for months, maintaining his innocence. Then four days before the trial, police officers interrogated Edward without his lawyer's knowledge or consent and threatened him with the death penalty unless he confessed to the rape *and* pled guilty. Edward did not understand that the death penalty did not even apply to his case. He was sentenced to life imprisonment plus twenty years on the basis of his "confession."

After serving twelve years in prison, Edward sought the assistance of the North Carolina Center on Actual Innocence (NCCAI). The NCCAI then sought the rape kit collected from the victim, but the police department said that it could not be located and had probably been destroyed. *Nine years later*, the police department and the district attorney's office again searched unsuccessfully for the rape-kit evidence and confirmed that it had been destroyed. Then in 2014, after another four years had passed with Edward behind bars, the North Carolina Innocence Inquiry Commission, using its statutory power to subpoena evidence, subpoenaed the rape kit. Only then did the rape kit miraculously appear.

The physical evidence, when tested for DNA, conclusively ruled out Edward as the perpetrator. In 2015, Edward's conviction was vacated, and he was released after serving twenty-seven years in prison. A review of the notes in the police file showed the details that Edward offered to the police when he confessed—after two prior interrogations in which he vehemently denied any involvement—were at odds with the account given by the victim. In light of Edward's impaired intellectual ability, and his inability to truly understand the full circumstances of the proceedings against him, it is unforgivable that the police threatened him with the death penalty unless he confessed. A civil claim brought on Edward's behalf settled for $4.25 million.

FLOYD LEE BROWN

Perhaps the worst case of police abuse of power in the context of a fabricated confession came in the case of Floyd Lee Brown. Like Edward McInnis, Floyd had diminished intellectual capacity and was taken advantage of by two North Carolina State Bureau of Investigation agents.

Floyd was first arrested and incarcerated in 1993 for the murder and robbery of Kathryn Lynch, crimes he did not commit. The only evidence against Floyd was his alleged confession, which two SBI agents claimed to have taken down "verbatim." No other evidence implicated Floyd in the crime.

Growing up, Floyd had significant difficulties with everyday life skills. He struggled to eat with a fork and keep himself from running into the street. He spent every day of his school years in special classes for children with an IQ between 30 and 50. When Floyd was fifteen years old and in high school, he functioned at a kindergarten level academically and socially. Even by the time he was sixteen, Floyd was unable to tell time, write his own name and address, or read basic words necessary for his daily survival, such as the words "boys" and "girls" on bathroom doors. He knew the order of the alphabet only up to the letter J. He did not know the names of colors, how old he was, or how many brothers or sisters he had. He could not begin to understand the concept of money. He could not tell right from left and did not know the name of the state where he lived. He could not even say what year it was.

Immediately prior to his arrest, Floyd was attending a sheltered workshop for the developmentally disabled at a local vocational center. At the time of the robbery and murder, Floyd lived with his mother in a house with no bathtub or shower. He earned spare change by planting flowers at a greenhouse and catching turkeys on local turkey farms. He had not experienced significant improvement in his cognitive ability since his teenage years.

On or about July 8, 1993, Kathryn Lynch was beaten and killed in her home in Wadesboro, North Carolina. She was struck viciously on the face and forearms with a blunt instrument until she was unconscious and was left to die in her bedroom.

SBI Agent Mark Isley was assigned to be the lead investigator on the case. Isley knew Floyd because Floyd used to hang out at the local courthouse with law enforcement and clerks. Isley was aware of Floyd's diminished mental capacity, which was readily apparent to anyone who interacted with him. Isley and another SBI agent, Bill Lane, inexplicably began to focus on Floyd as a suspect in the

Lynch murder without obtaining any evidence linking Floyd with the murder and without any suggestion by any witness that Floyd was the culprit.

Isley went to Floyd's house and had him sign a "Consent to Search" form. Floyd signed his name as "BWN." After not finding anything to incriminate Floyd in his home, the next day Isley drove to the vocational center where Floyd was attending his sheltered workshop to interrogate him about Ms. Lynch's death. After driving Floyd back to the police station, Agent Isley presented Floyd with a "Waiver of Rights" form, which Floyd was unable to understand or even fill out. Floyd signed the form, misspelling his own name on the signature line.

Agents Isley and Lane interrogated Floyd for approximately two hours and ten minutes. Isley did not take notes or reduce to writing anything Floyd said during this time until the interrogation had ended. Agent Lane made no notes of the interrogation at all.

The confession allegedly given by Floyd was written in the first-person voice. In the typed transcription of the statement, the section containing the text of what is alleged to be Floyd's confession is set apart from the rest of the document with quotation marks. Agent Isley testified under oath that the transcription he prepared was a "verbatim" account of what Floyd told Agents Isley and Lane during the interrogation.

The verbatim statement Agents Isley and Lane attributed to Floyd is as follows:

On Friday, July 19, 1993, my mama woke me up at 6 a.m., in the morning. After I got up, I took a bath and then walked outside. I live on Highway 742 near Highway 52 where they are building a bridge. When I walked outside, I started walking down towards Mark Cox's house. Mark Cox's house is located across the street from Ms. Katherine's driveway. Ms. Katherine [the victim] is my cousin.

When I was standing next to some mailboxes on the side of Ms. Katherine's driveway, I saw Hattie Little leaving the driveway in a blue Chevrolet. It looked like she had her children in the car with her. I think it was about 7 o'clock. After I saw Hattie drive away, I walked up the driveway to where Ms. Katherine lives. Ms. Katherine lives in a white house with a fence around it. When I walked up to Ms. Katherine's front door, the screen door was shut, but the front door was opened. I knocked on the screen door. Ms. Katherine came to the screen door and opened it for me. Ms. Katherine was my favorite cousin and she hugged me. We were standing in the doorway with the screen door against my back when she hugged me. I was at Ms. Katherine's house because I wanted to borrow some money from her and plus she told me to come back to see her sometime to do some yard work. Ms. Katherine invited me on into the house. We walked into the living room where a little brown heater was sitting. I sat in a red chair in the living room while Ms. Katherine sat behind me on a couch. Ms. Katherine told me to get the TV and bring it in the living room. I got the TV out of her bedroom and sat it on the heater in the living room. I had to move some stuff to plug in the TV. We were watching Andy Griffin [sic], but I didn't get to watch it all. While I was watching TV, I asked Ms. Katherine if I could have some water and she said for me to get it myself. I went into the kitchen and got a glass from the kitchen table. I drank the water while I was in the kitchen and put the glass back on the table. Ms. Katherine was drinking juice from a glass that had a straw in it. She was drinking from a straw because she ain't got no teeth.

When I walked from the kitchen, I asked Ms. Katherine for a dollar and she said she didn't have a dollar. When Ms. Katherine told me she didn't have a dollar, I hit her on the neck with a stick that I brought into the house. I held the stick with two hands when I hit her the first time. I hit Ms. Katherine again, but this time, on the right arm. Ms. Katherine threw her hands up in front of her when I was hitting her with the stick. One time when I hit Ms. Katherine, she tried to catch the stick with her hands. I didn't hit her that hard. While I was hitting Ms. Katherine, she fell back on the couch she was sitting on. After she fell down on the couch, I bent down and felt Ms. Katherine's chest to see if she was alive and still breathing. Her heart was still beating. I saw *blood on top of her head, but I didn't hit her in the head. After checking her, I helped Ms. Katherine to the bathroom because she had to use the bathroom. After getting out of the bathroom, Ms. Katherine told me to lay her on her back in her bedroom. I checked her chest again and she was still breathing. I left her between her bed and her dresser in her bedroom. Ms. Katherine was laying flat on her back. I even straightened her legs out.*

Before I left the house, I took twenty dollars from a dresser in her bedroom. I know ya'll [sic] aren't going to be believe me, but Ms. Katherine told me I could have her money if something happened.

I don't remember what I did with the stick when I left the house. After leaving the house, threw [sic] the front door, I walked back to my house and waited for the van to pick me up to take me to the McLaurin Workshop in Hamlet, North Carolina.

I wish Ms. Katherine was alive right now. If she was, she would tell you that I only hit her five times and that she was still breathing when I left the house.

I'm sorry for hitting her. I told you I made a mistake."

Even the state's own mental health professionals who worked with and evaluated Floyd in the years after his arrest uniformly agreed that Floyd could not possibly have given this statement. Dr. Bob Rollins, the former chief of forensic psychiatry and superintendent of Dorothea Dix Hospital, testified that the confession was "too educated, too sophisticated, too relevant, too cohesive for Mr. Brown." The chief of forensic services at Dorothea Dix, Dr. Mark Hazelrigg, pointed out, "As a whole, the alleged confession is too detailed and organized for even a normally intelligent person." It couldn't have come from Floyd because, as Dr. Hazelrigg noted dryly, Floyd "does not use complete sentences."

Floyd was incarcerated on the basis of this "confession," which could well have been given by an English major, but was deemed incompetent to stand trial because of his low-functioning cognition. Each year between 1993 and 2003, he was again determined to be incompetent and therefore unable to stand trial. During this time, he was imprisoned in the secured units at Dorothea Dix Hospital, an institution for people with severe mental illnesses. In many ways it was worse than a prison.

In 2003, a forensic psychologist at the hospital issued a report stating that Floyd was finally competent to stand trial. Shortly thereafter, in what I believe was another unfathomable abuse of power and wanton cruelty, the prosecution filed a notice of intent to seek the death penalty against Floyd. His lawyer had to explain to Floyd that the state was now trying to kill him for a crime he hadn't committed, after he'd been locked in a mental hospital for a decade. Fortunately, this did not come to pass. A year later, after a hearing, a superior court judge found that Floyd was "mentally retarded," and therefore that the state was barred from seeking the death penalty against him.

Finally, in 2007, the pending charges of first-degree murder and robbery against Floyd were dismissed. All told, Floyd spent over fourteen years in custody without any trial for a crime he did not commit. When the judge dismissed the charges, he concluded, over the state's objection, that Floyd's incarceration for fourteen years had violated his constitutional right to due process.

On Floyd's behalf, I brought a civil action against SBI Agents Isley and Lane, who of course denied that they had done anything wrong in procuring Floyd's improbable confession. I alleged that the SBI agents had fabricated Floyd's confession, and that from 1993 until 2007, the agents concealed the fact that the confession had been fabricated. I argued that by remaining silent year after year, they allowed Floyd's wrongful incarceration to continue.

The case resulted in a settlement to Floyd in the amount of $9 million. We made sure Floyd had a guardian, and a trust was set up to protect his assets. All Floyd wanted to do with the money was to buy a BMW for himself (although he couldn't drive) and a house for the sister who had stuck by him all the years he was incarcerated. He sent me a picture of himself sitting in the passenger seat of his used BMW 5 series, with a very big smile. And I recently got a copy of the plans for the house that is being built for his sister, with whom he is living. Nothing, however, can give him back the fourteen years he spent in confinement at Dorothea Dix Hospital.

JAMES BLACKMON

James Blackmon, a man suffering from a history of severe psychiatric illnesses, confessed in 1983 to killing Helena Payton, a student at St. Augustine's College in Raleigh. He was innocent, and the real perpetrator got away with murder.

It was a college student's worst nightmare. An outside door to the all-girls dormitory had been left unlocked overnight. Someone had gotten inside and made his way unseen to the sixth floor, where he waited quietly in the dark of the communal bathroom for someone, anyone, to come in.

It all happened in a matter of seconds.

At 6:10 on the morning of September 28, 1979, Helena Payton awoke and made her way sleepily out of her dorm room and across the hall to the dormitory's shared bathroom. It was her twenty-third birthday. Once in the bathroom, she turned to enter the first stall on the left. She felt the cold of the green and white tile on her bare feet. He heard her come in. Before she could turn around, he was there with her, grabbing her from behind. She screamed in terror. He drove a knife deep into the base of her neck, striking her carotid artery. Bleeding profusely from the wound, slipping in the blood, Helena escaped her attacker and ran from the bathroom back into her room across the hall, where she collapsed on the floor. Her roommate pressed a cold towel to her neck to stanch the bleeding while they waited for an ambulance to arrive.

Hearing Helena's scream, other girls on the hall opened their doors and came out to see what happened. Jackie Kelly was one of them. She saw a Black man wearing jeans and a maroon dashiki come out of the bathroom. He walked down the hall directly toward her, allowing her a good look at his face. He then passed by her and calmly walked down the dormitory stairway. Jackie told the police she could identify the man if she saw him again. Another student who saw the man believed she had seen him before but didn't know his name.

Downstairs, in the game room, the attacker dropped his knife, a wooden-handled Guardian 007, and fled out through the parking lot and into a wooded area beside the dorm. Once in the woods, he stripped off his blood-stained shirt—the maroon dashiki—and left it on the ground, where it was later found by investigators.

Helena was rushed to the hospital, where she underwent emergency surgery. The doctors said she was stable, but the stability didn't last the night. During a brief period of lucidity, she told her mother that she did not know the man who attacked her. She then fell into a coma that persisted for days and then weeks. Her mother, who was always by her side, refused to allow the hospital to remove Helena from the equipment that was sustaining her life, saying, "Anything is possible with God."

After Helena had been in a coma and unresponsive for more than a month, it became apparent that she could not be saved. The loss of blood had caused irreversible injury to her brain. Her mother let her pass on October 30. The college canceled classes for two days after Helena's death, flags were lowered to half-staff, and more than five hundred students attended a memorial service in her honor. The tragedy was felt far and wide. One newspaper wrote, "Just as the students were moved by the tragedy, North Carolina feels the same way. It has had a traumatic impact on all of us."

Investigators searched in vain for possible suspects. In the bathroom, the attacker had left fingerprints that were lifted by the police. Although a number of suspects were questioned, and their fingerprints compared to the prints found at the scene of the murder, all were ruled out. The case quickly went cold.

On February 8, 1983, some three and a half years after Helena Payton was killed, Raleigh police detective N. S. Lockey received a tip from an unidentified person at Dorothea Dix Hospital that a Black man who was a patient there had bragged about killing women in New York, New Jersey, and Raleigh. Detective Lockey subsequently received another anonymous tip that the man's name was James Blackmon. The police performed a fingerprint comparison between Blackmon's prints and the latent prints lifted from the bathroom stall door where Helena Payton was attacked, but the prints did not match.

Even though Blackmon was not the source of the fingerprints, the Raleigh police requested and received records from New York State, including from prisons where he had been incarcerated and treated in psychiatric units. These records revealed that Blackmon had been diagnosed with severe mental illnesses, including schizophrenia, organic brain syndrome, and delusional thinking. There was also testing that revealed him to have significant intellectual disability (referred to in the records at the time as "mental retardation" or "mentally defective"). The police also obtained Blackmon's medical records from his civil commitment at Dorothea Dix. The records reflected, among other things, diagnoses of paranoid schizophrenia and delusional thinking, which included statements by Blackmon that God and Satan were his fathers, that he could cause floods and earthquakes, and that he was going to marry the singer Diana Ross. He was reported to have a full-scale WAIS-R IQ of 69, indicating "mild mental retardation."

Other records from New York revealed that on August 24, 1979, little more than a month *before* Helena Payton was attacked in Raleigh, Blackmon had been arrested in Binghamton, New York, for disorderly conduct and possession of marijuana, and that on November 8, 1979, only five weeks *after* Helena Payton was attacked in Raleigh, Blackmon had again been arrested in Binghamton, New York, this time for trespassing. There was no evidence that Blackmon had traveled to Raleigh between his arrest in Binghamton on August 24, 1979, and his arrest in Binghamton on November 8, 1979.

The Raleigh police also met with Jackie Kelly at Fort Benning, Georgia, where she was serving in the army. She had been face-to-face with the attacker in the hall of the dormitory. The police showed her a photo array that included a photo of James Blackmon. She did not identify him, or anyone else, as the person who had attacked Helena Payton.

In the absence of any credible evidence that Blackmon was the killer, the detectives assigned to this cold case decided to interview him. Before doing so, they reportedly studied how his mental illness might affect him during the interview. They then proceeded to pretend to befriend Blackmon, interviewed him for hours, and actually brought him to St. Augustine's campus, and then inside the dorm where the crime had occurred. Blackmon's mental illness was on full display during the interrogation. For starters, he was wearing a blanket tied around his neck like a cape during the interview.

During the first thirty minutes of the interrogation, Blackmon told the police that he used "masonry," which he said was a form of magic, to cause a judge in Lumberton to "fall out of his chair." He told them that just the previous week he had healed a sick woman at Shaw University using "masonry," that he had learned how to do it "from the thoughts," and that he had been doing "masonry" his entire life. Blackmon also told them he had used "masonry" to remove "a bad spirit" from his friend Melvin and took it on himself, but it was now out of him as well.

Blackmon's delusions were further confirmed later in the interrogation, when he told the police the following:

". . . if I draw the moon, cut the moon out of a piece of paper and put a star there and a flying saucer, and then put the nine planets around that, you will see things at night."

"You see things move. You know like when you're watching on TV, right, watching TV, and all the electricity waves and volts, they is coming through to see the whole of the big picture, all over the world. I used the mirror for a focus, right? Penetration, sending things out. And I get it in my mind, and they come on into being."

"And concentrating to it at the same time, what I want to come about, you know, and as I look and get deeper into the details, the elements begin to move, you know. A lot of people don't know that. The mirror is the substance of reflection of time and place. And I'm the only one know how they work."

At one point Blackmon told the police, "I don't care how many flying saucers or UFOs are there, you know, or where the ships may be."

In the midst of these delusions, the police fed Blackmon information about the crime through leading questions, and ignored statements that were inconsistent with the physical evidence. They suggested that there was a "good James" and a "bad James," and that the body of the "bad James" went to places where the mind of the "good James" was not present. They also suggested scenarios where the "bad James" might have gone to St. Augustine's and hurt a girl in the dorm. The interview, which went on for hours over the course of two days, included the following questions asked by the police:

Do you think in body you might have been to one of these dorms at St. Aug.?

What do you think your body might have done in that dorm?

If your body were to be at St. Augustine College in the dorm where these women are, where would you go?

When your body, James, went to the dorms, and your mind was some other place but your body was there, how would you dress?

Say your body was over in the dorm, and something happened, what would you do?

Put your body on the time that you were over there at St. Aug. University in the dorms. Can you recall anything else, thinking in your mind now, 1979. You were at St. Aug. University.

Close your eyes again for me, James. Just think a minute, '79, St. Aug. University, you talking to a young girl. What time is this?

You think your body has been over there before, but your mind hasn't?

Does your mind communicate with your body at all, James, while you were over there, while your body is over there?

In the past when your body was over at St. Aug., does your mind see any lady getting hurt?

Does your body and your mind, do you see one of the sisters or some of the sisters getting hurt?

Your body was there. You were re-formed.

And something happened, James, something you had no control over.

And you know, somebody got hurt.

I want you to close your eyes and think of this other James Blackmon. Something happened on the sixth floor. You said a lot of confusion going on, a lot of screaming. . . .

Open your eyes now and just look a moment at this [the knife]. The other James Blackmon. Do you recognize this? The other James Blackmon we're talking about. Not this James Blackmon. The other James Blackmon, several years ago.

I'm talking about the other James Blackmon. I'm not talking about this James Blackmon. I'm talking about the old James Blackmon. Did he have a knife like that?

Did he have this knife with him when he was making love to the girl?

I want you to concentrate for me now, thinking, and just think before you answer, in your own mind as you see the other James Blackmon at St. Aug.

Okay. Now, I want you to concentrate and see if there is anything unusual about this lady that James Blackmon cut?

After the girl had been hurt by James Blackmon, and James Blackmon walked away, how long did he stay in the woods?

Did this thing that happened, happen by James Blackmon, the bad, vicious James Blackmon?

What did James Blackmon do to this girl as she started screaming?

Where on her body did—can the other James Blackmon remember where he cut the girl?

From this series of questions, the police eventually obtained "admissions" from Blackmon that served as the basis for charging him with Helena's murder.

They were not dissuaded when Jackie Kelly, the eyewitness, told them after a lineup that Blackmon was *not* the man she saw leaving the scene of the attack. When told by the police that Blackmon had confessed, she replied that he must be crazy, because it wasn't him she saw that morning in the dorm. This information was never documented or provided to the prosecutor or Blackmon's lawyer.

After he was charged, Blackmon denied killing Helena, and his attorney filed a motion to suppress the "confession." In 1987, the Court held a hearing on the motion to suppress that extended over four days. Finally, the Court denied the motion, making the confession admissible. In light of the ruling, Blackmon's attorney told him he was likely to be convicted and sentenced to life in prison, if he managed to avoid the death penalty. On the other hand, the state was offering a plea to second-degree murder, with eligibility for parole after ten years.

Blackmon had already served more than four years in pretrial detention and decided to follow his lawyer's advice and plead guilty to second-degree murder, provided he would not have to say that he had killed Helena Payton. Blackmon entered an *Alford* plea to second-degree murder. This meant he pled guilty, while at the same time maintaining that he had not committed the murder. It's a strange compromise that has been approved by the U.S. Supreme Court, designed simply to allow both sides, as a practical matter, to settle a case that they agree should be settled, without either conceding the other side's position is true. It's the same plea Michael Peterson entered thirty years later in another court.

An attorney from North Carolina Prisoner Legal Services, Beth McNeill, began representing James Blackmon in 2011, and the case was referred to the North Carolina Innocence Inquiry Commission the following year. The NCIIC asked the Raleigh police to search for any evidence that had been retained, and in July 2013, a latent fingerprint taken from the bathroom stall where Helena Payton was attacked was found. That print was then run through a database, which resulted in a "hit" for James Edward Leach. This was confirmed by a manual comparison. Leach's left thumbprint was positively matched to the print lifted from the bathroom stall.

Leach had no legitimate reason to have ever been in the bathroom stall of the sixth-floor bathroom of Latham Hall, an all-women dorm. He was never an employee or student at St. Augustine. He was not employed in any capacity on or before September 28, 1979, that would have caused him to be on the campus of St. Augustine.

Janice Bass, a former girlfriend of Leach's, was interviewed and stated that Leach carried a knife all the time. The knife had a brown handle and silver blade about four inches long that folded down. Cynthia Leach, Leach's former wife, stated that Leach carried a knife and once threatened her with a knife. John Leach, Leach's brother, stated that Leach carried a knife all his life. He described Leach's knife as a brown folding knife with a blade about six inches long. These descriptions matched the Guardian 007 knife found at the scene of Helena's attack.

On November 15, 2018, Jackie Kelly, the eyewitness, testified before the Innocence Commission. She identified a photograph of Leach as looking like the man she saw leaving the sixth floor of Latham Hall the morning Helena Payton was murdered.

The evidence showed that James Edward Leach, not James Blackmon, had likely murdered Helena Payton in 1979. Blackmon was found by a panel of three judges to be innocent and was released from prison. He had served thirty-five years and eight months for a murder he did not commit. We have filed a lawsuit on his behalf against the two lead detectives and the City of Raleigh.

During the time Blackmon was in prison for the murder of Helena Payton, Leach was convicted of committing multiple violent assaults on women and two assaults on law enforcement officers. And those are only the crimes for which he was arrested. It is not known how many women he attacked, raped, or killed for which he was not arrested. He was never prosecuted for the Helena Payton murder. By the time he had been identified as the likely perpetrator, James Leach had died.

26

ABUSING THE POWER OF SCIENCE

On Friday, December 6, 2001, just a few months after the attack on the World Trade Center Towers in New York, Michael and Kathleen Peterson received some good news. Michael's friend, David Perlmutt, a reporter for the *Charlotte Observer*, called to tell him that a producer in Hollywood was going to option one of Michael's novels for a movie. The next night, Michael and Kathleen decided to celebrate at their home in Durham. Michael rented a movie from Blockbuster, *America's Sweethearts*, and they settled into their den to watch the movie and drink wine. Around 10:00 p.m., Michael's son Todd dropped by with a friend, a woman the Petersons had known for years—a doctor who had recently completed her residency—to say hello on their way to a party nearby. The two couples exchanged pleasantries before Todd and his friend left, and Michael and Kathleen settled back in to finish the movie and their wine. The doctor later reported that the atmosphere at the house at ten o'clock was relaxed and normal.

Sometime later, after 11:00 p.m., the phone rang and Michael answered it. It was one of Kathleen's coworkers, calling about a project they were going to be working on the next morning. Michael gave the phone to Kathleen, and she briefly discussed what they would do the next morning. The coworker later reported that both Michael and Kathleen were their usual selves on the phone. There was no tension, and nothing seemed amiss.

That was soon to change, quite drastically. After Michael and Kathleen went outside by their pool to finish a second bottle of wine, Kathleen returned inside, as she had the work call the next morning. Michael stayed outside with the couple's two dogs, listening to the water fountain in the pool. He lost track of time, maybe even dozed off, and then went inside to go to bed. Upon entering the house, he found Kathleen lying in a large pool of blood at the bottom of a narrow back stairway that led to the couple's bedroom on the second floor. Their celebratory date night had turned into a nightmare, one that seemed to never end.

When the police arrived at the house around 3:00 a.m., they found a gruesome scene. Kathleen was lying dead at the bottom of the stairs. There was blood all over the landing, the bottom steps, and the walls inside the landing, going several feet up from the floor. Art Holland, the first detective to enter the house, came to an immediate conclusion: This was a crime scene. Kathleen Peterson had been murdered. Michael Peterson was the only suspect.

Holland left Michael with some other officers while he went to get a search warrant. He also called the North Carolina SBI to send their bloodstain-pattern expert, Special Agent Duane Deaver. When Deaver arrived at the Peterson house later that morning, Holland told him he thought that Michael had killed Kathleen.

Within ninety minutes of arriving at the Peterson home, and before performing any calculations concerning the origin of the blood spatter in the stairway, or examining any of the clothing worn by Kathleen or Michael, or doing much of anything except looking around and talking to Holland, Special Agent Deaver informed Holland that he agreed. The death was a homicide rather than an accident, and he set out to prove Holland's theory right from the start. His work would become crucial to the criminal prosecution of Michael Peterson.

I won't try to take you through all the incredible twists and turns of the case. The Netflix series about the case, *The Stairway*, is thirteen episodes long, and it still doesn't tell the entire story. Nor will I try here to convince you of what I strongly believed shortly after I got involved in the case, and have always believed ever since—that Michael Peterson did not murder Kathleen. Instead, I want to focus on Duane Deaver and the abuse of forensic science that he was guilty of committing, beyond any reasonable doubt, no matter your view of Michael Peterson's guilt or innocence.

That there was an enormous amount of blood in the stairway is beyond question. But the only thing that proved was that Kathleen had been bleeding profusely and moving around within the stairway for an extended period of time before losing consciousness and dying. All of the blood on the landing, the stairs, and the walls had come from the several wounds on Kathleen's scalp. As anyone who has ever had a scalp wound (or had a child who split open her scalp while playing) knows, the scalp bleeds profusely. It is the most vascularized part of the body. And the bleeding is hard to stop. It gets in your hair, which spreads the blood around whenever you shake your head. It can get in your nose and mouth and cause you to cough or sneeze the blood. So although the amount of blood made the scene look like a violent crime had taken place, it didn't prove Kathleen had been murdered. *The critical question was not what had caused the blood to be spattered as it was, but rather what had caused the wounds on Kathleen's scalp.* Was it some object that someone had hit her with, or had she fallen and struck her head on the stairs and landing? Deaver quickly realized this was the key, and he set about trying to prove that Kathleen's injuries resulted from an object swung by Michael.

Blood spatter, because it behaves according to the laws of physics, can provide some clues about the events that caused it. For example, one can determine the direction of the spatter, because as it hits a surface going in a particular direction, it will leave a "head" and a "tail," similar to how a sperm cell appears. The head shows where the spatter was heading, while the tail shows where it was coming from. If blood spatter on a floor is perfectly round, it indicates that the blood dropped straight down from above, without any directionality. Similarly, the size of the spatter can provide some general information about the force of the blow that caused it. If the spatter is extremely small, it means it was caused by significant force, like a gunshot. If it's large, it was caused by much less force, perhaps a slap or a punch. And if it's "not too large and not too small," like the bowl of porridge in the fairy tale, it becomes much more speculative, depending on the analyst's definition of "large" and "small."

But none of this really helped Deaver. He wanted to determine if the blood spatter had traveled from some stationary object, like a step or a wall, in which case it was consistent with an accidental fall, or if it came from an object swung by Michael, hitting Kathleen's head, in which case it was murder. In short, Deaver was determined to find a point of origin for the source of the blood that was "out in space," not from a step or a wall.

In theory, where blood originated can be determined by selecting certain *representative* spatters, carefully measuring the angle at which they hit a wall or other object, and then calculating, based on that angle, the path of the spatter. Once you do this with enough representative spatters, where the angles of all these come together and meet is where the blood originated. There are computer programs that can be used to do this calculation.

Deaver, however, didn't bother with computer programs. He used kite string, scotch tape, and a protractor. He selected blood spatters that would give him the result he desired. And then he "pulled the strings" to determine where they crossed. Using this methodology, Deaver concluded that there were three "points of origin out in space" (i.e., somewhere above the floor and the steps and away from the wall), rather than places where Kathleen's head might have struck the wall inside the stairwell. Since Kathleen Peterson's head had been struck by an object while it was "out in space," according to Deaver, it had to be murder. And that's how he testified at Michael's trial:

On the night I was at this scene, I gave Detective Holland a minimum
of four blows that occurred to the victim. The reason for that was that
I found three points of origin for impact. That means that the source
of blood, the back of the head, was struck three times. I add one to that
because there needs to be at least one blow that occurs to start bleeding.

One of the points of origin is nineteen inches up from step number
17, eight inches out from the east wall, and six inches out from the north
wall. The source of blood, the back of the head, is going to have to be
up, and be impacted in space, such that the blood spatters can go up the
walls and create the blood spatters that you see. . . .

He also testified that the scene in the stairwell was "not unlike"
other murder scenes he had investigated and was "not similar" to
the scenes of accidental falls he had investigated. Deaver's "expert"
testimony was central to the state's case.

But it was false. All the textbooks on bloodstain-pattern interpretation, and all the experts I consulted with, agreed. While it was
theoretically possible to determine an *area* of origin, it was scientifically impossible to determine a *point* of origin. The science was just
not that precise. The best one could do, under ideal circumstances,
would be to determine an *area* of approximately twelve by eighteen inches from where the lines intersected. That would have done
Deaver no good, since that area, even as he had calculated it, would
have included the steps and the walls. It would not have ruled out an
accident and established a murder. So instead, he got on the witness
stand and lied. He claimed the science allowed him to find a point
of origin. He stuck with that throughout the trial, claiming that the
textbooks I cross-examined him about and the testimony we offered
from our experts were just "wrong."

Deaver also conducted a series of so-called experiments designed
not to test any hypothesis using the scientific method, but rather to
prove that Michael Peterson's shorts had been "in close proximity to
a point of origin" and that the "wearer of [Michael Peterson's] shoes
and shorts was involved in impacting a source of blood, in this case

the victim. . . ." He delivered this testimony with an arrogant confidence and disdain for any contrary opinion.

Deaver's direct and cross-examination encompassed nearly a thousand pages of trial transcript. He was, by far, the most critical witness in the state's case against Michael. Without Deaver's testimony, there was no evidence that Kathleen's head wounds had been caused by a moving object, such as an alleged "missing blow poke," or that Michael Peterson was present in the stairway when Kathleen sustained the injuries to her scalp.

In their closing arguments, the prosecutors stressed repeatedly the importance of the blood-spatter evidence, Agent Deaver's opinions about that evidence, and his honesty and integrity. The state argued that for the jury to believe our defense experts, "you're just going to have to believe that Duane Deaver is just a liar." Deaver and the state's other witnesses were "tried and true. Tried and true. Because they work for us. . . . For our state." Based on his testimony, and despite our best efforts to impeach that testimony, Michael Peterson was convicted of first-degree murder and sentenced to life in prison without parole.

This was, without a doubt, the lowest point in my career. An innocent man I represented had just been put away for life. Intellectually, I could not bring myself to understand how any jury would not have experienced reasonable doubts about Michael's guilt based on the evidence presented at trial, especially after the alleged murder weapon had been found and ruled out as the source of Kathleen's injuries. The adverse verdict made me question everything I thought I knew; it made me rethink everything that I'd thought I understood about the criminal justice system. It shook me down to my foundations. Emotionally, I felt such incredible sadness and disappointment for Michael and his family, who had been through so much. I felt a deep sense of frustration that something so fundamentally unjust had happened—another tragedy, another loss, for the Peterson family—and that I was not able to prevent it. I was determined to correct the injustice if I possibly could. It would come in time.

In 2009, while Michael was in prison, things started to unravel for Agent Deaver. In October of that year, a U.S. District Court judge, in a habeas corpus proceeding involving a criminal case from 1993, concluded that Deaver had given misleading testimony in a murder trial regarding a phantom blood spot on a defendant's boot. The court found that Deaver "falsely portrayed to the jury that he conducted a test for blood that indicated blood . . . was on [the defendant's] boot," and that Deaver had presented "misleading evidence about the testing done on [the defendant's] boots being conclusive for the presence of blood." In that case, the defendant, George Earl Goode Jr., was being tried on two counts of first-degree murder. He claimed that he had witnessed the murders of Leon and Margaret Batten but had not committed them or participated in the killings.

A fundamental issue in the case was whether Goode had blood on his clothing and his boots. One of the victims had twenty-three stab wounds. The other victim had also been stabbed multiple times. If no blood spatter appeared on Goode's clothing or boots, it would be highly exculpatory and would support his account that he was not involved in the murders. Duane Deaver was called as a witness for the state at Goode's trial. He testified that although there was no *visible* blood on Goode's clothes or boots, a chemical test performed on one of Goode's boots revealed the presence of an "invisible blood stain."

The test he performed on the boot, however, was a preliminary chemical test that indicated only the *possibility* of blood being present. Deaver later claimed he had not performed the subsequent test that would have confirmed that the substance was in fact blood—or that it wasn't—although this was hard to believe. To not perform the confirmatory test violated the lab's protocols.

Deaver's testimony at trial allowed the jury to conclude that his test had *conclusively* determined there was blood on the boot. George Earl Goode Jr. was convicted and sentenced to death. The federal court that heard Goode's habeas petition determined that Deaver's misleading testimony did not likely change the outcome of the trial and therefore upheld his conviction, but it vacated his death sentence on other grounds. At the time, the Court had no reason to suspect that Deaver might not actually have run any tests at all, that his conclusion from the preliminary test might have been fabricated, or, even worse, that the confirmatory test result had been negative and was concealed altogether.

In 2010, a series of investigative articles into the SBI Bloodstain Pattern Analysis Unit—which was headed by Deaver—found that the unit operated without any written policies from 1988 until October 2009. The North Carolina attorney general suspended the entire unit in August 2010, noting that he was "concerned about the potential influence *of prosecutors* on the opinions of some SBI agents regarding this science." That same year, Deaver tried to get another SBI agent to testify untruthfully in the case of *State v. Gregory Taylor* that a stain depicted in a photograph was blood. Deaver repeatedly stated to the other agent that the defendant, Greg Taylor, was guilty. He subsequently provided "intentionally misleading" testimony to the North Carolina Innocence Inquiry Commission about the case, according to a contempt motion filed by the Commission against Deaver.

An independent review commissioned by the North Carolina Department of Justice and conducted by two former high-ranking officials of the FBI reported that in a sampling of files assigned to Agent Deaver from 1988 through 1993, as many as thirty-four reports prepared by Deaver that showed "indications of blood" from presumptive testing (as in the Goode case) *failed to mention that there were negative confirmatory tests.* There were five cases in which Deaver's conclusions were *completely inconsistent* with the results reflected in the internal lab notes. One of these cases involved a defendant who was executed.

Finally, a video surfaced in a murder case in which a defendant was charged with fatally slashing his wife's throat with a pocketknife. He told the police his wife attacked him first, gouging him in the thigh with a seven-foot spear—twice—causing a deep wound and barely missing his femoral artery. He claimed that the fatal wound inflicted upon his wife was an act of self-defense. The evidence from the scene included an unusual V-shaped blood stain on the defendant's shirt.

The prosecution's theory was that the defendant, a dentist from Kernersville, North Carolina, had killed his wife, and then faked the injury to his thigh so he could claim the killing was in self-defense. They posited that after the defendant had cut his wife's throat, he wiped the blade on his shirt and then proceeded to run an eighteen-inch blade from a spear through his own leg two separate times. Agent Deaver was called upon to help prove the state's theory. He wanted to show that the V-shaped pattern was the result of the defendant wiping the bloody blade on his shirt, and he set about to achieve this result.

Deaver attempted to re-create the V-shaped blood pattern by having the other agent wipe a "bloody" blade (with just the right amount of blood on it) across a shirt the agent was wearing in a way that was likely to reproduce the pattern. Thankfully, the "experiment" was videotaped. When Deaver and the other agent achieved the pattern they were looking for, Deaver announced, "Oh, even better, holy cow, that was a good one." Deaver then said, "Beautiful, that's a wrap, baby," as if he was creating a scene for a movie. It was the same kind of bogus "experiment" he had performed in Michael Peterson's case, but the videos we had received had no sound.

All of Deaver's misconduct that had come to light called into question his testimony in the previously discussed Goode case, as well as every other case in which Deaver testified for the state, including the Michael Peterson case.

After eight years of carrying the burden of Michael's conviction, I saw the opportunity to correct the forensic abuse that Deaver had perpetrated in Michael's case. I contacted Michael, and we agreed that I would file a motion to vacate his conviction based on Deaver's false testimony. He couldn't pay me anything, but that wasn't the point. We sought and obtained a court order requiring the SBI to produce all its files reflecting any work done by Deaver with regard to bloodstain-pattern analysis from 1988 to 2003. What we received pursuant to that court order was shocking. Deaver's perjury went well beyond the fake science and made-up experiments.

He testified under oath in Michael Peterson's trial that he'd been involved in five hundred cases involving bloodstains. The real number was fifty-four. He testified that he'd written two hundred reports involving bloodstain-pattern analysis. The real number was thirty-six. He had been to the scene of a potential crime only seventeen times in his entire career, and in only nine of those cases did he prepare a report about the bloodstains. Before being called to the Peterson home on December 9, 2001, Deaver had not conducted any bloodstain-pattern analysis for more than four years.

He testified in Michael's trial that he had been to a crime scene to do bloodstain-pattern analysis in fifteen cases in which falls were involved. It turned out that he had *never* been to a scene to conduct a bloodstain-pattern analysis to determine whether an accidental fall or an assault had occurred.

Deaver testified that he "typically" performed experiments for the purpose of analyzing bloodstain patterns at crime scenes. It turned out that the last "experiment" performed by Deaver prior to the Peterson case was in 1991, *ten years prior*. All told, he'd conducted experiments in only *three* cases, and one of them involved smashing pumpkins with a two-by-four to determine if a person present at the scene of a beating would have gotten blood on his clothing.

What I knew during Michael Peterson's trial, and what I tried to prove in court, was that Deaver's "experiments" were bogus and not based on real science. I argued at the time that it was scientifically impossible to determine precise and specific points of origin in three-dimensional space on the basis of bloodstain-pattern analysis. I also argued that it wasn't scientifically possible to determine whether an impact on a stairstep was due to an accidental fall or an intentional act, and that Deaver's testimony that the bloodstains on the steps were inconsistent with a fall was not scientifically valid or within the minimally acceptable standards in the field of bloodstain-pattern analysis.

The same was true of Deaver's conclusion that the shoes and shorts worn by Michael Peterson were in close proximity to an impact inflicted on Kathleen. From a scientific point of view, this was all nonsense. I objected and tried to keep the evidence out, but the trial judge, Orlando Hudson, disagreed. It all came in to be considered by the jury.

It was apparent to me during the trial, and conclusively established after the trial with all the new evidence that came out about Duane Deaver, that he did what needed to be done for the investigators and for the prosecutors who sought his so-called expertise. He was all too willing to set aside any scientific principles he knew, and his ethical responsibilities, in order to help ensure a conviction.

In 2012, Judge Hudson heard our new evidence regarding the multiple falsehoods that formed the basis of Deaver's testimony at trial. After a hearing that spanned several days, Judge Hudson determined that Deaver "deliberately and intentionally misled this Court at Mr. Peterson's trial about the scientific basis and acceptability of his opinions, methods and experiments." He also found that Deaver "exhibited a pattern of bias in favor of the State and against criminal defendants that was repeated over the course of twenty years" and that he had "committed perjury." Finally, Judge Hudson found that each of Deaver's violations "individually and cumulatively constitutes a violation of the United States Constitution that warrants that the conviction of Mr. Peterson be vacated and a new trial granted." Just writing this sends a chill up my spine, just as it did when I first heard the judge say those words in open court.

This moment was one of the happiest and most rewarding of my professional career. Michael was released from prison on bond, while the state decided whether to retry him. Although it took another four years to finally put the case to rest, Michael was home, and Deaver's abuse of power had been exposed. The system had not worked, as the prosecutor later claimed, but some measure of justice had finally been achieved—much too late, but better than never. Deaver was never prosecuted for his perjury.

27

LABORATORY SCANDALS

The abuse of science by "forensic experts" more interested in achieving a particular result than in practicing real science has occurred all over the country. In Massachusetts, a chemist named Annie Dookhan worked in the state crime lab. She was indicted in 2012 for perjury, tampering with evidence, forgery, and a host of other charges relating to her handling of drug evidence in criminal cases in that state. Taking a page out of Duane Deaver's book, she lied in court about her experience and credentials when testifying for the state, and she reported positive results on samples that had never been tested. Her fraudulent acts may have tainted as many as thirty-four *thousand* cases in Massachusetts, causing prosecutors to revisit the cases and dismiss charges against countless criminal defendants. Reverberations from Dookhan's wrongdoing are still being felt. In November 2020, a county prosecutor asked the court to vacate defendants' sentences in an additional 108 cases due to what she described as Dookhan's "egregious and reprehensible government misconduct." What's important here is not just the inconvenience to the prosecutors and courts that have had to clean up this mess. It's that hundreds, if not thousands, of individuals were wrongfully convicted based on fabricated forensic evidence. That is completely inexcusable.

A number of other states, including Texas, New Jersey, Oregon, North Carolina, and West Virginia, to name a few, have had their own crime-lab scandals. One of the best known involved a forensic expert named Fred Zain. It began with the arrest of Glen Dale Woodall.

On January 22, 1987, at 1:15 p.m., a man with his face hidden behind a ski mask abducted a woman from the Huntington Mall parking lot in Barboursville, West Virginia. He forced her into the passenger seat of her car and drove away from the mall. While threatening to kill her, he demanded that she keep her eyes closed as he drove through the rural county. Using a knife, he cut at her clothes. He pulled down her skirt and slashed at her underwear. At an unknown location, he brought the car to a stop and then repeatedly raped and physically abused the woman. He then pushed her out of the car and left her standing on the side of the road. The police had no reliable leads and were not able to identify a suspect or make an arrest.

On February 16, 1987, the man struck again, abducting another woman from the same mall parking lot. The modus operandi was the same as the first attack. He told the victim to close her eyes and informed her that "if you know who I am, or if you see me, I'll kill you." This time, he bound the victim's hands and covered her eyes with tape. He then drove to an unknown location and repeatedly raped her. After close to an hour, he taped her hands to the gearshift and left her alone in the car. When she finally opened her eyes, he was gone. She went directly to the hospital.

The police arrested Glen Dale Woodall for the crimes. He was twenty-nine years old on the date of his arrest, and was employed as the groundskeeper at a cemetery near the mall parking lot where the abductions occurred. The police stopped him on a bridge over the Ohio River as he appeared to be leaving the state. Glen was charged with first-degree sexual assault, kidnapping, and aggravated robbery, and faced multiple life sentences if convicted. He claimed he had nothing to do with the assaults and came forward with multiple alibi witnesses who averred that he was accounted for at the time the crimes were committed.

Still, there was some evidence that he was the assailant, albeit tenuous. The second victim believed Glen's voice matched that of her attacker. Glen had a "distinctive smell," which both victims recognized from the attack. Glen was not circumcised, which matched accounts given by the victims. Also, the second victim believed Glen's boots and jacket were similar to those worn by the attacker.

More significantly, however, the state crime lab claimed to have compelling evidence of Glen's guilt. Semen samples had been recovered from the victims, and serology tests showed it was consistent with Glen's blood type. This was before the days of readily available DNA testing, so the serology tests were arguably the best tests available. Strikingly, hair found in one victim's car matched Glen's beard hair, according to the lab.

The case went to trial, and Glen testified on his own behalf that he was innocent. The jury didn't believe his account, and he was convicted and sentenced to two life sentences, with a range of 203 to 335 years.

The critical state's witness was Fred Zain. He was, we now know, strongly biased in favor of the prosecution in Glen's case. This was problematic, because Zain was a forensic scientist working at the state crime lab in West Virginia. It was his responsibility to run blood tests and hair comparisons for the state. As a scientist whose job it was to examine evidence in criminal cases, he had an ethical and professional obligation to examine the evidence scientifically and impartially, and to do so without trying to achieve a particular result. In time, it would be clear that Zain did just the opposite, and he did it over and over again.

Zain worked for the crime lab from approximately 1979 until 1989. For part of this time, he was the lab's chief serologist. He was involved in more than 130 criminal cases, and his lab work and analyses contributed to dozens of convictions, including Glen's. The police and prosecutors liked having Zain perform their forensic examinations because he so frequently found incriminating evidence that could be used in prosecutions. He had a way of finding incriminating evidence in places where other forensic experts could not.

Zain left the West Virginia state crime lab in 1989 and found a similar job in a Texas crime lab. He was sorely missed by some police and prosecutors in West Virginia. After having evidence tested in their own state lab and being dissatisfied with the results, some West Virginia law enforcement officers would send evidence to Zain to be retested, believing him more likely to reach the desired results, whatever their accuracy.

One letter from a detective to Zain following his departure for the Texas crime lab reads as follows:

> Mr. Zain:
> This is the carpet that we discussed. . . . The W.Va. State Police Lab was unable to show any evidence of sperm or blood being present on it.
>
> The suspect was arrested for 1st Degree Sexual Abuse on a 5-year-old female. Any evidence you can find pertaining to this crime will greatly increase our chances of conviction.

True to form, Zain examined the carpet and was able to find evidence of semen the West Virginia crime lab had not found. It's reminiscent of Duane Deaver finding evidence of an "invisible blood stain" on a defendant's boot.

In Glen's case, Zain determined that Glen's blood type was consistent with the semen taken from the victims and that traits found in Glen's blood would be found in only six out of ten thousand men in West Virginia. At trial he went even further, testifying that "the assailant's blood types . . . were *identical* to Mr. Woodall's." Zain also concluded it was "highly unlikely" that the hair found in one of the victim's cars came from anyone other than Glen.

It was surprising, therefore, after his trial had concluded, when Glen was finally able to obtain a comparison of his DNA with semen taken from the victims, and the tests conclusively showed that Glen was not the source of the semen. Furthermore, it was discovered that the hair that Zain had testified had come from Glen's beard was in fact a pubic hair that had not come from Glen at all. Zain was aware that the hair was a pubic hair and not a facial hair, and he had written as much into his original report, but he later falsified the report to implicate Glen. In 1992, on the basis of the DNA test, Glen's conviction was overturned by the West Virginia Supreme Court.

Glen's case prompted an audit of Zain's lab work and testimony. The audit, which was overseen by a notable judge, found Zain responsible for an ongoing pattern of misconduct, all of which was deliberately geared toward implicating criminal defendants. The report concluded that "as a matter of law, any testimonial or documentary evidence offered by Zain at any time in any criminal prosecution should be deemed *invalid, unreliable, and inadmissible* in determining whether to award a new trial in any subsequent habeas corpus proceeding." The Supreme Court of West Virginia, when confronted with Zain's misdeeds, wrote: "The matters brought before this court [regarding Fred Zain] . . . are shocking and represent egregious violations of the right of a defendant to a fair trial. They stain our judicial system and mock the ideal of justice under law."

In light of Zain's pervasive misconduct, it was necessary for the state to review all the cases in which Zain had provided analysis and testimony. The same became true for Zain's work in Texas, which may have contributed to as many as 180 questionable convictions. Zain's employment with the lab in Texas was terminated in 1993, whereafter he faced criminal charges stemming from his misconduct in West Virginia. He died of liver cancer in 2002 still facing two criminal trials against him.

In 2011, Donald Eugene Good, on the basis of a DNA comparison, was convicted of the two 1987 Huntington Mall rapes for which Glen Dale Woodall had been convicted, and for which he served five years in prison. At the time of Good's trial, he was serving a life sentence for a murder he committed in 1992, five years after the Huntington Mall rapes. A sample of Good's DNA was uploaded to the national DNA database in 2009. After receiving a tip from a retired state trooper, prosecutors submitted DNA left by the perpetrator in the two Huntington Mall rapes for comparison with Good's DNA, and there was a match. Good's fingerprint impressions also matched those found on a victim's driver's license from the 1987 attacks. He was given two life sentences in addition to the life sentence he was already serving. Once again, a wrongful conviction had resulted in the true perpetrator being free to rape and murder other victims. This is the too-often-overlooked consequence that results from the abuses of power described in this book. The innocent go to prison, while the guilty go free. A greater perversion of justice is hard to imagine.

28

BEYOND THE LIMITS OF SCIENCE

Duane Deaver and Fred Zain are examples of so-called experts who intentionally fabricated incriminating forensic evidence out of whole cloth. They didn't just exceed the limits of science; they abused their position and power as experts to turn science into an instrument of injustice. While the Deavers and Zains of the world are the exception, there is a more pervasive, if less intentional, abuse of forensic science that occurs every day in courtrooms across America.

We know this to be true based on the hundreds of DNA exonerations that have occurred in recent decades. *More than four out of ten of these exonerations (43 percent) arose out of cases in which there was other forensic evidence of alleged guilt that turned out to be wrong.* These exonerations and the erroneous convictions that preceded them generally involved pattern-based forensic sciences, such as fingerprints, bite marks, tool marks, hair comparisons, ballistics, and others, all of which inherently involve a significant subjective component—the visual comparison of patterns.

For example, before DNA technology took center stage as a forensic tool, fingerprints were considered the gold standard of forensics. If the police discovered a fingerprint belonging to the suspect at the scene of a crime, and preferably on the murder weapon, it was case closed. It was common knowledge that no two fingerprints, like no two snowflakes, were ever identical. It was just a matter of finding enough points of similarity to call a match. Of course, different agencies used differing numbers of such points to determine a match, which should have been a clue of the extent to which the "science" was subjective. Still, prosecutors routinely used fingerprint evidence, judges routinely allowed such evidence, and juries routinely convicted based on such evidence. Then came the Madrid train bombing case.

On March 11, 2004, terrorists detonated bombs on four commuter trains in Madrid, killing nearly two hundred people. Spanish authorities found a fingerprint on a bag of detonators, and a digital image of the fingerprint, labeled as "LFP 17," was sent to the FBI for analysis.

The FBI ran the image of LFP 17 through its fingerprint database, known as the Integrated Automated Fingerprint Identification System (IAFIS). This produced a list of twenty potential matches, or "candidate prints." One of the candidate prints belonged to Brandon Mayfield, an Oregon attorney. An experienced FBI fingerprint examiner then did a side-by-side comparison of the points of similarity between LFP 17 and the twenty candidate prints, and determined that Brandon Mayfield was the source of LFP 17. The first examiner's conclusion was verified by a second FBI fingerprint analyst, and then confirmed by the chief of the FBI's fingerprint unit. There was no doubt that Mayfield was the source of the print found on the bag of detonators in Madrid.

The FBI launched an investigation into Mayfield and learned that he was Muslim, had married an Egyptian immigrant, and had once represented a convicted terrorist in court on a domestic matter. Although Mayfield had no criminal history, no apparent ties to any terrorist organization, and had never been to Spain, the FBI searched his home and his law office and investigated every aspect of his life. On May 6, 2004, Mayfield was arrested and detained. He was brought into court, where he denied that he had been involved in the Madrid terror attack. But he had no explanation for how his fingerprint might possibly have found its way to Spain on a bag of detonators. It appeared to be powerful evidence that, at the least, he was part of a terrorist conspiracy.

The Spanish authorities, however, had conducted their own comparison of LFP 17 and Mayfield's fingerprint and concluded that comparison of the two prints was "negative." There were too many points of "dissimilarity."

The U.S. court appointed a renowned fingerprint expert not associated with the FBI to review LFP 17 and Mayfield's fingerprint. He too concluded that the LFP 17 and Mayfield's print were a match. Yet *on the same day*, May 19, 2004, the Spanish National Police notified the FBI that the source of the print was not Mayfield, but rather an Algerian named Ouhnane Daoud. Mayfield was subsequently absolved and released. He was lucky. It could have turned out quite differently, but for the work of the Spanish fingerprint examiners.

Not just one FBI fingerprint expert, but *three*, had concluded that Mayfield was the source of LFP 17. Then, another fingerprint expert not associated with the FBI reached the same conclusion—but they were all dead wrong. How could this have happened?

The Office of the FBI Inspector General initiated an investigation to answer this question. The investigation found that the FBI examiners fell prey to "circular reasoning" in reaching their conclusion: after finding several points of "unusual similarity" between LFP 17 and Mayfield's print, the FBI examiners began to "see" other points of similarity between the two prints that didn't exist. As stated in the inspector general's report, the FBI experts "began to 'find' additional features of LFP 17 that were not really there. . . . As a result, murky or ambiguous details in LFP 17 were erroneously identified as points of similarity with Mayfield's prints." This is another way of saying that once the first examiner had erred, the rest fell victim to confirmation bias, which caused them to interpret the evidence consistently with their colleague—that Mayfield was the source of the print.

The initial set of examiners who concluded that Mayfield was the source of the print were not aware that he was Muslim, so this had no bearing on the initial erroneous conclusions. But the FBI's subsequent knowledge of Mayfield's religion and his marriage to an immigrant from Egypt contributed to the FBI's failure to adequately and correctly *reexamine* their conclusions even after the Spanish authorities notified the FBI that the FBI's print analysis was wrong.

There are several morals to this story. The first is that even the best-trained and most experienced forensic experts can make mistakes when it comes to pattern-based testimony. The second is that the same experts can easily succumb to psychological biases that interfere with and cloud their interpretations of pattern-based evidence. If three expert fingerprint examiners from the FBI and one court-appointed expert can each make serious errors regarding a fingerprint match in a case of international importance, imagine how often it happens when the fingerprint examinations are done by local law enforcement when there is pressure on them to provide forensic support for the prosecution of the perpetrator identified by a fellow law enforcement officer. Ironically, and most dangerously, the pressure is greatest when the other evidence of guilt is weakest.

Recognizing the importance of scientific advancements such as DNA technology in the world of criminology, Congress authorized the National Academy of Sciences (NAS) in 2006 to conduct a study on the various forensic sciences used in the criminal justice system.* The disciplines examined by the NAS were fingerprint examinations (friction ridge analysis), firearms and ballistics examinations,

---

* *Strengthening Forensic Science in the United States: A Path Forward.* National Research Council. © 2009, National Academy of Sciences.

toolmarks, bite-mark analysis (forensic odontology), impressions (tires, footwear), bloodstain-pattern analysis, handwriting analysis, hair-comparison analysis, DNA analysis, chemicals and toxicology (drugs), materials and fibers comparison and analysis, fluids analysis, serology, and fire and explosive analysis.

As you would expect, the NAS study found DNA analysis to be based on strong scientific principles and highly reliable. Many other forensic disciplines, notably fingerprint, hair, bloodstain, toolmark and bite-mark analyses, among others, were found to be much less reliable. Because these latter disciplines are not laboratory-based, but instead rely largely on the examiner's subjective visual interpretation and comparison of patterns between two specimens (i.e., do the characteristics of this fingerprint match the characteristics of the other; do the attributes of this hair correspond to the attributes of the other), they are subject to human judgment, and hence, to error.

Furthermore, the pattern-based disciplines lack standard protocols among practitioners for conducting the visual examinations, meaning that the outcomes of individual examiners cannot be reliably reproduced by other examiners. Another deficiency with these disciplines is that they have no population studies on which to rely—such as what percentage of people have a particular type of hair—making it impossible to say whether a specimen taken from the suspect truly "matches" evidence from the crime scene, or even what the probability is for a match. In the words of the NAS study, "The simple reality is that the interpretation of forensic evidence is not always based on scientific studies to determine its validity. This is a serious problem."

Subjective, visual forensic disciplines are at great risk of having bias influence the expert's observation and judgments, as happened in the Madrid bombing case. It is not uncommon for specimens to be sent to a crime lab with an instruction that encourages the lab technician to reach a particular result, sometimes explicitly and sometimes implicitly. Police have been known to make specific requests to the crime lab to implicate the suspect in the crime, such as, "Need to place the suspect in the victim's home," or "Any evidence you can find pertaining to this crime will greatly increase our chances of conviction," as in the case of Mr. Zain. But even where there is no such explicit request, if the form sent to the lab contains the name of a particular suspect, it would be clear to the examiner that the police are trying to prove that suspect to be the perpetrator. That by itself creates pressure for the lab to "deliver" the hoped-for result.

The NAS study concluded that with the exception of DNA testing and analysis, "no forensic method has been rigorously shown to have the capacity to consistently, and with a high degree of certainty, demonstrate a connection between evidence and a specific individual or source." This is a shocking conclusion. What this means is that for many forensic practices that are commonly used to convict criminal defendants, there is no sound scientific basis for saying that a particular individual was the person who "matched" the evidence from the crime scene, to the exclusion of all others. To make such a judgment with respect to pattern-based forensic disciplines simply exceeds the limits of science, and no data set has been compiled to allow such disciplines to make such pronouncements. Yet these forensic disciplines have been used myriad times in every jurisdiction to prove countless defendants guilty.

Microscopic hair comparison evidence, a pattern-based forensic technique that has been used in the prosecution of thousands of criminal defendants, provides a startling illustration of the problem. Hair-comparison evidence has been used in the American criminal justice system since the 1930s. Until about a decade ago, it was touted by its many practitioners to be roughly equivalent in reliability to other forensic criminal sciences, such as fingerprint examination. It was used in the Tim Bridges case in Charlotte to convict Tim on the grounds that two hairs found at the crime scene "matched" hair samples taken from Tim.

But are hairs unique to different individuals? Do they have special characteristics that can be microscopically examined, identified, and compared, based on established standards and population studies, such that the hair from one head can be "matched" to hair from another head? In 2012, three cases from Washington, D.C., raised questions about the limits of microscopic hair analysis, leading to a nationwide review of this forensic technique. This, in turn, again showed the significant limitations of pattern-based expert testimony.

In 1978, Santae A. Tribble, who was just seventeen years old, was accused of killing John McCormick, a sixty-three-year-old taxi driver. A police informant implicated Tribble in the murder, although her statements to the police were inconsistent. Another informant, who was under investigation for a separate crime, told the police that Tribble admitted to being involved in the murder.

John McCormick's wife was able to get a brief look at the attacker, and she told the police he was wearing a stocking over his head. A police dog found a stocking nearby, and an examination of the stocking found thirteen hairs in or on the netting. Of these thirteen hairs, an experienced FBI hair examiner concluded, after examining the hairs under a microscope, that one of the hairs belonged to Tribble. The prosecution took this information and argued to the jury that the chances of the hair belonging to anyone other than Tribble were *one in ten million*. The jury relied heavily on this information in convicting Tribble, and he was sentenced to twenty years to life.

Except it wasn't Tribble's hair on the stocking. In January 2012, Tribble's attorney persuaded a court to require DNA testing of the hairs from the stocking, including the hair that the FBI expert claimed came from Tribble. Luckily the hair contained enough of its root to test for DNA, and the DNA test conclusively established that the hair had *not* come from Tribble. The test also revealed that one of the hairs used in the FBI analysis was in fact a dog hair, and not a human hair at all. Tribble's sentence was vacated, and the charges against him were dismissed in 2012. In all, Tribble spent twenty-three years in prison based on the testimony that well exceeded the limits of science.

Following Tribble's case and two more like it in which criminal defendants who were convicted on the basis of microscopic hair analysis were later proven to be innocent through DNA testing, the FBI and the Department of Justice began a thorough review of cases in which FBI hair analysis testimony had contributed to a conviction. It was an extraordinary admission that the testimony of experts in microscopic hair comparison analysis might have been wrong and their conclusions scientifically unsupportable in important respects.

As of June 2018, the most recent date for which there is publicly available data, the FBI's review of cases involving hair-comparison evidence occurring prior to the year 2000 had found errors in a whopping 450 out of 484 cases (93 percent) in which an FBI expert had given testimony on hair comparison, with the review ongoing. Errors were found in the reports and testimony of thirty-one out of the thirty-five FBI hair examiners whose work was reviewed. This included more than thirty cases in which defendants were sentenced to death, and of those, fourteen defendants had already been executed or had died in prison. And these were the proverbial cream of the crop, forensic experts who had trained many hundreds of other hair examiners working for various state and local law enforcement agencies across the country.

Peter Neufeld, the co-founder and co-director of the Innocence Project, observed that the review of FBI hair-comparison techniques "confirm[ed] that FBI microscopic hair analysts committed widespread, systematic error, grossly exaggerating the significance of their data under oath with the consequence of unfairly bolstering the prosecutions' case." The key to what Neufeld is saying here is that the hair-comparison experts *exaggerated the significance of their data.* Forensic hair examination may, in the proper circumstance, be a valuable tool used to aid the police in *excluding* possible suspects— because such examinations can often determine that a hair from a crime scene could *not* have come from a particular suspect in cases where the hairs are too dissimilar.

The problem comes when microscopic hair analysis, which is at bottom based on the expert's subjective comparison of the similarity of two hairs under a microscope, is used to establish the statistical chances that the hair is a "match" to a particular suspect. The science is not sufficiently precise to be able to say that the chances of the hair belonging to anyone other than the suspect is "one in a million," as the FBI expert testified in the Tribble case, or any lesser probability. There is no science, and no studies, that back up such a statistical analysis. There is no database of hairs that can be relied upon by the hair-comparison expert to support such claims. The best a hair analyst can say is that the hair from the suspect has similar characteristics to hair found at the scene of the crime. That's it. In the Tribble case, the testimony well exceeded the limits of science and greatly overstated the significance of the hair analysis to the jury.

So did the testimony in Tim Bridges case, where the state's forensic hair-comparison analyst, Linus Whitlock, claimed that the hair found at the scene belonged to Tim and that the odds were *a thousand to one* that it came from anyone but him. Whitlock had been trained by the FBI; he had attended their two-week hair analysis training program. He was touted to the jury as having valuable expertise in this forensic "science." We now know that his testimony, and the statistical probability offered by Whitlock, simply had no basis in science. He admitted at a deposition in Tim's civil suit that he had essentially "guessed" at this ratio based on a study he had read. There were no scientific studies, population studies, or learned treatises in existence at the time this testimony was offered that supported Whitlock's conclusion, and that continues to be the case today. We also know that Whitlock's testimony was not only unscientific, it was also entirely erroneous, as the DNA testing in Tim's case subsequently established.

It is difficult to avoid the conclusion that Whitlock's testimony—that Tim's hair matched two hairs found at the crime scene—stemmed from the fact that, consciously or unconsciously, he wanted to help his colleague, Detective Horner, solidify her weak case. That is precisely why pattern-based expert testimony is so dangerous and subject to abuse. For all pattern-based forensic disciplines, there is always a significant danger that the analysis will be influenced by confirmation bias. This has occurred even at the most advanced and well-funded crime labs, like the FBI. Imagine how often this happens with a local underfunded and overworked police lab, when the detective has a particular theory and just needs some forensic evidence to shore up an otherwise weak case. It's frightening to consider how many travesties of justice must have occurred over the years based on testimony that exceeded the limits of real science, and how many are yet to come.

29

I SHALL BE RELEASED

*I see my light come shining / From the west unto the east /
Any day now, any day now / I shall be released.*

—Bob Dylan, 1967

Now that we've seen how police and prosecutor error and misconduct can result in wrongful convictions, let's revisit the case of Ray Finch, who was accused of killing Shadow Holloman in 1976. Ray was tried and convicted of murder, and sentenced to death, during the high point of lawlessness and corruption in Wilson County, North Carolina, at a time when the sheriff's department had no regard, and no respect, for the rule of law. At a time when the sheriff's department was operated as a wide-ranging racketeering enterprise, and persons with interests in local gambling, prostitution, and narcotics trade paid the sheriff for protection and thrived without fear of prosecution. Abuses of power by police and prosecutors, like those described in this book, were commonplace and done with reckless impunity. We know all this because of a two-year investigation by the FBI that resulted in the trial and conviction of the elected sheriff on corruption charges.

Ray claimed all along that his arrest was related to the corruption, and that he was prosecuted while the real killer was protected in order to safeguard the all-encompassing lawlessness in the county that was padding so many wallets. This wasn't just a bare allegation with no substance. Ray backed it up with corroborative details and the names of dozens of witnesses who Ray believed would confirm his theory. When the new sheriff asked the SBI to investigate Ray's claims only three months after the federal corruption trials in Wilson County had concluded, it seemed all that happened was an official whitewash. The investigating agent, Special Agent Alan McMahan, did not interview *any* of the witnesses identified by Ray, and likewise did not interview the former sheriff or his chief deputy, the very men Ray claimed were responsible for his arrest, or Lester Floyd Jones, the one eyewitness in the case. Instead, Agent McMahan concluded summarily and inexplicably that Ray could not substantiate his allegations of corruption—despite the conviction of the former sheriff on corruption charges—and he closed his file on the matter, leaving Ray incarcerated with diminishing prospects for release. Ray was not provided with a copy of Agent McMahan's report and would not learn of its contents for decades to come.

Years and years passed with no hope for Ray. He was shuttled from one prison to another, as the events of that February in 1976 slipped into the past.

Then, in 2001, Ray sent a desperate letter to the Duke Law Innocence Project, a student-led volunteer organization devoted to identifying wrongful convictions and investigating claims of innocence. The Duke Law Innocence Project was brand-new when Ray made contact, and his case was the very first case undertaken by the organization. Led by Professors Jim Coleman and Theresa Newman, students and attorneys at Duke Law School took on Ray's cause and began their own investigation. The Duke Law Wrongful Convictions Clinic would soon also join the fight on Ray's behalf. They would leave no stone unturned.

Their first goal was to track down and obtain copies of files related to Ray's prosecution that should have been maintained by the Wilson County Sheriff's Department, the Wilson County district attorney's office, and the SBI—files that might contain evidence that could be used to demonstrate Ray's innocence. What they discovered was that most of the evidence related to Ray's case was either missing or had been destroyed. What little evidence that remained was kept just out of their reach.

During a 2003 meeting between an attorney from the Duke Wrongful Convictions Clinic and the assistant district attorney (ADA), for example, the ADA displayed an inch-thick investigative file that he claimed was related to Ray's case. However, he refused to turn it over, maintaining that it belonged to the SBI. When the Duke Wrongful Convictions Clinic approached the SBI for a copy of the file, they were allegedly told the SBI would not release any materials or evidence in its possession related to Ray because the SBI would not help the Wrongful Convictions Clinic establish that a law enforcement officer had engaged in misconduct. The SBI did reveal, though, that it had conducted an investigation into Ray's case in 1979—the one by Special Agent McMahan—but then withheld the McMahan report from the Wrongful Convictions Clinic. Until that point, neither Ray nor the Clinic was aware that Agent McMahan had been assigned by the SBI to conduct an investigation into his allegations of corruption in 1979, and they had no way to know what was contained within the report. All Ray could relay to the Wrongful Convictions Clinic was a vague recollection of being briefly interviewed by an investigator about twenty years earlier.

Without files from law enforcement, particularly for a case that is decades old, it is exceedingly difficult to challenge a conviction, let alone establish someone's innocence. Witnesses are typically hard to find, or deceased, and those witnesses who can be located often have a hard time remembering the events of so long ago. And as the Wrongful Convictions Clinic often found, in most cases the relevant evidence has simply vanished or has been concealed or destroyed. But the Clinic directors and students persevered in the face of these obstacles for more than a decade and were able to make some headway in Ray's case.

They were able to establish, for example, that Shadow Holloman's death was not the result of a *shotgun* blast at close range, but instead was the result of as many as three separate *gunshots* from at least two different weapons. This was a critical discovery. It completely undermined the testimony of the key eyewitness, Lester Floyd Jones.

A shotgun wound and a gunshot wound are two entirely different things. A shotgun fires a cartridge that ejects a number of small round metal pellets. A wound from a shotgun will characteristically show a *cluster* of small holes from the pellets striking the victim simultaneously in an array. A gunshot wound, on the other hand, is the result of a single bullet (or slug) entering the victim's body. There is a single hole where the bullet enters the body, and another one where it exits the body, if it does.

The state's case at trial proceeded on the theory that Shadow had been shot in the chest with a shotgun at close range. Chief Deputy Owens reported to the *Wilson Daily Times* in the early-morning hours after Shadow's death that the victim had died from a "sawed-off shotgun blast" to the chest, and thereafter the state's theory never changed. This conclusion was echoed by the autopsy report, which stated that Holloman had suffered an "acute *shotgun* wound of the right upper thorax," with the probable cause of death being a "*shotgun* wound of the thorax." At trial, Lester Floyd Jones testified that Ray pulled out a sawed-off shotgun from under his coat and shot Shadow at close range, and the state put on evidence of a shotgun shell that was allegedly found in Ray's car. Remarkably, this is not at all what had happened.

A careful reading of the remainder of the autopsy reveals that Shadow had two, and possibly three, separate entrance wounds, each from a single projectile, each on a different trajectory. One small entrance wound was found at the base of Shadow's throat, near his right collarbone. Another was high on his back, on his right shoulder, as if it had been fired from someone standing above him as he knelt. A third small wound from a projectile was found on his back, near his right shoulder blade. None of these were consistent with a shotgun blast. The autopsy report also described fresh abrasions on Shadow's knees, which may have resulted from Shadow being forced to his knees by an assailant. Right away you could see, if you wanted to, that this evidence painted an entirely different picture than the one described in court at Ray's trial by the eyewitness, Lester Floyd Jones.

The Wrongful Convictions Clinic tracked down the medical examiner who had prepared the autopsy. To his credit, he admitted, under oath, that his conclusion as to the cause of death was erroneous. In an affidavit, he wrote, "All of these references [in the autopsy] to 'shotgun wound' are erroneous; each should have said 'gunshot wound.' The wounds suffered by Mr. Holloman were not caused by a shotgun." One mystery is why he wrote what he did. The answer may be that Chief Deputy Owens attended the autopsy and influenced the findings.

Given that this new information cast serious doubt on the account of the one eyewitness, this alone should have been enough to call Ray's conviction strongly into question. The district attorney, however, refused to consider joining the Wrongful Conviction Clinic's efforts to vacate Ray's conviction and withheld photographic evidence pertaining to Ray's case from the Clinic.

In August 2008, a lawyer representing Ray pro bono contacted the SBI in another effort to obtain evidence related to Ray's case. The general counsel for the SBI claimed in response that he had "requested a search of the files of the SBI be conducted for *any evidence* collected during the initial investigation, presented at the trial of Mr. Finch *or* evidence related to this case uncovered during the subsequent investigation by the SBI," and that "the search failed to uncover any such items of evidence, including photographs, related to Mr. Finch's case." However, two record-keeping notes found later in the possession of the SBI established that the general counsel for the SBI had been given the agency's full laboratory files related to Ray's case in early 2003, the same year the Wrongful Conviction Clinic first contacted him, but this information was not turned over to Ray's attorneys in 2003, nor was it turned over in 2008 in response to this subsequent request.

It wasn't until September 13, 2011, *more than eight years after* the Wrongful Conviction Clinic's first request to the SBI, that the SBI finally produced a microfilm copy of its Ray Finch investigative file, including a copy of Agent McMahan's report from 1979.

In reviewing Agent McMahan's report, attorneys for the Clinic came across something absolutely stunning. As part of his investigation, Agent McMahan had been given access to the police file on Ray Finch assembled by the Wilson County Sheriff's Department—a file that was subsequently lost, destroyed, or hidden. According to McMahan's report, the police file showed that Lester Floyd Jones, the sole eyewitness, had identified *someone else* as being present in Holloman's store that night, someone involved in the robbery and murder of Shadow Holloman. Someone, that is, other than Ray. Someone wearing a checked shirt, the same description that Jones had given the state trooper immediately after the shooting. Jones had picked this other man out of a photographic lineup in front of Chief Deputy Owens two days after the in-person lineup conducted at the jail, but Owens had concealed it from everyone, including the prosecutor. He sat on this information all through Ray's trial, even as the prosecutor argued to the jury that Jones had only identified Ray. This was a bombshell. It meant that critical exculpatory evidence, evidence that had been concealed from Ray, proved there was much more to the story than the jury had been told.

It also turned out that a week after the murder, Jones confided to a friend, Bobby Taylor, that he wasn't as sure about the identification of Ray Finch as he let on. He said the light was bad in the back of the store and that he wasn't able to identify the shooter. He even asked

Taylor what Ray looked like and told Taylor that he (Jones) had recognized another man—not Ray—in the store that night. Taylor was interviewed by the Wrongful Conviction Clinic and signed an affidavit to this effect.

Other parts of Jones's story fell apart under scrutiny. Jones told the police and the jury at trial that Shadow had closed the store early that evening and that Jones and Shadow were standing out-side *in their coats* on the cold February night when three men came walking up out of the darkness. In fact, two pieces of evidence inside the store suggested otherwise. First, as shown in photographs taken immediately after the murder, some condiments served by Shadow with the hot dogs sold by the store had not been put away or refrig-erated for the night, but instead were left sitting out on the counter. Was this just an oversight by Shadow and Jones? Second, the same photographs showed Shadow's coat draped neatly around the back of his chair behind the cash register. Jones's explanation was that af-ter Shadow was shot and moments before his death, as his lungs were filling with blood, Shadow took off his coat and arranged it over the arms of his chair in this way. Further, in light of the medical findings that Shadow had bullet wounds not only near his right collarbone but also high on his back right shoulder and on his back, the coat should have shown at least one bullet hole, possibly two, and likely a great deal of blood. However, the coat was evidently pristine and was not even collected as evidence by the police.

Two and a half years passed before the SBI surrendered even more evidence favorable to Ray. In 2013, the SBI relinquished a bal-listics report prepared by the SBI's firearms laboratory comparing one of the projectiles taken from Shadow's body with a pellet taken from the shotgun shell allegedly found in Ray's car following the shooting. The ballistics report showed it was not possible, even for the experts at the SBI lab, to determine whether the projectile from Shadow's body matched the pellets from the shotgun shell. Yet the prosecutor at Ray's trial argued to the jury that the pellets matched, just by comparing them visually in court, and that the shotgun shell allegedly found in Ray's car was therefore critical evidence of his guilt. Like other exculpatory evidence in the case, the ballistics report had been concealed from Ray, his attorney, and the prosecutor at trial.

Finally, the Duke Clinic was able to obtain photographs of the three in-person lineups that Chief Deputy Owens conducted on the night of Shadow's murder. The photographs showed Ray wearing a three-quarter-length black coat in each lineup. He was the only person wearing a coat of any kind.

As I described in Chapter 17, Lester Floyd Jones, the only eyewitness, identified Ray in three sequential lineups, one held right after the other. This was the basis of Ray's conviction in 1976. It was *the* critical evidence for the state.

When Jones wrote out his statement for the State Trooper who first arrived at the scene, he provided scant descriptions of the three men in the store that night. He didn't describe the assailants' height, weight, skin tone, or facial features. He only described "3 Black Males," one with "a Stocking over his head," one wearing "a Black cap," the other wearing "a Tobogen." Separately, he gave the state trooper an additional detail omitted from his written statement: One of the men was wearing a "checked shirt."

But according to Chief Deputy Owens, Jones told him at some point before the lineup that the gunman had been wearing a three-quarter-length black coat—although we don't know whether this detail was reported before or after Ray was arrested wearing precisely that kind of coat, or who provided the detail. Regardless, Owens made sure to put Ray in the lineup wearing the long black coat, and he also made sure that no one else in the lineup was wearing a coat to further bolster the odds that Jones would identify Ray.

Armed with all this new evidence, the Duke Law Wrongful Convictions Clinic filed a motion with the Court in 2013 to have Ray's conviction overturned. The goal was to demonstrate to the Court

Ray Finch is pictured here fourth from the left in a three-quarter-length black coat. Charles Lewis appears on the far right of the photograph.

In this photograph, Ray is the third person from the right. Charles Lewis appears on the far left.

In this photograph, Ray is second from the left, his coat plainly visible. He has been made by Chief Deputy Tony Owens to wear a hat for purposes of the third lineup.

that Ray's conviction should be vacated on the basis of the newly discovered evidence, including the fact that the lineup procedure used by Chief Deputy Owens was unduly suggestive and therefore constitutionally improper as a result of the coat Owens had Ray wear.

I assisted the Wrongful Convictions Clinic in preparing for the 2013 hearing and was asked to do the key cross-examination of Owens and the direct examination of the lead FBI agent who had investigated Owens and Sheriff Pridgen all those years before.

At the hearing, Owens initially made a convincing witness. It was clear that he'd had lots of practice testifying with all his years in law enforcement. He had aged well, his black hair was now silver, and his shoes were polished. He spoke with confidence and an air of condescension. It was obvious he was intelligent. Even though the case had occurred more than thirty years prior, he professed a clear recollection of the details from so long ago and appeared to have retained a strong command of the facts. He made one very costly mistake, though. He assumed, without knowing, that no one else had evidence of what transpired with the lineups that long-ago night in 1976. He was wrong.

Owens took the stand, and I began questioning him in an open-ended manner about how he set up the three lineups. He responded this way, referring to Ray's coat as a "pea coat":

> *We took the pea coat that Ray Finch was wearing and toboggan off of him and put it on another inmate. . . . And we set the lineup according to that. We brought in the witness, Lester Jones, and Lester immediately identified Ray Finch. . . . Even though he was not wearing the pea coat nor the cap or the toboggan. . . .*
>
> *We had him removed, Mr. Jones, changed everybody around, changed clothing again. . . . Took the jacket from the one that had it on, had some change clothes entirely with each other and had Mr. Jones brought back in and he once again identified Ray.*

I asked, "And was Ray wearing the jacket at that point?" Owens responded, "No." I asked, "Neither time?" Owens replied, "Neither time." He was going out of his way to make the point that Ray *wasn't* wearing the long black coat in the lineups. This made it immediately obvious that Owens recognized exactly what was at stake—the fundamental fairness of the lineups—and also that he was lying about not having Ray wear the coat in each lineup. I had to pin him down so that he couldn't backtrack on his testimony later, so I asked him this key question, a veritable softball. He swung at it and probably thought he had hit it out of the park:

Q. And why didn't you have Mr. Finch wearing the coat that the witness said he was wearing?
A. Well . . . if a man recognizes you, he recognizes you by your facial features, not what you got on. *Ray Finch didn't have that coat on.* The man identified him without the coat on. . . . *If the coat had been on him that would not have, in my opinion, been a fair lineup for Ray Finch.* So, therefore, I had the coat removed.

His delivery was convincing and assured. If the Duke Law Wrongful Convictions Clinic hadn't tracked down photographs of the lineups from that night, or if they had been destroyed along with much of the rest of the evidence in Ray's case, Owens's testimony might have carried the day. It would have been impossible to contradict.

But then I had the sort of "Perry Mason moment" all criminal defense lawyers dream about. I opened a folder on the counsel table and brought out the photographs of all three lineups. I showed them one by one to Owens. Each photograph showed Ray in the long black coat. The first photograph, State's Exhibit 1, was a picture of the first lineup.

Q. State's Exhibit Number 1, do you see that down there?
A. Yes.
Q. And Ray Finch is right in the middle there, right?
A. Correct.
Q. What's he wearing?

Owens appeared to be quite taken aback. After a moment, he composed himself, and our exchange continued:

A. He's wearing a black, appears to be leather coat.
Q. Three-quarter length?
A. Yes.
Q. And is anybody else wearing the coat in that photo?
A. No.
Q. Well, I thought you just testified that it wouldn't have been fair to Mr. Finch to have him there with a coat on.
A. I did.
Q. Well, then why did you do it?
A. I didn't think I did.
Q. I know you didn't think you did. But now we know you did, right?
A. Well, that's what these pictures show.

Q. So my question is, sir, if you knew it wasn't fair to have Finch there in a lineup with his coat on, why did you put him in the lineup with his coat on?
A. Well, I have no idea.

He was dead in the water, and he knew it. A faint look of disillusionment appeared in his eyes and never left for the remainder of the time he was on the stand.

I moved on to the photograph of the second lineup. Owens didn't even wait for me to ask the question.

Q. Let's take a look at State's Exhibit Number 2.
A. He's still got it on there. . . .
Q. Everybody else is still wearing the same clothes, right? You didn't switch any clothes around in that lineup. You just switched where people were in the lineup, right?
A. Okay, yeah. . . .
Q. And Mr. Finch is still wearing that jacket, right?
A. Yes, he is.
Q. And if it was unfair the first time, it was even more unfair the second time, wasn't it?
A. Well, not more unfair, no.
Q. Just unfair?
A. Just unfair.
Q. And now let's go to State's Exhibit Number 3. . . . He's still wearing the three-quarter-length coat; right?
A. Right.
Q. And not a single other person in any of these photo lineups, in any of these lineups . . . was wearing a black or dark three-quarter-length coat, right?
A. That's right.
Q. And it was still unfair the third time, right?
A. Yeah.

I had no further questions. Owens just sat there. He had admitted, under oath, that he'd had Ray wear the long black coat for all three lineups, that it was unfair to Ray to do so, and that he had known it was unfair. This was powerful evidence, and it went directly to the validity of Ray's conviction.

Next on the stand was the FBI agent who would testify about the corruption in Wilson County, the prostitution at the Forest Inn Motor Court and the other Wilson County brothels, the gambling houses, the payoffs to the sheriff, and the robbery ring that was run out of the sheriff's department around the time of Shadow's murder and Ray's arrest. In the middle of the agent's testimony, the judge brought an unexpected halt to the proceeding. He called a recess and left the bench, leaving us wondering what had occurred. When he came back into the courtroom, he announced quite dramatically that he was recusing himself from the hearing and said the case would have to be assigned to another judge. Then he left the courtroom, leaving us all stunned. I blamed myself for calling the ex–FBI agent to the stand at all. His testimony probably wasn't necessary after Owens's admission, but I hadn't changed my plan. It was my second worst moment ever in a courtroom, exceeded only by the jury's verdict in the Peterson case. My Perry Mason moment was gone in a flash.

We didn't know all this in 2013, but it turned out that during the FBI's investigation into corruption in Wilson County, the judge, who had previously worked as a defense attorney in Wilson, had represented three of the Wilson County sheriff's deputies, a madam of one of the prostitution houses, and one of the men in the gambling business with Gerry Frazier at the Clubhouse. The hearing, after all that preparation, came to an abrupt and disappointing end.

Despite clear evidence that Ray had been denied a fair trial, and that he was actually innocent, the state continued to fight against vacating Ray's conviction. A new judge was assigned to the case, but he hadn't been present for Owens's dramatic admission, and reading it in a cold transcript just wasn't the same. After considering it for several months, he eventually denied Ray's motion. The North Carolina Supreme Court affirmed that denial, and the federal trial court thereafter denied Ray's habeas corpus petition. It was one heartbreaking roadblock after another—but still the Wrongful Convictions Clinic persevered.

Six more years passed as Clinic continued to fight. Despite the adversity they had faced and the decreasing chances for success, they never gave up on Ray. Meanwhile, an aging Ray remained in prison as his health markedly deteriorated. His eightieth birthday came and went. He was diagnosed with cancer, and cataracts plagued his vision. He suffered a stroke that garbled his speech and made it difficult for him to be understood. Outside the prison walls, Ray's children, their father taken from them at so young an age, were now grown and had children of their own. They struggled to find reason to believe that freedom would come for their father with so little time left.

In 2019, at long last, a day of justice finally arrived for Ray Finch. The Fourth Circuit Court of Appeals, based on the information uncovered over a period of nearly two decades by the Duke Law Wrongful Convictions Clinic, reviewed Ray's case and vacated his conviction, declaring that he had overcome the exacting standard of "actual innocence." The Court concluded that Ray had "demonstrate[d] that the totality of the evidence would prevent any reasonable juror from finding him guilty beyond a reasonable doubt, such that his incarceration is a miscarriage of justice." Ray left prison in a wheelchair on March 23, 2019, forty-three years after his wrongful arrest on February 13, 1976. He saw his first blue sky outside prison walls as an enfeebled yet resilient eighty-two-year-old man who looked upon a changing world he no longer knew.

On behalf of Ray, I filed a civil rights lawsuit against Tony Owens, James Tant (the officer who allegedly found the shotgun shell in Ray's car), SBI Agent McMahan (for the coverup), and the SBI general counsel, John Watters, alleging he had intentionally or recklessly concealed critical evidence from the Wrongful Convictions Clinic. Predictably, all of them denied any wrongdoing, but in May 2020, Wilson County agreed to pay $2 million to settle the claims against Owens and Tant. Then, on June 16, 2021, the governor of

North Carolina issued a pardon of innocence for Ray, clearing the way for Ray to obtain additional compensation (up to $750,000) from the state for his wrongful imprisonment. None of this, however, came close to compensating Ray for the forty-three years of his life that he lost while incarcerated. I wanted to get him something—financial peace of mind; a recognition of the wrong that was done to him—when it would still be meaningful to him, and while he could still hope to enjoy it.

Ray Finch died on January 24, 2022, the day before this book was published. After spending almost half a century behind bars for a crime he didn't commit, Ray was able to enjoy less than three years with his family as a free man before his passing. Many of his final days were spent incapacitated in the hospital.

After Ray died, we continued his lawsuit against SBI Agent McMahan and SBI general counsel Watters on behalf of Ray's family. In June 2022, we obtained an additional settlement of $7.5 million from the North Carolina SBI and its insurance carriers. In a settlement agreement signed by the parties to the lawsuit, the North Carolina SBI still denied all wrongdoing.

The money paid to Ray's family won't begin to heal their emotional wounds or fill the void left by Ray's passing and his lifelong absence from their lives. Their pain makes me even more determined to fight the abuses of power that destroy the lives of innocent people and their loved ones. Rest in peace, Ray.

30

WHO KILLED SHADOW HOLLOMAN?

They had me in such a way that I couldn't speak out about Ray.
Something was attached to me.

—Otis Walston, Interview with the Duke Law Wrongful
Convictions Clinic, 2013

None of this answers the question of what actually happened on the night that Shadow Holloman was murdered, nor does it tell us *why* Ray Finch was targeted for the killing or why the evidence implicating him was so quickly and effortlessly gathered, while the evidence in his favor seemed so carefully concealed for all those years. Due to the persistence of the Duke Law Wrongful Convictions Clinic and the work of its lawyers and law students, I believe we now have a much clearer picture of what happened on the night that Shadow Holloman was murdered. An important piece of the story involves a man named Otis Walston.

Just before nine o'clock on February 13, 1976, a car slowed as it passed Holloman's store, then turned off onto a narrow back road that looped up and around to the west. Out of sight from the store, with woods in between, the car pulled onto the grass on the side of the road. This was near the house where Ray was living at the time with his aunt and uncle. Three men climbed out of the car. They set off on foot into the woods toward Holloman's store, a faint glow of light half a mile away.

Otis Walston was the driver of the car. Two months after Holloman's murder, he found himself in the Wilson County jail alongside Ray Finch for an unrelated crime. He knew Ray hadn't killed Shadow Holloman, and he told Ray about driving the car on the night that Shadow was killed. He conveniently claimed he had dropped off three men at the edge of the woods and that he had stayed with the car until the men eventually made their way back to the car from some errand unknown to Otis. He then drove them to a motel. Ray relayed all this to his attorney, Vernon Daughtridge, and Daughtridge called Otis as a witness at Ray's trial.

Otis was brought to court from the Wilson County jail to testify. He was a known criminal and drug user and was therefore not likely to be the most credible source of information, but it was worth putting him on the stand.

Ray's trial was not going well for him. He'd been positively identified in court as the shooter by Lester Floyd Jones, whose memory seemed to have grown sharper with the passage of time, and Chief Deputy Owens had given ironclad testimony that supported Jones's version of events. The prosecutor had argued to the jury that Jones had not identified anyone other than Ray (which we now know was untrue). When Daughtridge tried to introduce evidence that the two small blood spots on Ray's coat had been tested by the SBI and determined *not* to have come from Shadow, and that Jones had told Bobby Taylor he wasn't sure it was Ray who shot Shadow, the court blocked the testimony and the jury never heard it. The state was well on its way to proving that Ray had killed Shadow Holloman with a shotgun, as Jones alleged. Ray's prospects of an acquittal were slim.

After the state rested its case, Daughtridge called Otis Walston to the stand to show that someone else was responsible for the murder. But on direct examination, Otis was much less precise and sure than he had been when telling the story to Ray at the jail. He told a confused and meandering tale about that evening's events that did little to advance Ray's cause. He started by saying it was around 10:00 p.m. when he first drove past Holloman's store—well after the murder had taken place. He claimed there were no emergency vehicles in the parking area at that time, allowing for the possibility that it was even later than ten o'clock when he passed the store.

When asked for the names of the other men in his car, Otis at first offered three, and then four names—Alton Grooms, Tony Horton, William Rogers, and finally, Danny Rogers—the latter name having been supplied by Daughtridge, over an objection, after Otis failed to mention Danny. In recounting the events of that night, Otis had difficulty keeping track of who was allegedly in the car and what anybody might have said or done. When pressed, he'd pause and say, "Let's see . . . ," search his mind for answers, and then follow this uncertain preamble with what appeared to be invented details.

Otis claimed to have driven the men, at their direction, on a course that led them past Holloman's store and then back up and around, to just on the other side of the woods from the store. He claimed not to have known the purpose of the trip. Otis testified that once they arrived at the woods behind Holloman's store, two of the men got out of the car to do something—Otis wasn't sure what—but were back in the car in a matter of minutes. He then drove them to a motel, with no questions asked.

A most curious piece of testimony came when Otis told the jury what he claimed happened when he was dropping the men at the motel. As they exited the car, Otis said, he happened to see a shotgun and one other gun on the floorboard of the back seat. According to his testimony, the guns were removed from Otis's car and hidden in a nearby ditch.

It was hard for the jury to know what to take away from Otis's account. There was certainly a suggestion that the men might have had something to do with Holloman's murder, but his testimony didn't add up. Plainly, Otis was holding something back. The men whose names Otis had provided had not been charged with the murder, and no one—not even Daughtridge—was pointing an accusatory finger at them, which undermined any implication that they were actually involved. Most notably, Otis said he didn't drive by the store until well after Holloman had been killed. To the jury, it probably sounded like an elaborate red herring and a last act of desperation by Ray's attorney.

Still, it was intriguing enough to make the prosecutor cross-examine Otis about his story. On cross, Otis's unusual tale became even more muddled. He couldn't keep straight the details he'd just provided on direct. He even admitted talking to Ray in prison prior to the trial, and the prosecutor's questions fairly raised the inference that Otis was just there to save Ray's skin.

The prosecutor was on a roll, and Otis was in tatters on the stand. All the jury would take away from Otis's testimony was that he was unreliable and untrustworthy—a liar. The prosecutor could have, and should have, stopped while he was ahead. But he asked the proverbial "one question too many," a question to which he surely did not know the answer. He asked Otis if he had told anyone about the guns he saw in the back seat of his car that night. He assumed, I suspect, that Otis hadn't told *anyone* about the guns, because he thought the whole story had been fabricated to cast suspicion away from Ray. The answer he received could not have been the one he expected.

Otis responded that he had, in fact, told someone about the guns. He had told Captain Tom Smith of the Wilson Police Department. My sense from reading the transcript is that this was a fact that neither the prosecutor nor Ray's attorney knew at the time. It lent an unexpected air of legitimacy to that portion of Otis's testimony and hinted that there was more to the story that hadn't been told. Without any follow-up, the prosecutor ended his cross-examination.

Hearing about Otis's conversation with Captain Smith and likely not knowing exactly what to make of it, Ray's attorney cautiously explored this new information on redirect:

Q. You say you talked to Captain Tom Smith about this matter you just testified about?
A. Yes, sir.
Q. Did you talk to Mr. Tony Owens over here about it?
A. You know, we had a few conversations about it.
Q. You did, with Mr. Owens?
A. Yes, but not about the shotgun or nothing like that, but we talked and he asked me a few questions about the case.
Q. He asked you a few questions about it?
A. Yes, sir.
Q. Well, did you tell Mr. Smith or Mr. Owens about the shotgun?
A. I think I talked—I think Detective Smith.
Q. You told him about the shotgun?
A. Yes, sir.
Q. Did you tell Mr. Owens about the shotgun?
A. I don't remember.

Ray's attorney left it there and asked nothing further about it. This peculiar testimony, which at the time seemed tangential to the question of Ray's guilt or innocence, wound up having no bearing on the outcome of Ray's trial. He was quickly convicted and sentenced to death.

It wasn't until years later that its significance became more apparent. It was just one small piece of an elaborate puzzle that had to be slowly assembled, put together with other pieces that were discovered, bit by bit, piece by piece, over a period of many years, as the quest to establish Ray's innocence ground on. A day would come when the puzzle was complete and a picture of what likely happened on the night Shadow Holloman was killed emerged. Here are the other pieces of the puzzle.

One or more of the men who likely robbed Holloman's store that night went on to commit two additional armed robberies of small country stores in Wilson County *within five days* of the shooting at Holloman's store, then a third robbery the very next month, followed by others in Greensboro, one hundred twenty miles away. In each case, the modus operandi was the same. Store clerks were taken to a backroom of the store and forced on their knees at gunpoint while the store was robbed, as the abrasions on Shadow's knees suggested had happened to him. Each of these additional robberies occurred while Ray Finch was in jail. Chief Deputy Owens was aware of this information at the time of Ray's trial.

Three of the men whose names Otis Walston testified to in court—Alton Grooms, William Rogers, and Danny Rogers—appear to have had nothing whatsoever to do with the robberies. However, the story is different for one of the men named by Otis in court that day: Tony Horton.

The sheriff's department made no arrests in connection with the additional country-store robberies in Wilson County when they occurred. It wasn't until Tony Horton, along with a man named Ricky Reid, was arrested by the Greensboro police in June 1976 that Horton and Reid were charged in Wilson County in connection with the robbery of the three country stores that occurred in the days and weeks following the murder at Holloman's store. All of this happened *before* Ray's case went to trial. And even though the police now had circumstantial evidence that Horton, or Reid, or possibly both may have been involved in the similar robbery at Holloman's store, neither was charged in connection with that crime. Owens had already arrested Ray and had him identified by the eyewitness, Lester Floyd Jones.

Strangely, although Otis Walston admitted under oath that he had driven men who had firearms in their possession to a wooded area in close proximity to Holloman's store on the night that Shadow was murdered, and that the men had hidden the firearms after some nighttime excursion that Otis improbably claimed ignorance about, he had not been charged in connection with Shadow's murder. Logic and experience tell me it was not likely that Otis had simply stayed in his car while the other men went through the woods to rob Holloman's store. It's much more likely he would have approached the store with the others, although perhaps hanging back at some distance when they got there.

In April 1976, according to court records, two months after the Holloman robbery-murder and only two months before Ray's trial, Otis and another man from Wilson County allegedly attempted a robbery of their own, botched it, and wound up shooting someone in the head with a .25-caliber pistol. Fortunately for everyone involved, the person survived. Otis was charged with armed robbery and assault with a deadly weapon with intent to kill. Given the severity of the crimes and his past record, he was facing serious prison time if convicted. This, it turned out, was serendipitous for the sheriff's department, for it gave them an unexpected source of leverage over Otis when he testified at Ray's trial.

It is clear that when Otis got on the stand to testify at Ray's trial, he didn't tell the whole truth about who he drove to Holloman's store that night. He gave up Tony Horton's name, but the other names he supplied were fabrications. The key question, therefore, becomes why Otis was protecting anyone (other than himself), and whether it had anything to do with his conversations with Captain Tom Smith and Chief Deputy Tony Owens.

What Chief Deputy Owens knew at the time of Ray's trial was that Lester Floyd Jones had described a man with a checked shirt as being involved in the murder, and that Jones had identified this same man in a photographic lineup on the Monday following the shooting. He knew that the men with Otis Walston on the night of the murder had guns in Otis's car, and that the guns had been taken and hidden somewhere—which would only make sense if the guns had just been used to commit a crime. And, lastly, he knew that Otis Walston had been subpoenaed to court to testify at Ray's trial.

The evidence suggests that if Otis had told the whole truth, it would have established that Ray Finch wasn't involved in the shooting death of Shadow Holloman after all, and that Owens knew it. It would also have implicated the man the sheriff's department absolutely needed to protect.

"They got people to lie.... Telling people what to say.... I wasn't as truthful as I should have been." This is what Otis Walston said to the Duke Clinic's attorneys in 2013. "I couldn't speak out like I wanted to. They had me in such a way that I couldn't speak out about Ray. *Something was attached to me.*" That something was a charge for armed robbery and assault with a deadly weapon, along with his own involvement in the Holloman murder.

The other person in the car with Otis Walston that night besides Tony Horton, as he revealed to the Wrongful Convictions Clinic in 2013, was the person Lester Floyd Jones described to the police as wearing the checked shirt—the same person he identified in a photographic lineup three days after the murder, an identification that Owens concealed from Ray and his attorney. It was the same man that Jones told Bobby Taylor he had recognized in the store the night when Shadow was killed. And the same man who, after the shooting at Holloman's store, walked to the house where Ray Finch was living and asked for a ride back into town. The same man who lived at the Forest Inn Motor Court, who had witnessed all the corruption on display at the motel, and who knew that the sheriff of Wilson County was on the take: Charles Lewis. He had to be protected, even at the cost of another man's life.

EPILOGUE

The Roots of Resistance

For as long as I can remember, I've had an aversion to blind obedience to authority. I tend to question authority in all its forms. I'm sure this instinct developed from numerous experiences, but there is no question that I was fundamentally shaped by the times I grew up in, as were so many others of my generation. In high school I was awed by the courage of the leaders of the civil rights movement and the hundreds of college students, only a little older than me, who protested the Jim Crow laws in the South. I don't think I would have had the physical courage to ride a Freedom Bus to the Deep South to confront white-hooded Klansmen, even if I had been old enough to do so, but I was inspired by the protestors' willingness to risk their lives for a just cause. The abuses of power could be successfully resisted through nonviolent means. That was an important lesson for me, even if I didn't appreciate it at the time.

During the summer before I entered Rutgers University as an undergraduate, we were given a reading list for incoming freshmen. I chose *Escape from Freedom* by Erich Fromm, although I no longer remember why. This now-classic book examines Hitler's rise to power in Germany, but on a broader level, it explores the nature of freedom and authoritarianism. I read it in 1967, when the Vietnam protests were heating up. Fromm's book spoke to me then and has had a profound effect on me ever since. It helped me understand how and why authoritarian regimes come to power and the deceptions employed by despots to retain control. The danger arises because, on a fundamental level, most people find it easier to follow rules, whether imposed by religion or government, than to make the difficult choices freedom often requires.

Authoritarian regimes exploit this human tendency and make the questioning of their authority an offense to the greater good. It becomes "unpatriotic" to peacefully protest injustice. But when people don't question abuses of power and don't push back to assert their rights, the power of the state expands and the rights of the citizens, particularly those who are labeled "the others," erode and ultimately disappear.

Being in college with a student deferment during the height of the Vietnam War, and then being fortunate enough to draw a high number in the first draft lottery, protected me from having to choose between going to Vietnam or going to Canada. Many of my friends faced that dilemma, and I joined other young Americans in opposing the war. I was a junior in college when, on May 4, 1970, four students at Kent State University were gunned down by the Ohio National Guard. I was in Boston at the time of the shooting, surrounded by tens of thousands of college students who were protesting in and around Boston Common. Final exams were canceled almost everywhere. There was a palpable sense of disbelief that our government had killed college students for assembling and speaking out against the government. This was soon followed by the disclosures in the Pentagon Papers, which made clear we had all been lied to about the war. I grew even more distrustful of authority.

In September 1971, as part of my orientation at NYU Law School, the first-year students were given the opportunity to go on a tour of various legal "landmarks" in New York City, such as the Federal Courthouse at Foley Square or Wall Street. I chose to go on a tour of "the Tombs," the notorious New York jail where defendants awaiting trial in state court were housed, several stories high, in steel cages.

There were several female law students in the group, and when the male prisoners saw us they started banging on the bars of their cells and shouting. I felt like I was visiting a human zoo. It was degrading to everyone and appalling to watch, but the guards found it funny. It was my first direct experience with the criminal justice system, and I was shocked at the inhumanity and callousness I saw. I had not realized how the system treated people, even those who had not yet been convicted of any crime—who were just too poor to make bail while they waited for their day in court. It was dehumanizing, and the prisoners acted accordingly.

In the fall of 1973, when I was a third-year law student, I was shaken when news reports of the Saturday Night Massacre came across the television. Richard Nixon fired special prosecutor Archibald Cox and abolished the Watergate Task Force. The attorney general and the assistant attorney general resigned in protest. It seemed as if the rule of law was disintegrating before my eyes. Five months later, the *attorney general of the United States* was indicted for obstructing justice. Indictments across the White House staff led to Nixon resigning to avoid an impeachment trial. I was just starting my career as a lawyer. What was I to think? These historic events heightened my distrust of authority and my instinctive resistance to abuses of power. These powerful images remain with me to this day; they have been a defining part of my life and my career.

It would be easy to describe this series of events as the reason I question authority, but there is substantial evidence that it's in my DNA. In fifth grade I was sent to the principal's office after a confrontation with my teacher, Mrs. Jurow. I wasn't paying attention when she told us all to pick up our sneakers from under our desks, so she came along and, in what I now recognize as simply a misguided attempt to teach me a lesson, threw mine in the trash bin. As a ten-year-old child, I missed the symbolism she must have intended. "Those are *my* property, *you* can't throw them away," I still remember saying, as I marched up to the trash bin and took them out. My sneakers and I were quickly dispatched to the principal's office. My parents were summoned, and they were unimpressed with my assertion of property rights. They imposed their own form of "house arrest."

Whatever lesson they hoped to impart apparently didn't sink in. Two years later, in seventh grade, my questioning of teacher authority was still deemed unacceptable by those in charge at my junior high school. As a result, in an effort to understand my "acting out," and to help me conform and comply, my parents arranged for a battery of psychological tests at NYU to diagnose my "problem." The evaluation report—which I still have—described the root cause: "Strong-willed and intelligent enough to perceive the inconsistencies in discipline given by his parents, he is inclined to 'push the limits' of authority to find some 'rock-bottom' basis that he can respect." All these years later, I still am.

ACKNOWLEDGMENTS

This is a book I always wanted to write but thought I never would. The fact that it exists is the result of the influence, help, and encouragement of many, but there are some who deserve special recognition and my sincere gratitude.

First and foremost, my family: my partner in life and in the law, Sonya Pfeiffer, and my daughter, Zayne Rudolf, who have borne the brunt of my obsessive-compulsive "tendencies" (to put it gently) in recent years, and my sons, Matt, Josh, and Aaron, who bore the brunt years ago, when they were growing up and I was even worse. But especially Sonya, who is an amazingly talented person in her own right, and has been my best friend and trusted partner for the past fifteen years. None of this, the arc of my life, my continuing work, or this book, would have been possible without your support, occasionally grudging, usually willing, but always loving. You have made my life complete, and for that, thanks are not nearly enough.

The book itself owes its existence to my friend Webb Hubbell, the former Associate Attorney General of the United States during President Clinton's first term, who was himself the victim of an incredible abuse of power by the so-called Whitewater Special Prosecutor, Kenneth Starr. Webb introduced me to his literary agent, Michael Carlisle, who in turn introduced me to the two people responsible for helping me prepare a professional book proposal, Henry Ferris, Jr., and Barbara Feinman Todd. Michael, a well-respected agent with Inkwell Management in New York, then agreed to represent me, mostly on faith, since I had no books to my credit. Michael, in turn, connected me to Geoff Shandler, who was then the editorial director at Custom House, an imprint of Harper-Collins, who agreed to purchase the book and publish it—once again, mostly on faith. And so it often goes.

The finished product is the result of the talented editors and staff at Custom House, who have been incredibly helpful and supportive through the entire process. Peter Hubbard, who succeeded Geoff as the editorial director at Custom House, Molly Gendell, the editor who has worked most closely with me, Christina Joell, our tireless publicist, Danielle Finnegan, our marketing whiz, Andrea Molitor, our production editor, Ploy Siripant, who is responsible for the in-credible cover design, and Leah Carlson-Stanisic, who is responsible for the interior design. The entire team has been dedicated to the project from the beginning, and have improved the print version of the book in ways large and small. I am forever grateful for their help in bringing this to fruition.

Finally, there is one person I can truly say is most responsible for what is contained on these pages. Phillip Lewis, a lawyer and a successful author in his own right, joined my law firm because he wanted to help people in meaningful ways by focusing on civil rights cases. But it turns out the person he has helped the most (so far) is me. Phillip dug through my old files, did his own indepen-dent research, helped to refresh my memory of various events, and did first drafts for a number of the chapters or parts of chapters. I tend to be sparser in my language than Phillip, who took great joy in "painting" the various scenes that come alive with his descriptions, but we worked together seamlessly. He provided the structure, the discipline, and the perseverance to make this a reality, and deserves credit for how the book has turned out. I plead guilty and accept full responsibility for its failings.

INDEX